Implementing ISO 9000:2000

Implementing ISO 9000:2000

MATT SEAVER

Gower

Published by
Gower Publishing Limited
Gower House
Croft Road
Aldershot
Hampshire GU11 3HR
England

Gower Publishing Company
131 Main Street
Burlington VT 05401–5600 USA

Matt Seaver has asserted his right under the Copyright, Designs and Patents Act 1988 to be identified as the author of this work.

British Library Cataloguing in Publication Data
Seaver, Matt
    Implementing ISO 9000:2000
    1. ISO 9000 Series Standards
    I. Title
    658.5'62

ISBN 0 566 08373 6

Library of Congress Cataloging-in-Publication Data
Seaver, Matt.
    Implementing ISO 9000:2000 / Matt Seaver.
        p. cm.
    ISBN 0–566–08373–6 (hardback)
    1. Quality control--Standards. 2. ISO 9000 Series Standards. I. Title.

TS156 .S368 2001
658.5'62--dc21   00-069174

Typeset in Utopia by Bournemouth Colour Press, Parkstone and printed in Great Britain by MPG Books Ltd, Bodmin, Cornwall.

Contents

Preface

In writing this book I decided to forego any lengthy introduction to quality – how it is the key to survival and how important it is to be committed to it, and so on – on the basis that, since you are reading the book, you are already convinced of the value and importance of quality. In any case, you have probably read all that many times already, and it would not add anything to the impact of this book.

Nor have I included the history lesson on how the ISO 9000 standards were developed, which is usual in such a book. In my experience the reader of a book like this does not have the time for, and even less interest in, the details of how ISO 9000 came to its present prominence. What it does contain is a practical guide to setting up an effective but simple quality management system. The guidance is essentially a distillation of my own experience of quality management systems, starting in the pre-ISO 9000 days, through years of working with quality systems, first, as a quality manager in a manufacturing environment and, later, as a quality management consultant. My reasons for considering myself qualified to write a book on ISO 9000 are also based on the fact that I have been involved in the active development of the ISO 9000 standards as an *expert member* of the ISO Technical Committee 176 since 1992.

From the years I spent as a quality manager in industry I know that most managers do not have time to study the theory of management. What they most want is practical advice and help on how to manage their own operations. For that reason you will find very little theory in this book. I have tried to confine myself to what may be useful to a busy manager. All of the advice I offer is based either on my own, sometimes painful, experiences as a quality manager in the infant-food industry or that of clients in many different businesses, small and large, with whom I have worked closely over the years.

I have attempted to give equal emphasis to manufacturing and service sectors, and to pay special attention to the difficulties that small companies have in knowing how best to address the various elements of ISO 9000. I have not attempted to address, other than in passing, particular industry sectors. So, for instance, there is no treatment of standards such as QS 9000 or TL 9000, since the supplementary material contained in these standards is very specific to those industry sectors and not generally applicable. Nor have I specifically addressed total quality management. However, if the initiatives described in the book are adopted with commitment, then the organization is well on the way to total quality management. In my experience most companies gain quite sufficient benefits from a properly implemented ISO 9000 system.

This book does not pretend to give a comprehensive treatment of the topics covered. What it does present is a set of tools that a manager could usefully employ for implementing ISO 9000 while trying to get the normal business in hand completed. So, for example, the section dealing with finance offers just a few practical ways of getting a little more out of the financial resources that you deploy. If the reader wants a detailed treatise on the full range of techniques that are available, then a specialist text dealing with that subject should be consulted.

The book is divided into four main Parts:

● Part A: An introduction to the ISO 9000 standards, which includes guidance on how to manage the ISO 9000 project.

- Part B: A commentary on all the clauses of the ISO 9004 standard. This contains specific advice on how to implement the various quality initiatives described in the standard. In this section of the book I have followed the ISO 9004 sequence of paragraphs, since ISO 9004 is broader in scope, and includes some topics not covered by ISO 9001. The reference at the top of a paragraph, therefore, is to ISO 9004. Where there is a difference between the two standards this is noted.
- Part C: A sample quality manual. As required in ISO 9001 this quality manual contains references to specific procedures. Where I have considered it helpful I have included an example among the Help documents. See below.
- Part D: A set of 'Help documents' consisting of procedures, forms and guidance notes. These are examples which are referred to either in the general guidance section or in the sample quality manual.

Finally, a word about the terms *product* and *service*. At each stage of development of the ISO 9000 standards there has been a very serious academic debate among the experts about how to deal with the concept of a service in the ISO 9000 family of standards. For many years the official ISO definition of product has included the idea of a service. Product has always been defined in terms of the processes that generate it. Since processes can generate intangible as well as tangible output the purists proposed that the term *service* should not be used in the standard, as the readers would automatically understand that it was adequately covered by the term *product*. In fact, a ballot was held among ISO member bodies and they concurred. It seems that service providers still do not have a sufficiently loud voice. However, I prefer to think that most people in business are more concerned about the practicalities than about familiarizing themselves with abstruse definitions and, consequently, I have not refrained, heretically, from using the term *service* when appropriate.

MATT SEAVER

Introduction to ISO 9000

CHAPTER I

What is ISO 9000?

Everybody is familiar with the concept of a standard. A standard is simply a definition of how something should be. In the case of a physical object the standard might include such things as physical dimensions, colour, hardness and functional properties. There are also standards for services, often called codes of practice. There are many thousands of standards for physical products, produced by national standards bodies, industry groups and individual companies. Of all the standards produced by the International Organization for Standardization the ones that are most widely known are those of the ISO 9000 series. A standard is intended to be used as a set of criteria against which the quality of an item or service can be measured. So, for example, when a company purchases an item it can specify that the item must comply with a certain standard. We get the supplier's agreement on that and if he or she cannot meet that standard we will purchase the item elsewhere.

But what happens if there is no standard for the item in question? Or if we are buying a mass-produced item in a shop or from a distributor? Is there any way that we can have confidence in the quality of the item? Traditionally, a manufacturer always thought that if sufficient inspection was carried out on the finished product it would be guaranteed to meet quality requirements. In the extreme case the items could be subjected to 100 per cent inspection, and this would absolutely guarantee quality in the product sent to the customer. But 100 per cent inspection is not nearly as effective in detecting faults as it might seem. Even though a quality inspector is looking at the fault and knows what he or she is looking for, it may still go unobserved. Typically, 100 per cent inspection is only about 90 per cent effective. For an inspector coming to the end of an eight-hour shift the figure may be much lower. Its inadequacy is demonstrated by the simple visual test shown in Figure I.1.

So, if we cannot rely on inspecting every item how are we to guarantee quality? The answer is to ensure that the product is right before we get to the inspection at the end of the line, by building quality into the product at all stages. If we do that, then even before we test it we will already know that the output meets the quality standards. In order to achieve this we must organize ourselves at all stages from the purchase of the raw materials right through to the delivery of the finished product to the customer. The way we organize ourselves we call the quality management system.

THE FINAL FORMULA IS THE RESULT OF TEN YEARS OF SCIENTIFIC RESEARCH COMBINED WITH THE EXPERIENCE OF MANY PEOPLE.

Figure I.1 Imagine that the letter 'F' represents a faulty item that can be visually identified as such, and the letters in the text passage represent a sequence of items for inspection. Take about ten seconds to count the number of F's. Many people fail this test in the time allowed.

What should such a system consist of? That is the role of ISO 9000. In order to bring uniformity to quality management systems the International Organization for Standardization formalized a standard for such a management system, which was based on various existing national and industry standards. This standard encompasses all the quality activities that are needed to provide assurance about the quality of the finished product or service.

However, it is important to understand that the ISO 9000 standards address only the system that operates in the company and does not directly assess the quality of the product itself. Thus, a company which properly operates a quality management system to the ISO 9000 standards is *likely* to produce a product that meets customer requirements, since its activities are organized in an effective way, as described in this book. On the other hand, a company that does not have an effective management system in place may produce a quality product, but it will only do so by good fortune or inconsistently. The customer, therefore, has a much better chance of receiving a quality product from a supplier who operates an effective quality management system.

ISO 9001 AND ISO 9004

There are several standards in the ISO 9000 family, the most important ones being ISO 9001 and ISO 9004.

ISO 9001 is entitled 'Quality management systems – requirements'.

ISO 9004 is entitled 'Quality management systems – guidelines for performance improvements'.

A third standard that the reader should be aware of is ISO 9000 itself, entitled 'Quality management systems – fundamentals and vocabulary'. This standard, as well as giving definitions of terms that have different usage to the normal dictionary definitions, also contains some useful, though not very detailed, discussion on selected topics related to quality management systems.

Note that ISO 9002 and ISO 9003 no longer exist, having been incorporated into ISO 9001:2000. As well as referring to a specific standard, the term 'ISO 9000' is often used as a convenient way of referring to the entire family of related ISO 9000 standards. Thus, we may speak of an 'ISO 9000 quality management system', meaning that the system is based on the principles outlined in ISO 9000, was designed using the guidance in ISO 9004 and complies with the requirements of ISO 9001.

When the standards were first published in 1987 it was intended that ISO 9004 should be the first port of call on the journey towards excellence. The quality management system was to be based on it, rather than on ISO 9001 or ISO 9002. With the demand for ISO 9001 and ISO 9002 certification, however, organizations started to take the minimalist approach and designed their systems on the much narrower requirements of ISO 9001 or ISO 9002. This resulted in many companies being disappointed with the level of benefits that they derived from ISO 9000, and frustrated at what they saw as the inordinate effort that had to be put into maintaining the certification.

ISO 9004 addresses the entire range of initiatives that you should consider when setting up a quality management system, and this is where you should start. While ISO 9001 is primarily concerned with ensuring customer satisfaction, that is, product or service quality, ISO 9004 strives to create an organization that is successful in all aspects of its operation, including financial success. ISO 9001 describes the minimum requirements for a quality management system if it is to be effective in ensuring customer satisfaction, whereas ISO 9004 gives broad guidance on all aspects of the quality management system.

To understand the difference between ISO 9001 and ISO 9004 consider how you look after your car. ISO 9004 is like the car technical manual. It contains every detail of all repair and maintenance tasks and schedules. In practice few of us do absolutely everything that it recommends, but if we are to keep the car in good condition and maintain its resale value we will do more than the minimum required to keep it roadworthy. We attend to the essential items like brakes, but we also change the oil at the recommended frequency, keep the upholstery in good order, clean the car and have it serviced from time to time.

ISO 9001, on the other hand, is more like the checklist for the statutory test for roadworthiness, which is essentially concerned purely with road safety. These are the requirements you must comply with if the car is to get its certificate, but it does not assess how well you have maintained it or if its resale value is protected. Similarly, ISO 9001 identifies certain minimum requirements that all quality management systems must meet in order to ensure customer satisfaction. But that is not to say that compliance with these requirements gives you the most effective system, or even a comprehensive system. In fact, so long as the customer is satisfied ISO 9001 does not care if the organization goes bankrupt! Not so ISO 9004, since it concerns itself with satisfying all interested parties.

It is very important to understand that ISO 9004 does not give guidance on how to comply with ISO 9001 requirements. To quote from ISO 9004 itself: 'ISO 9004 is recommended as a guide for organizations whose top management wishes to move beyond the requirements of ISO 9001 in pursuit of continual improvement of performance.'

Since it was first published, in 1987, ISO 9000 has had an extraordinary impact on companies worldwide. It is no exaggeration to say that most, if not all, persons engaged in business are aware of this family of standards. The standards were first revised in 1994. That revision was a fairly minor affair, considering the amount of work that went into the revision over about five years. I first became involved in the standards development field during the latter stages of that revision.

The first revision did not really address the principal criticisms of the 1987 version, which made necessary a second revision involving a total rewrite. As companies became more and more familiar with the requirements of the standard, many found that ISO 9000 presented less and less of a challenge and, consequently, delivered fewer and fewer benefits. Companies wanted to generate improvement in their performance, and wanted more from ISO 9000 than mere compliance with minimum requirements. The revision of 2000 attempts to address this, and stresses the need to take the quality approach in all aspects of the organization's business. Of course, there were companies who struggled to knock their systems into shape in advance of each impending audit, but these companies usually had very low expectations of ISO 9000 anyway. These were the companies whose sole motivation in adopting ISO 9000 was to obtain a certificate. The revision of 2000 also addresses another criticism, namely, that the earlier versions were aimed primarily at large manufacturing companies, and were difficult to interpret for service companies and small manufacturing companies.

THE SYSTEMATIC APPROACH

It hardly seems necessary to justify the idea of adopting a systematic approach to managing your business. There must be very few companies who would openly admit to being totally disorganized, though people often jokingly say that this is the case. In practice, however, there are many companies who are disorganized in a systematic sort of way. I have seen large companies with plenty of paper to show that they had systems in place, and yet the problems were constantly there. The tragedy of many of these situations is that it is the same problems that crop up time and again, since no real effort is made to identify and address the root causes.

Companies who have need of a management system often suffer from at least some of the following problems:

- There is insufficient time to sit back and take an overview of the situation.
- There is never time to read relevant articles.
- Silly mistakes are being made all the time.
- There is a high level of scrap product.
- The level of scrap product is not known.
- Customers are forever complaining.
- Staff morale is low.
- A great amount of time is spent at crisis management meetings.
- Improvement never seems possible.

THE CULTURE CHANGE

Adopting a quality-centred approach to management, which is what ISO 9000 advocates, often requires proprietors and managers to change completely the way they interact with their staff. In the past, managers managed and workers worked and there was no need for one to know very much about what the other did. We are more enlightened nowadays. Or are we? Unfortunately, there are still residues of the old approach, and often this impacts negatively and very strongly on a company's ability to deliver a quality service to its customers.

In this new world of total quality we will all be relying on each other to deliver on commitments we have given. Managers will depend on operators to do the job properly, probably with less supervision than before. Operators will be expected to report problems, perhaps even to correct them themselves. They may even be given authority over their own tasks, in effect becoming managers of their own units or cells. But they, in turn, will look to management to supply training and make the appropriate resources available. Furthermore, people now expect the organization to look after their welfare and invest in their personal development.

This culture change can be particularly difficult in the case of smaller owner-managed companies that have operated successfully for many years in the older management style. In many of these companies the management style can most charitably be described as autocratic. Two aspects of management that characterize the difference between progressive companies and the others are delegation and blame. Delegation is often an unknown or misunderstood concept, with managers feeling that nobody can do the job the way they can. That approach is no longer viable. The modern manager must delegate. The old saying 'If you have a dog, there is no need for you to bark' is often quoted with amusement, but more often ignored. The effective manager operates on the principle that if people are properly trained they can do the job. It might not be quite as well done as the manager would do it, but the difference may not justify spending valuable management time on the task in question. Management time is much more profitably spent managing the organization than doing jobs that can easily and appropriately be done by subordinate staff. Managers should do what managers are paid to do.

If the quality management system is to work effectively there must not be a 'blame culture' in the organization. When a loss occurs the most important thing, surely, is that it should be prevented from happening again. That means establishing the full facts. However, if the person at the centre of the problem is going to be blamed irrespective of the circumstances, then he or she is more likely to cover up all problems, and the organization as a whole will be the loser.

It is not easy to make the change, and many companies have spent a great deal of effort breaking down the barriers that have built up over the years. But it must be done if the organization is to prosper.

ISO 9000 AND TEAMWORKING

Traditionally, companies have been organized on the basis of separate functions or departments. Thus, one department, with a manager at its head, is responsible for central purchasing of all goods and services for the entire organization. A different department, under a different manager, is responsible for dealing with customer complaints. Yet another department attends to the repair and maintenance of equipment, and so on. Overlaid on that arrangement is the hierarchical structure – chief executive, senior managers, middle managers and supervisors. Nowadays, however, more and more companies are moving towards working with cells or teams, in which a group of perhaps eight to ten people take responsibility for all aspects of product realization,[1] from planning the order and purchasing the necessary materials right through to final delivery to the customer. The benefits of this approach are that the team members are totally in control and responsible, and are therefore motivated to produce a quality output. The team is smaller and more flexible than the larger organization and, consequently, can react more quickly to changes in orders and specifications, and they can implement speedily any improvements that they identify. Finally, this type of structure usually results in a significant reduction in overall costs.

It has always been assumed that the departmental type of management structure is what ISO 9000 has in mind. In earlier versions of the standard the actual structure of the standard itself may have contributed to this misunderstanding, with its 20 clauses dealing with separate aspects such as purchasing, design and development, inspection and testing, and so on. In fact, everything that the ISO 9000 standards contained could be implemented for both individual teams and the organization as a whole.

Irrespective of the overall structure there will be a senior management team, and they will have certain responsibilities that will exist whether the product realization is carried out under a hierarchy or by individually empowered teams. The numerous references in the standard to 'top management' do not, therefore, imply any particular form of structure.

Because most organizations are still structured in a generally hierarchical manner, I have adopted this model in the book. That is purely for the convenience of the majority of readers and should not be taken as an endorsement of that approach rather than team working. In a team situation many of the Help documents would have to be reworded. For example, QM-11 in the sample quality manual (see p. 124) would need to be totally restructured to give the managers more of a monitoring role and to pass responsibility for the actual tasks to the team members. Apart from that, most of the Help documents would require little modification to be applicable to teams.

NOTE

1 Product realization is the routine activity of producing a product or delivering a service. See page 58.

CHAPTER II

Setting up the ISO 9000 system

PRELIMINARY WORK

The first thing to do is to purchase copies of the ISO 9001 and ISO 9004 standards. Then, before you embark on the project, find out as much as you can from others who have already done it. Speak to people who have experience with ISO 9000. In particular, find out about the level of commitment that is necessary and what difficulties others have encountered. The more input you get the more informed you will be. You should speak to people who have had a positive experience with ISO 9000. Try to find what factors made it work for them. Listen carefully, also, to people who have complaints about bureaucracy and paperwork. Try to establish the root cause of their difficulties, and identify what you can do to avoid these problems. When you have heard both sides you will have a broad vision of the benefits and pitfalls. If you have adequate expertise within the organization, you will not need to employ a consultant. If you do not, then you will have to consider this option. If you decide to use a consultant, select one who comes well recommended by somebody whose opinion you value. The standard of service and knowledge is as varied among consultants as it is in any other field. It is vitally important that the system you eventually end up with is practical and can be implemented with the minimum disruption of the normal activities. Many of the problems that arose in the past resulted from cumbersome systems that were transplanted from other organizations without any regard for the difficulty in implementing them. If you use the services of a consultant who is not totally sure of the correct interpretation, you risk being advised to implement procedures that are unnecessarily detailed and cumbersome just to cover for the consultant's insecurity. There is an adage in the aerospace field: 'Anybody can design a structure that is strong enough. It takes an expert to design a structure that is *just* strong enough.' This principle is particularly apt for quality management systems and the consultants who design them.

The question often arises, if one engages a consultant must it be somebody who is technically familiar with the industry sector involved? Usually it is not necessary for the consultant to be expert in the technical field in question, since a quality management system is more about managing resources effectively than about technical knowledge. In any case, you surely know the technicalities of your process better than any external expert. What you are probably lacking is a broad knowledge of the range of solutions for the various management problems that can arise in any organization. Therefore, unless the subject matter is highly specialized and technical, it is likely that your real requirement is for somebody who has a comprehensive understanding of ISO 9000 and how it is best interpreted and implemented, and who can suggest practical ways of managing your business most effectively. There are cases, of course, where a certain amount of technical knowledge is highly desirable, if not essential, but generally the gap in the consultant's technical knowledge can usually be filled by the organization's own technical experts. So, it may be better to engage a consultant who may not be familiar with the technicalities of your business or process but who has a proven record of providing practical and effective management methods, rather than a consultant who has direct experience in your field but has an undetermined knowledge of practical solutions. The risk is that you could end up with a cumbersome system based on the limited knowledge circulating within your own industry sector, rather than tapping into the general body of management experience from a wide range of sectors.

PRODUCE A QUALITY POLICY

Once you know what is involved you are in a position to set out a policy that will genuinely mean something. Your policy must recognize that achieving customer satisfaction is central to the success of the organization, and that all quality activities must be geared towards satisfying customer expectations. Indeed, you should aim to exceed expectations – 'delight your customer'. Your policy should commit your organization to real improvement in performance, both in the quality of the product or service and the performance of the organization. You should also consider making a commitment to the whole question of developing your personnel by providing the resources to help them develop their personal skills to the benefit of both them and the organization. An example of a quality policy is given in the sample quality manual included in this book.

APPOINT A PERSON OR GROUP TO CO-ORDINATE THE PROJECT

To ensure that the ISO 9000 project is implemented as quickly and efficiently as possible you should appoint somebody to co-ordinate the project. If yours is a small organization, that person may have to work alone in setting up the system. In larger organizations it may be more appropriate to set up a project group with representatives of the different functions. In either case it is critical that the person or group driving the project receives support from everybody in the organization. Make sure that this person or group keeps everybody else informed of progress. Hold regular briefing sessions for other staff.

If possible involve a number of people in the project. This is recommended for several reasons. First, there is a lot of work involved in writing procedures and, perhaps, trying out different controls and organizing people to make changes to the way they operate. It is very difficult for one person to do all this except in the smallest organizations, whereas a group can share the work, making the whole project easier to complete. Second, and more important, the more people who are involved the more commitment there will be throughout the organization. If a person is involved in setting up a system he or she will be more likely to implement it, and cannot easily raise objections later on the basis that it has been imposed or is impractical.

DEMONSTRATE COMMITMENT

Senior management must be committed, and must demonstrate that commitment. Adequate time and resources must be devoted to the project. The person or group co-ordinating the effort must be supported to demonstrate its importance. Senior management must be very conscious of the messages that their actions give to all employees. Apart from giving support in terms of resources, senior managers must be willing to participate frequently in routine project activities, particularly attending meetings, briefings and training sessions whenever practicable.

IDENTIFY YOUR PROCESSES

Before starting to write procedures you must first examine all your activities and organize them into processes. A process is a sequence of activities that convert inputs (materials and information) into outputs (a product or a service). You have an overall process representing whatever business you are in, such as selling fast food, designing buildings or manufacturing steel bolts. You have your customer at both ends of the process. The customer starts the process by placing an order, thereby telling you what you need to do to give satisfaction. The customer is also present at the finish, receiving your product or service and expressing an opinion on how well you have met his or her expectations. What happens in between is your principal process. This can be further divided into sub-processes. Very often these sub-processes represent units or departments within the overall structure of the organization. The sub-processes can often suggest the structure of the quality management system documentation.

DECIDE ON A STRUCTURE FOR THE SYSTEM

The typical ISO 9000 management system documentation is structured on four levels, usually depicted as a pyramid (Figure II.1). On top is the quality policy, from which all quality initiatives derive. Underneath the policy comes the quality manual. This is the principal manual in the quality management system, and describes the overall system in general terms.

Beneath the quality manual are the detailed manuals containing the operational procedures. The number of such manuals will be determined by the size and complexity of the organization. In a small company it may be sufficient to have one manual containing all the procedures for individual key tasks, which could be called the procedures manual. This manual contains all the procedures, both high-level procedures relating to the operation of the quality management system itself and detailed procedures for operational tasks. For convenience it could be divided into sections that suit the nature of the operation. See Help document 4.2–6 for an example of what such a manual might contain.

In a large manufacturing operation, on the other hand, there might be ten or more operational manuals, identified on the basis of the various functions or departments. Each manual would contain the procedures specific to the department concerned. In addition, there will still be some procedures that apply throughout the organization, for example, control of documentation, and procedures that

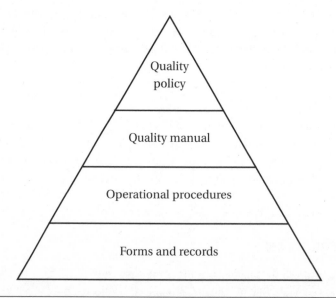

Figure II.1   The quality system documentation can be regarded as a hierarchy. The structure is founded on the routine activities that are captured in the records, but everything is determined at the highest level by the quality policy.

involve a number of different functions. It may, therefore, be convenient to have a general management procedures manual containing such procedures, and this manual would be copied to all departments. The actual manner in which the documentation is structured and circulated is entirely at the discretion of the company, and should be chosen on the basis of effectiveness and convenience. In all cases the circulation of documents should be restricted to those who need them, to prevent excessive paperwork.

The bottom level of the documentation hierarchy contains the working forms and record sheets that are used to capture the history of routine events and activities. Examples are job sheets, service records, material usage records, training records, refrigeration temperature check records and goods inwards inspection sheets.

No two systems are identical, and only you can decide on the best one for you. The best system for you is the one that works most effectively and comfortably for you. If it works well for you, then it is correct for you.

MANAGEMENT STRUCTURE

The structure of the quality management system depends largely on the management structure in the organization. In the traditional management structure there are individual managers for each major division of responsibilities. QM-11 of the sample quality manual (see p. 124) shows the typical titles. Each such department will probably have its own manual. In smaller companies, however, such titles and division of responsibilities may not make sense. There is no requirement to have any of the functions listed. In most very small companies (and some very large companies) there will not even be a quality manager. What is important is that you have identified the critical tasks that must be carried out in order to manage quality effectively, and have assigned those tasks to individuals. It does not matter what titles those individuals have or how the tasks are shared out. The smaller the organization the fewer titles there will be and the simpler the organization chart will look.

DETERMINE THE SCOPE OF THE SYSTEM

The system you set up will depend entirely on your particular circumstances – the number of employees, whether family owned or part of a large multinational enterprise, whether public or private, the culture within the organization, the physical size of the premises and such like.

ISO 9001 allows you to define the scope of your system. Requirements that do not apply to your operation, that is, those that are not appropriate or cannot be applied, do not need to be addressed in your system. However, there are two conditions that apply to this:

- You may not exclude any requirement if its exclusion affects your ability to supply a quality service or product.
- You may only exclude requirements given in section 7 of the standard.

For example, the requirements for calibration of equipment could be ignored in the case of an accountancy company. But it is not permissible to exclude something simply because you think it is too much trouble! In the case of an organization that subcontracts the manufacture of a finished product or the delivery of a service, the standard specifically states that such subcontracted operations must be controlled, and the controls must be identified within the quality management system.

DOCUMENT WHAT YOU DO CURRENTLY

Existing methods need to be documented in the form of procedures. There are two principal reasons why this should be done. First, there may be a number of different ways in which a task can be performed. If one of these ways is better than the others in terms of the likely effect on customer satisfaction, then this should be defined as the way in which the task must be done, so that everybody uses this method. Until such time as somebody comes up with an improvement, this is the way that the task is to be done. This will ensure a consistency to the output. The concept of consistency is sometimes regarded negatively, and is considered to limit the urge to improve. It is better to think of consistency as setting the minimum level of acceptability, and improvement as the raising of this minimum level. Second, documented procedures can be invaluable as a training aid to supplement the instruction given. This is particularly useful in the case of induction of new employees.

If you are running a successful business, you are probably doing most things right. So, start by documenting your existing procedures and methods, and then see what needs to be changed. Use your own experts, namely the people who actually perform the tasks. Do not make the mistake of getting somebody, either internal or external, to write the procedure that you would *like* to operate. Do not change your existing method unless there is clearly a problem with it, either because it is not effective, or because it does not comply with the standard. Leave *improvements* until later.

There is no reason why documenting a procedure should result in inflexibility or stunt creativity. Proper wording of the procedure will allow you to maintain the level of control that you define as desirable or necessary, and at the same time allow the operator of the procedure to use whatever discretion is appropriate in the circumstances. For example, it may be possible to allow a person to experiment outside the scope of a procedure, but the conditions for doing this would need to be specified. Of course, this cannot be done in isolation from other aspects of the system, and would impact on such elements as responsibilities and authority, training and competence, risk assessment and record-keeping.

Think of the documented procedures not as a method externally imposed for control purposes, but as the current recommendations of the person carrying out the task on how best to do it. ISO 9001 only requires those procedures that are necessary for the effective operation and control of the processes. Furthermore, the amount of detail that is appropriate in the procedure will depend on the complexity of the task, the methods used, and the skills and training needed by personnel. In other words, you only have to have a written procedure *where it is necessary*.

Do not be discouraged when you see the number of Help documents in this book. You may think that you will not have time to do any real work if you are expected to juggle all of those in the air at the same time. You do not! I always remind people that the procedures are not like a pet dog, which has to be fed and exercised every day. In general, once a procedure has been written it will not need any attention for a considerable time and, indeed, may never need changing. From an administrative point of view the really hard work will have been done when the documents have been written, approved and put into use. Thereafter, the task will be to implement what you have written down.

For that reason, it is essential that you should only write down in your procedures what you are prepared to do. If you write it down, then you have to do it! Do not include aspirations posing as facts. The only place where you are allowed aspirations is in your objectives, and even then the aspiration should be achievable, with some effort.

The Help documents at the back of the book will give you ideas on how to implement the various ISO 9000 initiatives, but the actual procedures and rules you end up with must reflect the reality for you, irrespective of what the examples show.

You have to put in the effort yourself into setting up the system. There is no easy way, no instant solution. You may be tempted to purchase a ready-made system, where you fill in the blanks, or to copy somebody else's system. While these may seem to be cost-effective options you will pay many times over later on. Such a system can *never* be fully right for you!

INTEGRATE YOUR ACTIVITIES

There is a movement nowadays towards integration of the various management systems within the organization. The three principal areas involved here are Quality, Environment, and Occupational Health and Safety (OHS). The first two are largely discretional, whereas the third is determined by law. The quality management system, enshrined in the ISO 9000 series, was the first to be adopted widely by companies. The second to become widely used was the environmental management system, with its separate ISO standards, the ISO 14000 series. In parallel with this the European Union operates the Eco-Management and Audit Scheme (EMAS). More recently has come the OHS management system, though some of the more progressive companies have been actively managing OHS for many years. In the UK this first appeared as BS8800, and more recently as a certifiable specification OHSAS 18001.

Looking at these three management systems more closely it can be seen that they are essentially three different manifestations of a single overall requirement. This requirement can be stated simply as the need to define, control and improve a particular aspect of the organization's operation – customer satisfaction, impact on the environment, or the health and safety of the organization's employees and others who come into contact with it.

Looking at it more closely, we see that each of the three addresses the following core issues:

- definition of the requirements to be met (for example, customer satisfaction (Quality), elimination of hazards to health and safety (OHS) and minimal impact on the external environment (Environment));
- definition of what constitutes nonconformity (for example, product rejection (Quality), personal injury accident (OHS) or uncontrolled discharge of harmful effluent to the external environment (Environment));
- control of critical information;
- documenting the methods of keeping control;
- training of personnel;
- control of inputs to the operation;
- control of processes;
- monitoring of activities and results;
- control of outputs from the operation;
- dealing with nonconformities;
- implementation of corrective action;
- identification of preventive action;
- auditing of the system;
- review of the system; and
- improvement.

Consequently, it makes sense to have a single basic system with common methods of dealing with the generic problems that arise. This can be achieved in several ways. At one end of the integration spectrum there is the single totally integrated system, in which every (written) procedure addresses quality, environmental concerns and health and safety. At the other end you could have separate documented systems for the three aspects but a single approach to managing all the processes and tasks involved. In this case the individual systems, though separate, are fully compatible, and ideally have a recognizably related structure. For integration the important thing is to have a single company-wide approach to managing the different aspects, understood and implemented by all employees.

TRY IT OUT

As you progress through the process of formalizing your activities you should start to implement them immediately. Do not wait until everything is ready. I have seen companies experience difficulty through waiting until everything is ready before 'launching' the ISO 9000 system. Sometimes this can indicate a certain reluctance to actually face the difficulties that may arise in the early stages.

Your management system must become a dynamic entity, one that works effectively to help you achieve your objectives, both your overall company objectives and those at every level in the organization. You must, therefore, get used to the idea of making changes to suit changing circumstances. You must facilitate the introduction of necessary changes, but without losing control. This is a very fine balance. Make it too difficult to introduce changes to the system and you will find that the changes are made anyway, but unofficially, and without control. On the other hand, if it is too easy changes will be made without adequate consultation and deliberation.

Your system should deliver benefits. If after serious and informed deliberation you decide that a particular initiative is not beneficial, then it is sensible to drop it altogether, or amend the way in which you implement it. Remember that whatever you do should deliver benefits. If it does not work change it. Keep working on it until you find a practical way that suits your circumstances.

AUDIT THE SYSTEM INTERNALLY

The typical set-up period for a reasonably complex ISO 9000 system is about 12 months, though much depends on the resources that you can deploy in the development stage. When your system (or a substantial part of it, even) has been running for a period of about three months you should consider carrying out an audit. You will have to do this before certification anyway, but doing it at this point can help you to identify any remaining gaps. Review the audit findings and try to find the most practical way of resolving the problems.

REVIEW THE SYSTEM

It is a requirement of ISO 9001 that your management team should carry out a review of the system to see how effective it is in achieving the objectives set by the organization. This makes sense, considering the resources you have invested in setting up this system – management time, finance, training and perhaps even lost production time. So, you need to know if it is delivering the benefits promised or expected. If the review identifies deficiencies in the system you must take the necessary action to correct the problems. Later, the review will have improvement as its main objective, but in the early stages you will be satisfied if it highlights gaps or defects.

HAVE A PRE-ASSESSMENT AUDIT CARRIED OUT

When you believe that you are complying completely or substantially with the requirements of ISO 9001 you may consider it useful to engage an external auditor to carry out a pre-assessment *consultancy* audit. There is one significant difference between this audit and the later certification audit. For the pre-assessment audit you should be as open as possible with the auditor, and facilitate him or her in finding all significant non-compliances. In this case the auditor is working for you, and you should make the best use you can of the audit. Make sure your personnel understand in what way each non-compliance identified contravenes the standard. After the audit you may be able to obtain some suggestions for corrective action from the auditor, though this is not normally part of the auditor's brief. It is then for you to decide how best to correct the non-compliance. You should have an arrangement with the auditor whereby he or she will review your corrective action afterwards and confirm if it solves the problem.

SELECT A CERTIFICATION COMPANY

ISO 9000 certification is controlled in each country by a government-sponsored agency. In the UK this is the United Kingdom Accreditation Service (UKAS), which was formed by the amalgamation of the National Accreditation Council for Certification Bodies (NACCB) and the National Measurement and Accreditation Service (NAMAS). In the USA it is the Registrar Accreditation Board (RAB). These are the agencies that monitor the certification companies, also called registrars, working in the ISO 9000 and other fields. An accredited certification company must comply with certain specified requirements in exactly the same way that an individual company has to comply with ISO 9001 requirements in order to achieve certification. By selecting a certification company that has accreditation from an agency such as UKAS you can be reasonably sure that it will act responsibly and fairly. It also ensures that the certification company has the competence to carry out audits in your sector.

However, in order to achieve UKAS accreditation a certification company must first show a track record of certification. That means it must find a number of client companies who are satisfied to accept non-accredited certification. Everybody has to start somewhere! Before selecting your certification company you must decide how important accreditation is for you – and for your customers!

Whether the certification company you select is accredited or not you should make sure that it will give you the quality of service you require. You should interview the prospective certifiers and make sure that you can work with them. In particular, you need to know how they approach the auditing process:

- Which companies in your sector have they audited previously?
- What do they regard as a major non-compliance?
- What level of detail do they expect in your written procedures?
- Will they accept corrections to non-compliances that are made during the audit?
- What is their appeals procedure?
- How often will they carry out surveillance audits?

Remember that you will probably be dealing with these people for a number of years, so it pays to select a certification company with which you can develop a long-term relationship.

THE CERTIFICATION AUDIT

When the system has been operating for about four to six months you might consider yourself ready for the certification audit. This period is necessary in order to demonstrate that you have a practical system that you can operate over a long period. If you have only been operating the system for a short period an auditor might think it possible that you are making a huge effort to keep the system running and that you would not be able to maintain that effort in the long term. The actual period will depend on the circumstances. Many companies have been keeping the majority of the necessary records for much longer than a few months, for example, production records, product testing and release records and training records. What may have been missing are records for activities such as management review, supplier review and internal audits. In this case one could argue that a system complying with most of the requirements of ISO 9001 had actually been operating for a long time. It is quite acceptable to have records dating from earlier than the dates on the procedures. Thus, the manuals might date from only a few weeks before the audit, but if there were adequate records dating back a number of months, that should be quite satisfactory.

The certification audit itself is dealt with in more detail in Chapter III.

MAINTAINING THE SYSTEM

Once the initial certification audit is over there is a great temptation to relax in a haze of self-congratulation. If this lasts too long you may find that the implementation of the system has slipped – records not completed, training or induction not carried out in all cases, documents changed without going through the correct procedure etc. If this happens it will take an effort to bring it back under control. But, more importantly, the message will have gone out that ISO 9000 is not so important after all, and you will have established the classic cycle of Audit–Relax–Panic–Audit, so familiar in many companies.

Once the initial audit is out of the way you simply have to continue to follow procedures and routinely implement the controls. Nothing will change until you identify some areas for improvement. If you have set up a system that is practical and beneficial, you should be able to maintain it without too much pain. If you find that the pain is not worth the benefit, you have probably got the wrong system for your circumstances and must set about correcting the situation.

Although the certified system is stable and will not change much in the short term, it is not fixed for ever and must evolve with the organization. If it does not change with changing circumstances, it will in time come to act as a brake on progress. Circumstances do change, and you should review your system regularly against the broader guidance given in ISO 9004 to see if there are useful elements that are not currently part of your system.

Finally, remember that the system should be working for you – not the other way round!

CHAPTER III

The certification audit

The first certification audit can be one of the most stressful experiences in a quality manager's career. Although the project may have been a team effort and everybody will take credit if it goes well, should it go badly it is the quality manager who will be blamed. It is an occupational hazard of the job. However, if everybody has put the required effort into the project, and the advice taken in the design stage has been good there should be no serious problems. This chapter contains some advice on how to make the experience easier for everybody concerned.

PREPARATION FOR THE AUDIT

The final days before the audit should be devoted to polishing up the system. If you find yourself printing out the manuals for the first time, as I have seen several times, then you are not ready for audit. If the procedures and manuals are as new as that, people will not be familiar with them and this will be obvious during the audit.

Hold a briefing meeting for key people a couple of days before the audit. Any person who holds a manual of procedures should know thoroughly his or her manual. Each individual should know where the procedures or manual relevant to him or her are physically located, and check that they are actually there.

Tour the entire site. Check for things that may have been overlooked, such as old documents that pre-dated the ISO 9000 system, uncontrolled copies from the development phase of ISO 9000, unlabelled materials and unacceptable physical conditions. Check that all manuals are in place.

Check that all records are available and can be accessed within about ten minutes if requested during the audit. This is particularly relevant if records are locked away or stored in another location.

Each manual 'owner', that is, the person responsible for the *content* of a manual, should check each page in his or her manual to make sure that it is signed as required by the document control procedure. In the case of physical stock, check all materials as far as practicable to ensure that everything is labelled as it should be. Take particular note of any non-conforming materials and make sure that all relevant documentation is available and complete. I never complete an audit without selecting some non-conforming material and tracing its history back through the process. If there is any weakness in the system it is most likely to show up in the case of non-conforming product.

Each manager and supervisor should brief his or her team on what to expect during the audit and how to cope with it.

Be familiar with the standard, and understand the underlying concepts and principles.

If, during the course of the final preparation for the audit you discover something that needs to be corrected but there is insufficient time, record the fact on a nonconformity report and be ready to present that if the issue arises during the audit. In that way you can demonstrate that you had found the problem before the auditor did. After all, one purpose of the quality management system, surely, is to reveal shortcomings and facilitate their elimination. One difference between quality companies and non-quality companies is not that one makes mistakes and the other does not, but in the way the two react to the mistakes. Of course, if the nonconformity discovered represents a serious non-compliance with an ISO 9001 requirement you cannot expect to get away with it simply by having recorded the fact that you had discovered it.

Realize that the certification company actually wants you to pass the audit, as you will then be a client and a source of income to the certifier. That does not mean that they will be in any way lenient, but it does mean that they are not leaning the other way, contrary to what you might think.

You could fail the audit even before the audit starts. Auditors are only human and react to what they see like anybody else, even though they are trying to be objective. So, for example, if the exterior of a food premises is badly kept or dirty, the auditor may wonder how the company could be committed to producing a safe product and whether the company could implement process control properly. If a solicitor's office is full of mountains of paper with no apparent order the auditor may form an immediate subconscious opinion that the place is not organized. This subconscious opinion may manifest itself in the form of a strictness on the part of the auditor that might not otherwise be there.

THE AUDIT TEAM

The audit is usually carried out by a team of two or more auditors. Only in very small companies is a single auditor able to carry out the full audit in a reasonable time that does not cause intolerable inconvenience to the company. One of the auditors will lead the team and make the final decision on the audit outcome. While the audit is essentially non-technical and concerns itself with the management of quality, the team will usually contain one person who is familiar with the technicalities of your operation.

THE AUDIT

The purpose of the audit is to establish whether the quality management system meets all applicable requirements of ISO 9001. That implies that the system includes the appropriate documented procedures and that the necessary activities are being carried out routinely. The main thrust of an audit is, therefore, to look at the documented procedures that describe what is to be done, and then to check the records and other available evidence to see if this has actually been done.

If a procedure is not being followed according to the method documented, a non-compliance will be recorded. That is not unreasonable, since the procedures represent *your* definition of the correct way to do things. If something is prescribed in a procedure it must be something that *you* consider important for quality. That consideration should be a great incentive to people writing procedures to keep these short and only include what is really important for quality. The more unnecessary detail you include, the higher the risk that somebody will be found not following a procedure.

The audit normally lasts from one to three days, depending on the size and complexity of the operation. That is really a very short time in which to know everything about the way the company operates. Since the auditors can only directly examine what is actually happening on the day of the audit, when everybody is on their best behaviour, records assume a supreme importance. It is only by looking at records that the auditor can form an opinion about how the company operates at other times.

The programme for the typical audit is as follows:

1 Opening meeting with the management team to explain the audit procedure and schedule.
2 Brief tour of the site.
3 Meeting with the chief executive or the most senior manager on site.

4 Brief preliminary review of the various operational manuals.
5 Detailed interviews with relevant personnel. Inspection of relevant manuals, procedures, drawings, records, physical conditions, and stored materials and products.
6 Private meeting of the audit team to write the audit report.
7 Closing meeting with management team to discuss the results of the audit and present the audit report.

AUDIT GUIDES

You will be expected to provide a guide to accompany each auditor. The guides should know the general features of the quality management system and, in particular, should know where to find information. They do not themselves need to know all the details of every procedure, since the personnel dealing with the activities being audited will know those details.

The guide should act as a 'fixer', taking notes of any non-compliances that arise and comments made by the auditor, seeking clarification from the auditor, alerting the manager who is co-ordinating the audit at the earliest opportunity in case the problem can be resolved immediately, and generally acting as a communications link between the auditors and the rest of the management team.

MEETING WITH CHIEF EXECUTIVE OR MOST SENIOR MANAGER

The purpose of this meeting is for the auditor to get a sense of how committed the senior manager is to quality. The auditor will want to assess how this manager knows what the current level of quality is. For example, what sort of formal reports on quality does the manager receive routinely? Is he or she familiar with the current situation regarding complaints and the level of reject product? What sort of meetings are held covering quality? Does this manager actively support quality initiatives taken by subordinate managers? How does he or she approach the provision of resources necessary for quality? In other words, is quality being led from the top of the organization?

COPING WITH THE AUDIT

1 To the auditor this is just another day's work. You can help yourself by making it as easy as possible for him or her to carry out the audit. You already know what questions you will be asked, since the audit is based strictly on the ISO 9001 standard, so be prepared with the answers. It is very irritating to an auditor when the auditee is taken by surprise to be asked for something that is clearly demanded by the standard. One has to wonder if the person has read the standard.
2 Do not try to waste time with long lunches, or to distract the auditor with promotional films or detours to look at fancy new equipment. The auditor will know what you are trying to do, and will merely be irritated by your action. This is not in your interest!
3 Answer the auditor's questions fully, but do not volunteer unnecessary or irrelevant information. It is a popular ploy of auditors to fall silent at the end of an explanation from the auditee. The latter then feels that the answer has been inadequate and gives more and more detail, often saying more than he or she intended, and leading the auditor down a path that might be better left unexplored! Note that this is where the certification audit differs from the pre-assessment consultancy audit.
4 If the auditor asks for a particular document that is not available at that moment, but you agree to retrieve it and present it later in the audit, the auditor may not ask for it a second time. Do not then assume that the auditor has forgotten. If you do not present the document this may appear in the final audit report as a non-compliance – the document was 'not available'.

5 Do not argue with the auditor. You can never win an argument with an auditor! There is an adage that says 'Arguing with an auditor is like wrestling in mud with a pig; after a while you realize that the pig is the only one enjoying it!'. On no account should you lose your temper or act unprofessionally in any way with the auditor.

6 If a non-compliance is found during the audit it may be possible to correct it on the spot. For example, if the auditor finds that a particular responsibility should have been documented you should amend the relevant document before the audit is finished and present it to the auditor. *However, make sure that you carry out the amendment according to the document control procedure!* The auditor may or may not accept it, depending on the policy of the certification company in question.

7 Do not try to defend the indefensible. If the auditor finds an undoubted non-compliance you must show that you realize the significance of it. If you try to argue that it is not a problem, you may be simply showing that you do not know or understand the requirement of the standard or the principles on which it is based. It would be much better to show that you realize the significance of it and commit yourself enthusiastically to correcting the problem.

8 Be alert for the auditor's 'hobby horse'. Many auditors have a particular subject that they consider to be more important than the others, and this usually reflects a personal interest, perhaps related to the auditor's own previous career. For example, some auditors from an engineering background may be very strict on calibration, and may gloss over other aspects provided you have met the minimum requirements. When you sense that the auditor has reached a topic of personal interest to him or her you simply have to try to present as much information as will demonstrate that you have done at least the minimum required by the standard.

9 Do not try to pull rank on the auditor. You may be an important person in your own organization, but the auditor will not be impressed by a show of authority on your part. You have to decide what you want – a successful outcome to the audit or to demonstrate your own importance.

10 Do not be flippant with the auditor. The auditor is taking the audit seriously, and expects you to do the same.

THE CLOSING MEETING AND AUDIT REPORT

The closing meeting is the point at which you discover your fate. The audit team presents its findings and lists the non-compliances found. The overall result of the audit may be delivered before or after the non-compliances are presented.

During the closing meeting you may find yourself promising to do anything in order to pass the audit. Later, you may realize, too late, that the corrective action you promised to implement is not practical. You then have the situation that your quality management system is forcing you to do something that is not useful. This should never happen. Remember, the system should work for you, not the other way around!

If the auditor asks you to implement something that seems to you to be impractical or unnecessary when you are satisfied that your procedures give you the appropriate level of control for your circumstances, choose your words carefully. Instead of saying that it is ridiculous ask the auditor to explain why it should be necessary. With that explanation you may be able to propose an alternative course of action that will give an equivalent control in a more practical way.

NON-COMPLIANCES

The audit report classifies non-compliances into major and minor categories. A major non-compliance is a failure to control a significant aspect of the requirements. For example:

- a number of uncontrolled copies of quality system documents would indicate that there was a general problem with document control;
- a person carrying out a critical task with no training, experience or qualification for the task;
- absence of a specification for a product where this was considered essential;
- no management representative appointed;
- failure to implement a specified testing plan; and
- failure to measure customer satisfaction in some way.

Minor non-compliances are less serious breaches of ISO 9001 requirements. For example:

- a single instance of a document with no signature, but otherwise document control in order;
- absence of a training record for one individual, which did not seriously jeopardize quality, all other training records being satisfactory; and
- failure to record an instance of corrective action.

In addition to non-compliances, there may be some 'observations'. Perhaps there is no definite breach of an ISO 9001 requirement, but there is some question mark over the situation. For example, there may be some doubt about the effectiveness of a testing plan, or the company may need to gather more information about something before the full implications of the situation are known. The company is usually expected to make a written reply to observations, providing further information or explanation as to why the organization considers that the situation is satisfactory.

THE AUDIT OUTCOME

The auditor will state at the closing meeting what the outcome of the audit is. The auditor does not have the authority to award certification but only makes a recommendation to the awards board of the certification company. You will be told what recommendation the auditor intends to make. Several different overall outcomes are possible from the audit. All involve the correction of any non-compliances listed in the report, whether major or minor. The possible outcomes are:

1 Full compliance. Certification will be recommended.
2 One or a few minor non-compliances. Certification will be recommended, subject to receiving a written undertaking to correct the non-compliances. These will be audited at the first surveillance audit. See below.
3 One or a few major non-compliances. Certification will not be recommended until these are corrected. Depending on the nature of the non-compliances the auditor may be satisfied with a written confirmation with supporting documentary evidence within a short period that they have been corrected. Often, however, an audit of the corrective action is required.
4 A significant number of major non-compliances. Certification is refused outright on the basis that the system is seriously deficient. A full re-audit is demanded. This is disastrous, and will involve major overhaul of the system.

The actual arrangements and conditions that apply vary between certification companies.
 It should be noted that a sufficient number of minor non-compliances can justify overall failure,

since it can indicate a general inadequacy of the system, and therefore call into question its capability to manage quality effectively.

SURVEILLANCE AUDITS

From time to time you will be subjected to brief inspections from the auditor to confirm that you continue to comply with ISO 9001 requirements. This usually lasts not longer than one day, and in small companies may only be half a day. These audits address selected parts of the system and aim to cover the entire system over two or three years.

As an alternative to periodic surveillance audits some certification companies carry out a complete re-audit after three years. Most certified companies prefer to have the more frequent surveillance audits which are less daunting, and have the benefit of focusing people's attention on ISO 9001 for a period leading up to the time they are expected.

CHAPTER IV

A few popular ISO 9001 myths

Over the years many myths have grown up around ISO 9000. Here are just a few.

ISO 9000

1 *ISO 9000 allows you to produce rubbish, so long as you have a procedure for it and you keep records.* This is usually said by people who have decided that they don't like ISO 9000 for some other reason. Consider the facts: ISO 9001 has always required you to take corrective action to prevent a recurrence of non-conforming product. How can that square with the myth? You cannot comply with ISO 9001 requirements and continue to produce rubbish. If by 'rubbish' is meant something which is less than superlative in its design or finish, then this is to confuse quality and excellence. Not everybody needs, or can afford, the top-of-the-range item. Provided a product meets the customer's expectations it is not rubbish. Finally, ISO 9001 demands continual improvement.

2 *ISO 9000 is nothing but bureaucracy and unnecessary paperwork.* For some companies this is actually true. The blame for this state of affairs, however, rests not with the standard, but with some consultants who did not fully understand ISO 9000. It was never the intention of the authors of ISO 9000 that companies should drown in a sea of paper. Over the years people were encouraged by consultants to think that written procedures were required for everything (see Documentation, below). If a consultant is not sure of the position, the safest thing to do is to get the client to produce a procedure. That way, the consultant cannot be blamed for non-compliance over absence of a written procedure. A consultant needs to be sure of his or her ground before saying to a client that something is not necessary. Remember, 'anybody can design a structure that is strong enough; only an expert can design a structure that is just strong enough'. Hence, it is necessary to select a consultant carefully.

3 *ISO 9000 stifles creativity. It does not allow any flexibility.* There is no reason why creativity should be curtailed. Creativity can easily be built into the system. This objection is often raised by people who do not like to have to work in a disciplined manner and simply prefer to be disorganized. There is nothing to prevent you giving complete discretion to somebody if they are qualified to handle such flexibility. To comply with ISO 9000 you would ask them to record what they had done and to evaluate it properly, to communicate effectively with the relevant people, and so on. That is not curtailing their creativity in any way, but it is forcing them to be organized in their creativity. Equally, it is quite acceptable to allow managers the authority to take such action as is necessary to assure customer satisfaction, even if that action is totally contrary to procedures! They would still have to record what they did, and to justify it afterwards. Such incidents could well result in the procedures being changed to address those circumstances in the future.

4 *ISO 9000 only works for a strictly hierarchical management structure, and is unsuited for situations where people work in teams.* There has never been anything in ISO 9000 that prescribes how the management of the organization should be structured. The only specific function mentioned is that of management representative, and the duties of that function are not worded in a way that suggests hierarchy. There are numerous references to 'top management', meaning the team of

senior managers who take executive decisions, but this team will exist in all companies, however the overall management is structured.

All of the controls required or recommended in ISO 9001 and ISO 9004 can operate just as beneficially for an individual team or cell as for the organization overall (see page 7).

INTERNAL AUDIT

1 *A corrective action request (CAR) must be raised for every internal audit non-compliance.* There is no mention of a corrective action request in ISO 9001. In many respects the idea that corrective action must be requested is not in keeping with the spirit of corrective action. It is more sensible to use a nonconformity report, where the details of the nonconformity and the corrective action are captured. Indeed, it is quite acceptable to record the nonconformity and the subsequent corrective action in a diary rather than to use a preprinted form. The only requirements are that there should be procedures for nonconformity and corrective action and that appropriate records are kept to be able to demonstrate that you took corrective action.

2 *Individual audit non-compliances must be signed off by the auditee.* This is not in the least important. What matters is that the problems are recorded, and effective and permanent corrective action taken.

TRAINING

1 *Copies of all qualifications, degrees, diplomas and certificates must be on file.* This is nonsense. ISO 9000 places great emphasis on training and the need to keep people's skills up to date. In many cases a qualification that a person received ten years ago is not relevant or necessary for the job they are doing now. Only in special cases, such as a surveyor or engineer in a construction company, might this be necessary. Much more important is the recent training that a person has received for the tasks currently being done. It is this training that is important, and this must be recorded.

2 *Trainees must sign off the training record.* It is certainly preferable to have the trainee's signature. However, sometimes the trainee is unwilling to sign, for whatever reason. In that case the signature of the person's manager or the trainer is sufficient evidence that the training was provided.

3 *Internal auditors must attend an accredited auditor training course.* The requirement of ISO 9001 is that auditors are trained. That means that evidence can be produced that they have been trained and that the training was adequate. As with all training the proof of adequacy is in the evaluation of the trainee's work afterwards. If the auditors can be shown to be able to carry out an effective audit, then the adequacy of the training is proven. It is the quality of the auditing that is the objective, not the auditor training.

DOCUMENTATION

1 *There must be detailed procedures for all quality related tasks.* There are only six places where ISO 9001 calls for documented procedures. In all other cases procedures are only required where the absence of a procedure would jeopardize the quality of the output or customer satisfaction. Whether a procedure is needed depends on the circumstances, such as the level of supervision, the experience and training of the people concerned and the complexity of the task. Of course, there is no way that anybody would be able to get away with only six procedures, but it does demonstrate

the falsity of the above premise. The members of the working group that produced the ISO 9001 standard were adamant that the 2000 version would place less emphasis on documented procedures in order to counteract some of the misconceptions that had arisen in this regard.

2 *All documents must have the same titles as mentioned in the standard.* You must be able to produce the documentation that will answer the auditor's questions. The title you put on those documents is of no importance.

3 *Controlled documents must have revision numbers.* Many people think the 'revision status' means 'revision number'. A document must contain sufficient information to enable the reader to identify if it is the current version. That is what 'revision status' means. This may be done quite satisfactorily using the revision date alone. This is covered in detail later in the book.

4 *You must keep a file showing the revision history of all controlled documents, including reasons for changes, approval of changes, etc.* Sometimes this file is attached to the document and is many times thicker than the document itself! In fact, there is no requirement in ISO 9001 to maintain such a file. There is no requirement to maintain *any* records in relation to ISO 9001 documentation. You simply need to have a procedure that addresses the defined requirements and be able to demonstrate that you have followed that procedure. That means having all documents adequately identified and not having any obsolete documents in circulation. Of course, there are reasons why it can be useful or necessary to maintain records of document revision, and most organizations do maintain such records. But they can be very brief. A single spreadsheet alone can store all the revision history that may be needed.

PURCHASING

1 *Suppliers of critical items must be audited.* There are many ways in which you can assess a supplier without actually visiting them. Of course, if auditing is a practical option then it should be seriously considered. This is covered in detail later in the book.

2 *You must test for everything on the purchasing specification.* A simple example illustrates how this cannot be true. A purchasing specification will often state that the material must comply with all relevant statutory requirements. In most cases it would simply be impossible for the purchaser to test for everything covered by all items of legislation. In such situations a certificate of conformance or an affirmation by the supplier that the material conforms to requirements is usually quite sufficient.

3 *You cannot purchase from a supplier not on the approved suppliers list.* Suppose your three approved suppliers for a particular material are, respectively, shut by a labour dispute, shut for their annual summer holidays and experiencing technical difficulties. Does ISO 9001 require you to cease operations until one of your approved suppliers comes back on stream? Absolutely not. In fact ISO 9001 does not state anywhere that you have to purchase from approved suppliers. It states that you must control your purchasing process, and that you must evaluate and select suppliers based on their ability to supply quality product. You probably will not approve a supplier until you have purchased at least one order to assess the material. How can you do that if you are forbidden to purchase from a non-approved supplier!

4 *A supplier's ISO 9001 certification is sufficient evidence of capability to supply a quality material.* Not necessarily. Certification merely demonstrates that the supplier has an effective quality management system in place. There may be any number of technical problems that can arise in producing a material to your specification, and the supplier may or may not be able to overcome these difficulties. These issues would all have to be resolved before you could be fully satisfied.

Furthermore, it is an unfortunate fact that there are rogue certification companies who issue certificates to companies that do not merit them, and you need to be aware of who the reputable certification companies are.

HEALTH AND SAFETY

1 *Occupational health and safety must be addressed.* There are no requirements relating to health and safety in ISO 9001. The only situation in which health and safety aspects would be relevant is where it might affect quality. For example, a person working in stressful conditions or operating a dangerous machine without adequate guarding could hardly be expected to produce a quality output from his or her work. This would be regarded by ISO 9001 as a quality issue, and therefore within its scope.

COMPLIANCE WITH GENERAL LAW

1 *Any instance of non-compliance with the law justifies refusal of certification.* There are probably very few companies in the entire world that can truly claim to comply with every item of law, and very few companies would qualify for ISO 9001 certification if this approach were adopted. For example, if the road tax on a vehicle has expired this is not a non-compliance of ISO 9001 requirements on the basis that legal obligations in relation to transport of product have not been adequately addressed (see page 61).

INTEGRATED MANAGEMENT SYSTEMS

1 *If you have integrated other aspects of management, such as health and safety, into the quality system documentation, non-compliance on these aspects can be the cause of refusal of certification.* Refusal of certification can only be on the basis of ISO 9001 non-compliance. If you have incorporated other aspects of your company activities into your quality documentation, and you are not yet fully compliant on those aspects, this is not, in itself, sufficient reason to fail an audit for ISO 9001 certification. Of course, you can make the situation easier by highlighting those non-quality aspects in the documentation and, in effect, warn off the auditor by appropriate statements in the quality manual.

CALIBRATION

1 *All instruments used for making a measurement of the process performance must be calibrated.* Only those instruments that are used to make a decision on product or service quality, *without any other corroborating evidence*, need to be calibrated. In other words, you must be relying *totally* on this instrument for the decision on whether quality requirements have been met. It follows that in the event of finding an instrument out of calibration you may be faced with a product recall situation. This thought should help clarify the situation. If you take too broad a view on what instruments need calibration you will end up having to consider product recall for trivial measurement inaccuracies. This subject is covered in detail later under clause 7.6 (see page 74).

2 *All instruments must be labelled with their calibration status.* This is the most common approach. However, there are other options, such as maintaining a calibration log near the instrument readily available to users of the instrument.

FINANCE

1 *Finance is/is not covered in ISO 9001.* Whether an auditor has a right to look at financial activities depends on the circumstances, and how you define quality and customer satisfaction in your situation. What ISO 9001 does not look at is financial performance, and therefore an auditor would have no right to see project costings, customer invoices and such like. What could be relevant are controls for preventing errors in accounts documents going out to the customer, since these could be thought of as affecting the customer's perception of the organization's quality. However, as a general rule, these elements can usually be omitted from the ISO 9001 system, since they would not normally affect the customer's satisfaction with the product or service supplied. Note, however, that finance is addressed in ISO 9004.

Commentary on the ISO 9001 and ISO 9004 standards

INTRODUCTION TO PART B

This part of the book consists of a detailed commentary on the clauses of the two standards. It is structured to the ISO 9004 standard, since that is broader than ISO 9001, and all quality management systems should contain at least some of the supplementary initiatives covered in ISO 9004 but not required by ISO 9001. You will note that in some cases there are no requirements in ISO 9001 corresponding to clauses of ISO 9004. For example, 6.5 Information, 6.6 Suppliers and partnerships, 6.7 Natural resources and 6.8 Financial resources appear only in ISO 9004.

Where the same subject is covered in both standards the authors of the standards have attempted to align them as far as possible. In all cases this is so down to the first decimal clause. However, there are some instances where the clause numbering in the two standards differs at the next level down. For example, Internal audit appears in 8.2.1.3 in ISO 9004, but in 8.2.2 in ISO 9001.

There are no specific initiatives that need to be addressed in sections 1, 2 or 3 of either standard. The issue of the scope of the system is dealt with in clause 1.2 of ISO 9001, but this has been addressed already on page 11.

Each chapter begins with the list of headings from both ISO 9001 and ISO 9004. The headings are only given to the third level. In the case of ISO 9004 clauses 6.2.2, 7.1.3 and 8.2.1 go to a fourth level, but these are not listed at the start of the relevant chapters.

Throughout the text there are references to 'Help documents'. These documents are found at the back of the book and are arranged according to the section of the standard to which they principally apply.

The detailed requirements of ISO 9001 are not reproduced in the book, and the reader should obtain a copy of the standard and read it in conjunction with the book.

> **Specific products or industry sectors may have particular legal requirements. These will supersede anything suggested in this book. For example, retention times for particular records may be specified in law.**

CHAPTER V

The standards: Section 4
The quality management system

ISO 9004
4.1 Managing systems and processes
4.2 Documentation

4.3 Use of quality management principles

ISO 9001
4.1 General requirements
4.2 Documentation requirements
  4.2.1 General
  4.2.2 Quality manual
  4.2.3 Control of documents
  4.2.4 Control of records

MANAGING SYSTEMS AND PROCESSES (4.1)

In the past quality management systems tended to be based firmly on ISO 9001, since certification was often the primary or even the sole objective of the ISO 9000 quality system. This sometimes resulted in a set of ad hoc initiatives that did not form part of any recognizable whole. Thus, an organization may have carried out some training activity, some inspection and some purchasing controls, but often there was no sense that they formed part of an overall co-ordinated effort. Nevertheless, if all the ISO 9001 requirements were being met certification was assured.

Now, however, we must consider our entire business as a process rather than as individual, discrete elements. A process is defined as a set of activities that uses resources to convert inputs into outputs. What does all that mean in practice? A typical medium-sized organization has various departments such as Personnel (or Human Resources), Accounts, a main section engaged in the product realization process, that is, the principal activity of the organization (which may be manufacturing or delivering a service), Quality, Maintenance, Purchasing and, perhaps, a few more, depending on the nature of the business. Often they act totally independently. Sometimes they even work against each other! However, if you look at the overall organization you can see that they all rely on each other. A Production or Servicing department becomes redundant if the sales team does not generate orders. Equally, the sales team is in trouble if the customers are seriously dissatisfied with the design of the product. The design team cannot function if it is not given reliable materials by the purchasing team, and so on.

Only by regarding the business as a set of processes and sub-processes can you get a real overview of all the activities. When you can see clearly what is happening then you are in a position to make improvements.

You should include in your quality manual (see page 115) a brief description of how the process approach is applied in your particular circumstances. This is usually done by including flow charts for the various processes and sub-processes that make up the routine activities of the organization. It is particularly important to show the interaction of the sub-processes, particularly where the output from one sub-process becomes the input for another sub-process. This aspect is closely related to the question of authority and responsibility (see page 43).

See Help documents 4.1–1 and 4.1–2.

Where a company subcontracts the manufacture of a product or the delivery of a service there is a requirement to control this activity adequately. You might think that if you simply co-ordinate the sourcing of various services and act as the main contractor you have no obligation to comply with many of the requirements of ISO 9001, since they are not part of your operation. However, the standard is quite clear – you must control those operations to a sufficient degree to satisfy yourself and your customer that quality products and services are being provided. Your quality management system must contain adequate controls in this regard, and your quality manual should give a full overview of this aspect of your operation.

Finally, the quality management system must be a dynamic entity. Too often in the past, companies have set up quality management systems documented in impressive bound manuals destined never to be changed. There is a requirement now that your system should improve with time, and that it should improve continually. In fact, the term 'continual improvement' has become a mantra among quality gurus, to the extent that the word *improve* without the 'continuous' qualifier hardly appears in any of the ISO 9000 family of standards.

DOCUMENTATION REQUIREMENTS (4.2)

One essential feature of the ISO 9000 quality management system is that it is documented. The core elements of documentation that are required are a quality policy for the organization, objectives in relation to achievement of quality, a quality manual and records relating to quality. All these are addressed later in detail. Some people query the need to have at least some procedures documented. Without written procedures errors are often made because of confusion that could have been prevented by an appropriate document. Somebody fails to perform a task because it is not clear who is supposed to do it. Or a task is performed incorrectly because the correct way has not been defined. Or a change is introduced and not everybody implements it, or different people implement it in different ways.

However, contrary to what people used to think, it is not necessary to have 'a procedure for everything' (see page 24). During the drafting of the current standard the members of ISO Technical Committee 176 who were working on the ISO 9000 family of standards were determined that there should be less emphasis on documented procedures. The result was that there are only six instances where there is a stated requirement to have a documented procedure. Apart from those cases, if the absence of a document could put the quality of product or service or the level of customer satisfaction at risk, then a procedure must be provided. Otherwise, it is probably not necessary. This principle can also be applied when considering what level of detail to put in the documents. People have gone to silly extremes when this was neither necessary nor useful. When writing a procedure you should consider the following:

1 The criticality of the task – what are the consequences of not doing it correctly?
2 The difficulty of the task – if the task is so simple, maybe everybody knows how to do it without a written procedure.
3 The competence of the person – has the person achieved proven competence by virtue of formal qualification, and is this qualification a prerequisite for carrying out this task? Note that competence is dependent on the individual involved. You could not decide that a document is unnecessary solely on the basis that the person currently carrying out the task has particular experience or skills. If you do this you must specify the qualifications for that particular job. Then

the procedure might not be necessary. For example, you do not need to provide qualified computer graduates with rules for handling computer hardware. But if at some later time you decide that this level of formal qualification is not necessary you will then have a gap in the documentation, since untrained people would not intuitively know how to handle this material.

Important: some tasks may legally only be carried out by persons qualified to do so. Clearly, in those circumstances no amount of documenting procedures can justify an unqualified person carrying out the task.

4 The level of supervision – is the person under constant supervision, so that any errors or deviations would be immediately picked up and corrected? In that case, it may not be necessary to provide a procedure to the person carrying out the task. Rather the supervisor might need one.

Documents can be in different formats, not necessarily paper. More and more organizations are working with paperless quality systems. However, the same basic principles apply irrespective of the medium used.

See Help document 4.2–1.

QUALITY MANUAL (ISO 9001: 4.2.2)

The quality manual is essentially an overview of the entire quality management system and contains a brief description of the various elements of the system. It is usually structured strictly along the lines of the ISO 9001 standard. There is no actual requirement that it should follow the ISO 9001 structure, but it is strongly recommended. If you adopt a different structure you are causing yourself unnecessary difficulty during external audits, since the auditor will be using an audit checklist based on the ISO 9001 standard. You would, therefore, have to produce a cross-reference guide for your own convenience to show where and how the requirements of the standard have been addressed in your system.

The quality manual is a high-level document, and usually contains very little detail. It is the sort of document you could use as promotional material submitted as part of an application for a contract. You should not include anything that is confidential.

If you have excluded any requirements of ISO 9001 from the scope of your system because they are not relevant to your operation you must define these in the quality manual. However, see page 11 for the conditions that apply to any such exclusions.

Under each clause heading of the standard your manual will contain references to specific individual procedures. In some cases the reference will be to another manual rather than to an individual procedure. For example, it is quite acceptable to state: 'Individual procedures for sales staff are contained in the Sales Procedures Manual', without listing the individual references.

The quality manual must contain an overview of the different processes of the organization showing their interaction. This is most easily done by including a flow chart of the organization's principal process showing how the various sub-processes interact. If the system contains lower-level manuals for the different sections of the organization the individual flow charts for the sub-processes will be shown in those manuals.

A sample quality manual can be found in Chapter XII.

CONTROL OF DOCUMENTS (ISO 9001: 4.2.3)

Control of documents refers to the precautions you must take to ensure that important documents are kept up to date and circulated to those who need them, and that no obsolete documents are in use. It is one of only six instances in which ISO 9001 demands that you have a written procedure. Serious nonconformities can occur directly as a result of failure to control documents. For example, product can be made to an obsolete specification or product tested using an outdated test method. Document control is often seen as the epitome of bureaucracy and used to damn ISO 9000. Certainly, there are organizations that have cumbersome and impractical document control procedures, where as many as ten signatures are required before a document can be changed. In most cases there is no justification for this. It may seem like a good idea to have as many people involved as possible, but in practice this will slow the change process to the extent that people will not wait for approval but will implement the change anyway. When that happens the document control procedure loses credibility and the entire ISO 9000 system is at risk of being discredited. If truth be told, the only reason for insisting on several signatures is because somebody is trying to avoid taking responsibility.

There are two distinct responsibilities that need to be defined in relation to document control:

- responsibility for the words on the page; and
- responsibility for the distribution of the documents.

The first lies with the *owner* of the manual, usually the manager of the department whose activities are described in the manual. This person is responsible for the accuracy of the documents and ensuring that these will control the activity adequately. Many people may be holders of a manual, but it has only one owner who is totally responsible for all aspects of it. The quality manual should contain a list of all manuals and their owners.

The second responsibility lies with the controller of documents in general, the person who keeps the manuals up to date. Often this person will not understand the technical content of the documents, since the role of document controller is simply to ensure that the documents that have been approved by the manual *owner* are distributed to the correct people.

The basic requirements for document control are that:

- it should be clear that the document has been authorized for use, and by whom; and
- there should be a clear method of knowing whether a document is currently valid.

Use the label 'Approved by ...' for the signature of the 'owner' of the document who takes responsibility for the accuracy and adequacy of the document. You do not need to indicate who issued or circulated the document, nor who drafted it. However, some people like to identify the person who issued the document, and this can be done using the label 'Issued by ...'.

Some companies produce specially printed paper for the quality system documentation, but the simplest format is to use the header/footer function on a word processor to print the document control information, leaving a space for signature or initials of the person authorizing the document's use.

The simplest document identification system is as follows:

- Include every controlled document in one of the manuals of the system.
- At the front of each manual list all the documents it contains, with unique reference number for each document and the date that the *current* version was issued.
- On each document include the following:
  - reference number (this should appear on every page of the document);
  - document title;
  - signature of the person who authorized or approved it (the 'owner');
  - date of issue of the current version (on every page); and
  - individual page numbers and indication of the total number of pages ('Page 1 of 2').
- Reference to the contents page immediately shows the date on the current version.

- The contents page of the manual is itself a controlled document.

There is nothing you can write on a document which by itself can prove its validity. You can only check a document's validity by reference to some other document, which is usually a master list – often the contents page of the manual in question.

However, documents only need to show either a date or a revision number. Contrary to what many people think you do not need both. There are several possible methods for indicating the revision status of documents:

- date of creation of the original document *and* the revision number of the current version;
- the revision number of the current version alone; and
- date that the current version was issued.

The date of revision indicates how old the document is. It does not, however, tell how many times the document has been changed since its first issue. On the other hand, the revision number tells you how many revisions there have been but not when it was last revised. You must decide what information is useful for your circumstances. Confine yourself to that information. The simpler the information, the simpler the control procedure (see also page 66).

No document in a quality system manual should ever be copied without being immediately marked (physically or electronically, as appropriate) 'Uncontrolled copy'. An uncontrolled copy is one that has been made outside the scope and control of the document change procedure. As such, its existence has not been recorded and it cannot be relied on, since it will not be updated in the event of revision. There is seldom any justification for having uncontrolled copies of documents. If a document is to be used at all you must be able to rely on it being up to date. If you need a document you should be on the normal circulation list for the document and receive a controlled copy automatically. One situation in which an uncontrolled copy would be used is where a supplier requests a copy of a purchasing specification for costing purposes in advance of detailed discussion or agreement to supply.

Normally all system documents will be contained in manuals, and the manuals will be circulated to the appropriate people. A need sometimes arises to have additional copies of individual procedures, perhaps for posting up at a particular workstation. Such procedures must be controlled. There are two simple ways of doing it:

- Record on the contents page of the manual that document reference number so-and-so is copied to such-and-such a location.
- Record the same information on the bottom of the procedure itself.

Either way, when the controller of documents revises the document the extra copy will be updated. See Help documents 4.2–1 and 4.2–2.

Electronic documents

It is perfectly acceptable to have the entire quality management system information on computer, without any hard copies of procedures. The same requirements for control apply, though the practical application of those requirements may pose its own difficulties. Some of the issues that must be addressed in the paperless system are listed below:

- How are the users alerted to the fact that a document has changed, that a document has been added or deleted? This is particularly important in the case of experienced people who do not need to refer to their procedures regularly, and might not consult their computer screens frequently.

- How is access to make changes restricted to an authorized document controller?
- How does the document controller manage draft documents in the pre-approval phase?
- Is it permitted to print off hard copies? If so, how are these controlled and replaced in the event of a revision?

Changes to documents

When a document is changed it is essential to remove all obsolete versions from use. Sometimes the document controller has the job of collecting and destroying the obsolete copies, and sometimes the responsibility is placed on the manual holders to do this. Either approach is acceptable. There is no requirement to retain copies of obsolete documents for reference. Sometimes, however, it is useful. For example, it is advisable to retain copies of old product specifications and old test methods. If you decide to retain such documents for reference you should mark them clearly so that they cannot be used inadvertently.

There is also no requirement in ISO 9001 to maintain a record of changes to controlled documents. Some people attach an additional sheet to the back of a document every time it is modified, showing the details of the change. Often this attachment is many times larger than the document itself. To comply with ISO 9001 requirements all you need is evidence that you have maintained control over changes to documents. That means making sure that all documents in circulation are the current versions and that they are properly presented in terms of identification and approval. If this notion is violently different from what you have always been told, consider this: suppose you ask the auditor to present evidence that you have *not* complied with ISO 9001 requirements, where can he or she find such evidence if you have a written procedure showing how document control is achieved, and all the documents in circulation are valid, demonstrating that the procedure has been followed? In practice, most people want to keep such a history. It is often essential to be able to trace the history of the changes and to understand the thought process behind each change. In that situation you would keep a record of the changes because it is useful to you, not because you have been told you must do it.

There is a requirement in ISO 9001 to identify changes to revised documents. This is very helpful to the recipient, who does not have to pore over the document to see what changes have been made. There are several ways in which this can be communicated. The change can be marked in the margin. It can be accompanied by a covering note stating what the changes are, or the information can be communicated in person, by a team leader, perhaps. As a matter of good management the background to the change should be explained to the users of the document, so that they understand the reasons, and are therefore more likely to implement the changes fully.

See Help documents 4.2–2 and 4.2–3.

Miscellaneous documents

Document control extends into areas that might not seem relevant at first. For example, every packaging design should have an identification reference printed on it. That way, changes to the text can be implemented without fear of mixing up the designs. This can be particularly important when dealing with packaging printed in foreign languages, or even scripts with which the packer is not familiar.

Copies of blank quality record sheets should be included in the appropriate system manuals in the same way as procedures or other controlled documents. This will ensure that the blank forms themselves are controlled. For example, it may be decided to increase or decrease the inspection level, or the specification for a test may be altered. If the record sheets are not controlled there is a risk that at some future stage the obsolete form will re-enter circulation and result in the changes being reversed inadvertently.

It is possible that some documents that originated outside your organization need to be controlled. The most obvious one is the actual ISO 9001 standard itself. It is unlikely that you are working to an obsolete version in this case, but there are many other instances where serious mistakes can be made because of failure to control external documents. There may be codes of practice or statutory instruments that apply to your operation. It is likely that customers supply you with specifications, which they may change from time to time. It is critical that the relevant people know at all times which specification is the current one. The simplest way to control these is to assign internal reference numbers to them, include them in some appropriate manual and treat them as internal documents. It is not necessary to transcribe the information into the same format as the internal documents just for the sake of appearance.

Review of documents

If the quality management system is going to be dynamic it will be necessary to review the documentation to ensure that it is maintained up to date. The standard contains a requirement to 'review and update as necessary and reapprove documents'. This should be taken to read 'review, update and reapprove, as necessary'. Clearly, there is no point in reapproving documents that are perfectly good, however old they are. The requirement to review documents should be included in the defined responsibilities of the appropriate managers. In practical terms, a simple way to review a document is to request the users of the document to confirm that the written method does reflect the actual situation. To make a record of this review simply make an uncontrolled copy of the contents page of the manual and get the reviewer to initial the margin opposite the document reviewed.

CONTROL OF RECORDS (ISO 9001: 4.2.4)

Control of records is another of the six instances where ISO 9001 prescribes a documented procedure. Keeping records in relation to quality aspects is important for a number of reasons, particularly product release, improvement, audits and legal defence. Records permit a comprehensive assessment of the product prior to its release. In Chapter VIII we will look at how the control of the process usually impacts on the quality of the final output. Therefore it is logical that some evaluation of the process is necessary for a comprehensive assessment of product quality. The risk assessment of the process will have identified a number of critical points that need to be controlled if quality is to be assured in the final product or service. These points need to be monitored to confirm that the process remains in control, and the result of this monitoring should be recorded for examination as part of the release of the final product. Release of final product should not depend on the mere examination of final product testing records. Help document 7.5.1–1 shows an example of such a final check for a service – in this case a management consultancy project involving the installation of a quality management system with a view to ISO 9001 certification at a future date.

Records facilitate effective management of the operation. They provide the history of how the operation and processes have performed in the past, and by analysing the information they contain it is possible to identify trends in relation to improvement, deterioration, gaps in knowledge, cost-effectiveness, profitability, customer satisfaction and such like. Without accurate records, properly analysed, the organization is simply drifting from day to day, and the full picture can never be seen clearly to enable major improvement to be made.

You need to keep records for audit purposes. On the day of an audit the auditor can observe whether people are following procedures and keeping physical conditions in order. However, this is only a snapshot of the management of the organization. The auditor needs to know how the organization was two weeks or two months previously, and how it is likely to be in two weeks time when everybody has relaxed after the audit. The only way to gauge this is by examining the records. As an auditor, I know that what I see on the day of the audit is just a carefully stage-managed display of control. I need to know that on every other day the situation is not too different.

There are two principal situations in which an organization can find itself defending a legal action: prosecution by the authorities for breach of regulations or litigation on the part of a customer who claims to have suffered loss or damage caused by the product or service supplied. In either case, records will be crucial to putting forward a strong defence. If you can produce documentary evidence to show that you did everything that could reasonably be expected of you, then this may be sufficient for success. But, without doubt if you do not have comprehensive records you have little chance of winning your case. Quality records should be made in a disciplined manner and clearly legible. All entries should be signed or initialled by the person making the entry. Afterwards the information the records contain should be evaluated for its significance.

Records must be kept secure and protected against damage or loss so that they are available for examination and analysis throughout the period of retention. The disposal of records must be a carefully controlled exercise, and authority to dispose of them should be defined and severely restricted.

Help documents 4.2–4 and 4.2–5 give guidance on records.

USE OF QUALITY MANAGEMENT PRINCIPLES (4.3)

Eight principles of quality management have been identified as the basis for quality management. A dictionary defines a principle as *a fundamental truth or a primary element*. The eight principles are:

1 *Customer focus.* All quality effort should be directed towards ensuring customer satisfaction, then to exceeding customer expectations. Overall success for the organization depends fundamentally on how well you satisfy your customer's expectations.
2 *Leadership.* The quality system is only as good as the people who lead the effort. That lead must come from the managers of the organization. Without leadership and a firm commitment to quality by top management all efforts are bound to fail. The senior managers define the atmosphere in the organization and this will determine the attitude of all other employees in the organization.
3 *Involvement of people.* The organization depends on people to operate it. Without the co-operation of all persons involved there is little chance of objectives being met. People must be involved at all levels, and must feel that they have an interest in the success of the enterprise.
4 *Process approach.* Any assignment or project is more effectively carried out if it is treated as a process rather than as individual, discrete tasks.
5 *System approach to management.* The business of an organization can be managed more effectively if the various processes involved are controlled as part of an overall system. Managing the interrelation of the processes ensures that each process contributes to achieving the objectives of the organization.
6 *Continuous improvement.* We should not be content to operate at the same level forever. Consistency is fine, but improvement is even better. Competitors are constantly improving. We need to improve also if we are to maintain or improve our position relative to them.
7 *Factual approach to decision-making.* Too often critical decisions are taken on the basis of intuition

or emotion. It is much more effective to collect and analyse relevant data and facts, and to base the decision on this.

8 *Mutually beneficial relationships with suppliers.* Quality and reliability can be greatly improved and significant financial benefits achieved by developing strong relationships with trusted suppliers on whom you can rely. This topic is developed further in the section on purchasing in Chapter VIII.

CHAPTER VI

The standards: Section 5 Management responsibility

ISO 9004	ISO 9001
5.1 General guidance	**5.1 Management commitment**
5.1.1 Introduction	
5.1.2 Issues to be considered	
5.2 Needs and expectations of interested parties	**5.2 Customer focus**
5.2.1 General	
5.2.2 Needs and expectations	
5.2.3 Statutory and regulatory requirements	
5.3 Quality policy	**5.3 Quality policy**
5.4 Planning	**5.4 Planning**
5.4.1 Quality objectives	5.4.1 Quality objectives
5.4.2 Quality planning	5.4.2 Quality management system planning
5.5 Responsibility, authority and communication	**5.5 Responsibility, authority and communication**
5.5.1 Responsibility and authority	5.5.1 Responsibility and authority
5.5.2 Management representative	5.5.2 Management representative
5.5.3 Internal communication	5.5.3 Internal communication
5.6 Management review	**5.6 Management review**
5.6.1 General	5.6.1 General
5.6.2 Review input	5.6.2 Review input
5.6.3 Review output	5.6.3 Review output

GENERAL GUIDANCE (5.1), ISO 9001: MANAGEMENT COMMITMENT

The various manuals, procedures records and quality activities that are part of every ISO 9000 system represent the operational end of ISO 9000. The organization will invest a considerable amount of resources in the quality management system – management time, money and training. It will be repaid many times over by the resulting benefits once a proper system is in place. However, if the system does not work, then all these resources will have been wasted. Worse than that, the credibility of any other quality initiative in the future will be much more difficult to establish.

If the system is to deliver benefits it must be driven enthusiastically by top management, and their role is critical to success. If they do not actively support the quality effort it is doomed to certain failure. Their commitment must be demonstrated by giving real support to the people who are implementing the system at the operational level.

ISO 9001 specifies five ways in which top management are required to demonstrate support for quality. However, these are high-level, strategic activities, which are not visible to most personnel. To show active support for quality senior managers should be visible and be seen to be participating in quality-related activities. Some easy options are:

- attending quality-related meetings;
- attending training and awareness presentations (to listen!);
- entering the organization in quality award schemes and product quality assurance schemes;
- regularly touring the organization.

As with all elements of ISO 9001 you must show the evidence that this commitment exists, and that usually means records of some sort. What records can you keep that demonstrate commitment? One simple way is the minutes of meetings. Whenever a management meeting is held minutes should be kept. The person writing the minutes should be aware of the importance of recording evidence of management commitment and ensure that the minutes capture all instances of this commitment. Commitment is demonstrated by discussion of the appropriate issues, by top management becoming actively involved in quality initiatives, where appropriate, but mainly by providing the necessary resources to facilitate the quality effort.

See Help documents 5.1–1 and 5.1–2.

NEEDS AND EXPECTATIONS OF INTERESTED PARTIES (5.2), ISO 9001: CUSTOMER FOCUS

ISO 9004 addresses all interested parties, whereas ISO 9001 simply requires that top management ensures that *customer* requirements are determined and met with the aim of achieving customer satisfaction. This issue is vitally important to the success of the system. Every organization exists in order to generate benefits for its stakeholders. This benefit is derived from the transactions between the organization and its customers. Anything which increases this interaction improves the benefit to the stakeholders; anything which reduces this interaction decreases the benefit. Since customers are generally free to choose whether they do business with you or not, you should make the customer the focus of your business.

Since this is so important you should make special mention of it in the quality manual, with an indication of how this can be seen in practice. In particular, you should outline the specific activities that prove top management's commitment to customer focus.

See Help document 5.2–1.

QUALITY POLICY (5.3)

The quality policy is the highest-level element in the entire quality management system. Everything else flows from it. ISO 9001 mentions just two things that must be included, namely, a commitment to complying with requirements and a commitment to continual improvement of the quality management system. The policy must also 'provide a framework for establishing and reviewing quality objectives'. You should, therefore, also mention quality objectives in the policy.

The quality policy should also include references to the welfare of the employees, provision of adequate training, and a commitment to comply with all legal requirements. It may also be appropriate to give a commitment in relation to minimizing the impact of the organization's activities on the environment or the local community. The latter issue is not strictly within the scope of ISO 9000, but there is no reason why it should not be included in the quality policy.

The policy is usually included in the quality manual. It is useful to do this for purposes of document control, though document control of the quality policy has been deliberately omitted from the standard, since some experts considered it impractical to subject it to the type of control applying to the other documents in the system. Many organizations display the quality policy in prominent locations, usually in the reception area. This can be a useful public affirmation of the commitment to quality.

You are required to communicate the quality policy internally. Displaying it is one practical means of doing this, but it would not be sufficient simply to display it and expect people to read it. You need to take active steps to communicate it throughout the organization. There are several options for this:

- including a copy with the wage slips, perhaps once a year;
- using a newsletter to refer to different points in the policy over a period of time; and
- covering the various points in the policy during team talks, or refresher training. It should, of course, be covered in induction for all new staff.

Whatever method you employ keep a brief record of what you did. For example, keep a copy of the note that accompanied the policy when it was circulated.

Finally, the policy must be reviewed regularly. The simplest way of ensuring this is to do this as part of the management review.

See Help document 5.3–1.

PLANNING (5.4)

QUALITY OBJECTIVES (5.4.1)

The quality policy is a very important element of the quality management system, since it sets the whole scene for quality within the organization. In itself, however, it would not be sufficient to motivate personnel at all levels in the organization. People need something more immediate and concrete. For that reason ISO 9001 requires that you set objectives for relevant functions and levels of management within the organization. Each level of management and each department or function within the organization should have its own objectives, specific and relevant to the local circumstances. Objectives can, and should, be set at all levels down to the individual. To be effective an objective must be set in such a way that it can be used as a standard against which to measure performance. If objectives are purely qualitative, phrased in terms such as 'To provide a top quality service' then it is almost impossible to determine afterwards if the objective has been met. On the other hand 'To achieve a customer satisfaction rating of 95 per cent' or 'To achieve 55 per cent repeat orders' are quite specific and measurable.

Where relevant, the objectives must include meeting the requirements for the product. For example, personnel delivering a service directly to the customer or manufacturing a product should have specific objectives that relate directly to the quality of the service or product. Top management must ensure that objectives are set, but the objectives may be set locally in each area if that is more appropriate. A convenient way of doing this would be for each manager (or individual in the case of a small company) to produce a set of objectives for approval at a management review.

See Help document 5.4.1–1.

QUALITY MANAGEMENT SYSTEM PLANNING (5.4.2)

Planning is a theme that runs throughout the ISO 9000 standards. In section 7.1 (Chapter VIII) we shall be looking at the planning of the actual product realization, that is, the manufacture of the product or the delivery of the service that you provide. Here, however, we are considering the top-level planning that results in a management system that will direct the overall effort of the organization. Having set the objectives for the organization it is now necessary to plan how those objectives will be met. That planning involves an assessment of requirements for the product or service, the provision of adequate resources to ensure a quality output, the definition of the management controls that need to be put in place and the procedures for monitoring the effectiveness of the system.

In practice, your quality manual is the visible proof of your planning with regard to the quality management system. For that reason it is important that the quality manual contains a reasonable degree of detail about the various elements of the system. This planning is closely linked to the regular management review. However, it is possible that a need to review or even modify the quality management system could arise outside the context of the management review. This might happen when there is a period of upheaval in the organization, perhaps when major new equipment or processes are being installed, at times of company mergers or takeovers, or in the aftermath of a serious accident, for example. A classic example of such circumstances is where there is an unforeseen rapid growth in demand for the product. In that type of situation many companies have come to grief by failing to manage quality in parallel with quantity.

There are certain controls that you would absolutely insist on, no matter what the circumstances, and these must be strictly enforced. Other controls you may have to forgo in certain extreme situations. Proper planning at times like that will ensure that you maintain at least the minimum level of management control that will ensure customer satisfaction until normality has been restored.

See Help document 5.4.2–1.

Risk assessment

Under quality planning, ISO 9004 mentions risk assessment. All planning should include an in-depth examination of the processes involved to ensure that potential hazards to quality are identified and managed. Risk assessment entails identifying all possible hazards that could arise in any foreseeable circumstances, assessing the likely frequency or probability of the hazard coming to pass, and the severity of the resulting problem if it should come to pass. The combination of these two factors is called the risk. Help document 5.4.2–3 describes a simple approach to risk assessment, based on a scale of one to three (High, Medium and Low) for both frequency and severity.

In many cases risk assessment is more an art than a science. Nevertheless, many people think that by using numerical ratings it can be turned into a mathematical exercise. For example, sometimes probability and severity scales of 1 to 10 are used and the resulting product of the two factors taken as a percentage risk. In some cases the probability of non-detection is taken as a third factor, giving an overall risk assessment of 1 to 1000. In such situations it is easy to come to believe, mistakenly, that the figures truly mean something in the mathematical sense. In fact, the object of the whole exercise is simply to prioritize the preventive action so that the most serious risks are eliminated soonest, and the simple scheme described in the Help document is quite adequate for that.

See Help documents 5.4.2–2 and 5.4.2–3. See also section 8.5.3 (Chapter IX) on preventive action.

RESPONSIBILITY, AUTHORITY AND COMMUNICATION (5.5)

The quality management system cannot grow spontaneously from the bottom of the organization up; it must be designed and built by the management of the organization as a planned project. The system must contain all the administrative controls that are necessary for operating the system and that will facilitate the smooth operation of the system.

See Chapter II for further guidance on setting up the system.

RESPONSIBILITY AND AUTHORITY (5.5.1)

To ensure smooth running of all activities it is essential to define responsibilities and authority of all persons whose duties can affect quality. In simple terms, defining responsibility is identifying the person who must ensure that a particular task is carried out. Defining authority is identifying the person who is permitted to make a decision. As a general rule, if authority has not been given then a person does not have permission to make the decision. Too often one can see the result of failure to document responsibilities, when critical tasks are not done because two people each think that the other is doing it. Failure to document authorities can also result in wrong decisions being made by persons not competent or not knowing the full facts.

In practice, you should ensure that anybody mentioned in any document within the system has his or her responsibilities and authority defined. In particular, authority should be defined for all decisions in relation to quality, for example, approving suppliers, granting a waiver for non-conforming product, assessing records or setting quality standards.

The simplest way to do this is to produce a document containing all the principal responsibilities and authority for every person whose job can impact on customer satisfaction, from the chief executive to individual operatives. Examples are given in the sample quality manual (QM–11).

MANAGEMENT REPRESENTATIVE (5.5.2)

A member of management must be appointed to be the guardian, or champion, of the quality management system. He or she is given the title 'management representative' in ISO 9000. The intention is that this person is sufficiently senior to be able to resolve quality management issues. This role can actually be held by any member of management, including the proprietor or chief executive, though it is more usually assigned to the quality manager or other equivalent manager. Do not think of this person as somebody who is 'responsible for quality', since there should be no such role in your organization. Quality is a complex mosaic of responsibilities, with each person responsible for a part, even if that is only to perform simple tasks such as delivering documents from one office to another.

The duties of the management representative are to:

- ensure that the system, as defined in the documented procedures, is being implemented. This is a monitoring function, and does not imply that the representative is required to carry out routine quality control activities. Quality of product or service must be firmly the responsibility of line managers. The person who has the status and the salary for achieving the output must be held responsible for the quality of the output. In most cases the management representative does not have authority over the process, and cannot therefore be held responsible for the quality of the output;
- report to top management on the performance of the quality system, and suggest improvements. In order to do this the management representative will have to set up a programme of monitoring activities. Examples of such activities are attendance at regular, frequent management meetings, reviewing summary reports from individual managers and analysing the results of internal audits; and
- ensure that awareness of customer requirements is promoted throughout the organization. The management representative may carry out this promotion or it can be passed on to line managers and supervisors. Possibilities for this include:
  - use of a newsletter or noticeboard;
  - presentation to managers at management meetings;

– participation in refresher training for managers and operatives; and
– team talks by managers and supervisors.

In most organizations the role of management representative is a part-time one, and the holder of the position will have other duties. These other duties must not conflict with the duties of management representative.

See Help document 5.5.2–1.

INTERNAL COMMUNICATION (5.5.3)

Good internal communication contributes significantly to achieving quality. Although the ISO 9001 standard actually only requires you to communicate in respect of the effectiveness of the quality management system, you should extend your communication to all activities within the organization. Unless your organization is very small, less than ten people, for example, and all in one location, you should set up some formal channel of internal communication to address both the quality system and the routine activities.

How complex this internal communication is will depend on the circumstances of the organization. In a large organization with a number of different departments there could be a hierarchy of meetings – top management meeting, interdepartmental operations meetings and intra-departmental meetings. An effective meetings structure will facilitate the rapid communication of information upwards and downwards through a large organization.

When setting up a system of management meetings be careful to set strict rules in relation to how meetings are conducted. Without clear guidelines meetings can be a serious waste of time and a cause of great frustration to those involved. The principal rules for success of routine meetings are:

● a preset agenda;
● attendance only by those who need to attend and who can contribute usefully;
● a fixed time and day – one hour before lunch time is very effective;
● a maximum duration – this is essential;
● all participants prepare beforehand;
● discussion is limited to issues that can be resolved during the meeting. Other issues, such as analysis of information, are assigned to sub-groups for resolution outside the meeting;
● if a participant cannot attend, a deputy is sent;
● the meeting always goes ahead irrespective of which participants can or cannot attend.

In the case of a routine operations meeting covering a range of topics, all of which would not be relevant to everybody, it is useful to have a timed agenda so that people can come and go as required. For example, the daily meeting might start with a short production planning session led by the production planner in which the production plan for the next 24 hours is set out. That completed, the planner might not need to wait for the remaining topics such as discussion of maintenance issues or investigation of nonconformities. Equally, the maintenance person might not need to be there at the start of the meeting to hear the planning details.

See Help document 5.5.3–1.

MANAGEMENT REVIEW (5.6)

By the time the quality management system is in place and operating, a lot of resources will have been invested in it. You need to know if those resources have been well used – is the system delivering all the benefits that were promised? The management review answers this question.

The first management review is normally held some months after the system has been operating fully. It is possible to review the system before it is complete; this can be very useful as an interim review of progress towards implementation and can identify gaps that remain. But an effective review is not possible if large sections of the system are not operating.

The review is to be carried out by top management. In a small service organization that might consist of the owner of the company and the office administrator, whereas in a large manufacturing company it would certainly involve the chief executive or most senior manager and the heads of the major functions in the company – for example, Quality, Production, Engineering, Human Resources, Materials/Logistics and Finance.

The review will be held regularly. The frequency for this review is not specified in ISO 9001, but it is usual to hold it annually. However, it may be necessary or appropriate to do it more often. The particular circumstances will determine what is appropriate. The frequency should be defined in the quality manual.

REVIEW INPUT (5.6.2)

To be effective the review should have a preset agenda. ISO 9001 lists a number of items that must be addressed, and ISO 9004 suggests others that should be considered as inputs to the review. These lists can form the basis for the agenda, with additional relevant items added and anything which is not appropriate or relevant deleted.

It is important to remember that this review is a high-level activity, and will probably not address details. For example, it is unlikely that individual complaints or individual problems highlighted in an internal audit will be discussed. Instead, the discussion should centre on summary information. The format for the different summaries should be specified, so that the information is presented in the way that is most suitable for the review team to analyse quickly. Individual managers should be instructed to prepare the analysis of the relevant data in this format. So, for example, the quality manager or the customer services manager might be asked to produce a summary of the complaints received since the previous review under the appropriate headings, such as complaints per million units sold for the different product categories, month by month, with explanations for any obvious anomalies, or the number of complaints per 100 services categorized by geographical region.

See Help documents 5.6.1–1 and 5.6.1–2.

REVIEW OUTPUT (5.6.3)

The output from the review is essentially an assessment of the current status of the quality management system and a list of actions designed to facilitate improvement of performance in the areas of product performance and customer satisfaction, process performance, control of risks and the provision of resources. These corrective actions need to be implemented quickly. To ensure that this is so, the procedure for management review should cover not only the actual review meeting, but also the period following the review, up to and including the completion of the corrective action. That means assigning responsibility to somebody to monitor the implementation of corrective action and report to top management. This usually falls to the management representative. For each individual element of corrective action the responsibility for its implementation and the deadline for its completion should be assigned.

See Help document 5.6.1–3.

CHAPTER VII

The standards: Section 6 Resource management

ISO 9004

6.1 General guidance
  6.1.1 Introduction
  6.1.2 Issues to be considered
6.2 People
  6.2.1 Involvement of people
  6.2.2 Competence, awareness and training
6.3 Infrastructure
6.4 Work environment
6.5 Information
6.6 Suppliers and partnerships
6.7 Natural resources
6.8 Financial resources

ISO 9001

6.1 Provision of resources

6.2 Human resources
  6.2.1 General
  6.2.2 Competence, awareness and training
6.3 Infrastructure
6.4 Work environment

GENERAL GUIDANCE (6.1), ISO 9001: PROVISION OF RESOURCES

Resources are the means by which the process converts the inputs into the outputs. The quality of the output will depend partly on the quality of the inputs, and partly on the availability of adequate resources and the manner in which they are deployed.

The requirements of ISO 9001 cover those resources that must usually be provided in order to ensure a quality output and to derive full benefit from the quality management system. Many organizations have an ad hoc approach to the provision of resources. Sometimes resources are made available on the basis of the loudest demand. Sometimes it is based on the most recent crisis. Too often resources required for quality purposes do not get the priority they deserve, perhaps because the person putting the case for quality does not have the necessary status within the organization. To be effective, however, there must be a systematic approach. Resource needs change constantly, and you should have a formal mechanism for evaluating these needs and providing promptly the essential resources. The simplest way to manage resources is regularly to review the issue. It must be covered in the formal management review of the system, but it can usefully be included as a routine item on the agenda of regular senior management meetings.

Clearly, resources need to be provided for meeting customer requirements, as currently known, but you must also try to anticipate future needs, and plan to provide the necessary resources in advance. For example, you may foresee that expansion will result in a considerable increase in the workforce in some months' time, which will require significant induction and training activity. If there were insufficient personnel to carry out the training considered necessary, you might plan to recruit or train additional trainers first, so that when the new recruits arrive an induction programme would be ready.

PEOPLE (6.2), ISO 9001: HUMAN RESOURCES

It is a cliché, but nonetheless true, that people are the greatest resource and the greatest strength that an organization has. But strangely, many organizations are reluctant to spend money on this 'greatest resource'. Usually there is a serious imbalance between the amount spent on new equipment and new employees. A machine may only cost half the average annual wage in the organization, and may have a useful life of only five years, yet we will spend many hours evaluating options and carrying out trials to make sure it is the right machine. Once in place we will set up maintenance and servicing schedules, and take great care to look after it well. The employee, on the other hand, who may be with the organization for many years performing highly critical tasks and making decisions that affect the entire future of the organization, is often appointed on the basis of an interview lasting a few minutes and may be expected to 'pick up' the skills and information needed for his or her duties, without any formal induction.

INVOLVEMENT OF PEOPLE (6.2.1), ISO 9001: GENERAL

The reason that people are considered the most important resource is that things do not just happen in the organization; people make them happen. It is important, therefore, that people are motivated to make sure that their actions are for the good of the organization. That means making sure that you have the right people to start with, understanding their needs and then satisfying those needs as far as practicable. People have many different needs, and this book could not attempt to cover this issue in depth. However, a basic need for most people is to be performing jobs to which they are suited, and that is primarily determined at the recruitment stage.

COMPETENCE, AWARENESS AND TRAINING (6.2.2)

The investment in personnel should start with the recruitment process. Once an unsuitable person has been recruited a loss will already have been incurred by the organization. Even if there is a probationary period for the new employee, significant resources will have been wasted if he or she has to be dismissed and replaced. This situation can often be prevented by a little thoughtful preparation. Start by determining for each job the minimum requirements that all candidates must possess in terms of formal qualifications, experience, skills and knowledge, if any. In that way you can be reasonably sure that the new recruit will be competent and qualified for the tasks he or she will perform. Competence is the overall result of the combination of education, training, experience, skills and self-discipline.

Formal academic or skills qualifications will only be required for very specific, usually technical, functions. For example, a life assurance company will need to employ qualified actuaries for certain positions, and a food manufacturing company would probably require a qualified microbiologist for a post of that title where a technical knowledge of microbiology was required. However, a person being recruited to manage a quality department that included the necessary technically qualified personnel might not need a formal technical qualification, but could be qualified on the basis of experience with quality management systems in other fields.

Take a look at the job itself, the tasks that the new recruit will perform and the environment in which he or she will work. A 'person specification' defining the personal characteristics that are optimum or essential for the job can be a useful tool in certain circumstances. Companies sometimes draw up such a specification for occupational health and safety reasons. This is designed for the benefit of both the company and the prospective employee, and prevents a person taking up a job that could be damaging to his or her health. For example, a person with a fear of heights would not be suitable for a job that involved work high above the ground, nor would such a person wish to have that job. A similar approach may be appropriate for quality in some situations. Colour blindness might make it impossible for a person to carry out work that involved comparison of colours. A person with poor general vision might find it extremely unpleasant and stressful to have a job that involved close visual inspection of small items. However, do not confuse this issue with the need to provide a safe working environment. It would not be permissible to refuse a position to a person suffering from asthma on the basis that the environment was too dusty. In that situation the law requires you to remove the health hazard rather than discriminate against the individual.

If people are to produce a quality output from their work they must be trained adequately. Training should start with an induction programme the moment the new employee arrives. This induction can be carried out in one or more phases, depending on the size of the organization. General induction should be given on *the first day*, and consists of an introduction to the organization and its activities, general rules in relation to quality, health and safety, environmental issues, disciplinary matters, the importance of meeting quality objectives and how the recruit can contribute to the achievement of the objectives. This might only take 30 minutes and be given by the proprietor in a small company. In a larger company it might last a full day and be given by a team of specialist trainers.

Where there is a departmental structure the new recruit would then be passed on to the head of the section, where the second phase of induction is given. This covers the issues specific to that area in which the person will work. The recruit is now ready to be trained in the particular tasks that he or she will perform.

See Help document 6.2.2–1.

Training

There is no definition as to what constitutes acceptable training. There are no strict requirements as to how training should be carried out, or by whom. It is at the discretion of the management how this should be done. However, you must be able to justify your method, and demonstrate that it is adequate for the purpose and that the output of the training is satisfactory. The simplest form of training is for the new recruit to learn by observing an experienced worker performing the job. The 'talk-back' method is very effective in this situation:

- The trainer shows how the task is performed.
- The trainer repeats the task, explaining at each step why it is done in a particular way.
- The trainee carries out the task and explains at each step why it is done that way.

Where on-the-job training is given the trainer needs to be competent. That means being competent at the job and competent as a trainer. The trainer should certainly have a documented procedure for the tasks, even if these are not strictly required under ISO 9001. The trainer's work needs to be assessed from time to time to ensure that he or she remains competent at performing the task itself. Trainers should be designated as such, and this should appear on their own training records. The training status of every trainer should be reviewed and renewed regularly.

Training resources

Sometimes it is not sufficient or appropriate to do on-the-job training, and a classroom setting is required. The most important resource needed for that is a suitable location. Ideally this should be off-site, since training carried out on-site is often subject to interruptions by the routine work. However, if there is a room with adequate space for the trainees to sit comfortably at tables, away from noise and other distractions, then this may be suitable. There must be no distractions. A canteen where there is constant activity is not a suitable location.

Depending on the nature of the training you will need to provide some form of training materials or aids. Training aids can be as simple as a flip chart, or as sophisticated as high-tech audio-visual equipment. The circumstances will determine what is appropriate.

Consider whether it is useful to provide the trainees with some form of handout to remind them of what was covered in the training. Where there are written procedures for the tasks being covered this may be sufficient.

Whether training is done by internal or external trainers you should keep a record of the course content. External trainers should be asked to provide an outline of the training showing the details of the topics covered. This should be filed as an attachment to the training records for the trainees involved.

Identification of competence needs

Induction and training do not last forever. Circumstances change – people get 'stale' and lose their enthusiasm, new products or services are introduced, customer attitudes change, the company grows, and people are required to take on new tasks. All these give rise to changing needs, and the organization must ensure that it identifies changes in needs and provides training to meet those needs. As with everything else in ISO 9000 you should plan this methodically, and not simply in response to the latest training brochure that arrived in the post.

A review of competence needs is best carried out by a person's immediate superior. Usually competence needs are fully addressed by providing training. In order to carry out a review of needs, managers and supervisors should be given a guide-list of items that could help identify training needs, and asked to assess each member of their teams against this list. In addition, they can ask the individuals if they themselves can identify areas where they feel they need training.

When the training needs of all personnel have been determined the results can be collated to give an overall picture of the organization's training needs. This should then be translated into a company training plan. Typically, this would be done once a year. The annual training plan will ensure that training is provided on the basis of actual needs. Of course, it will not always be possible to meet every element of the plan on time, but that is no reason to abandon the plan. If a training element has to be cancelled simply write a very brief explanation on the plan and reschedule it. If the need for a particular element disappears make a note on the training plan and cancel the entry.

See Help document 6.2.2–3.

Evaluation of training

Because of the importance of training, not to mention its cost, you need to know that it has been effective. That means evaluating each element of training when it has been completed. There are two questions to be answered by this evaluation:

- Is the trainee now able to perform the tasks competently?
- Was the training itself satisfactory – value for money, no unnecessary disruption, training materials satisfactory, suitable for other trainees?

These two questions apply whether the trainer was internal or external.

To evaluate the effectiveness of training it is necessary to examine the work of the trainee some time after the training has been completed. Ideally this should be done in several stages. Depending on the tasks involved the person's immediate superior might observe the trainee one day, one week and one month after the training. Only if all three observations are satisfactory is the trainee regarded as trained. The training record should show that the training was evaluated and indicate that the trainee is now competent in the tasks covered by the training.

It can happen that the trainee has successfully learned the necessary information and skills from the training without the training itself being fully satisfactory. It is important for the organization to know whether it has received value for the money spent on the training. You should regard external trainers as suppliers under section 7.4, and evaluate them as you would any other supplier of a critical material or service. There are two principal ways of assessing how satisfactory a training course is. The first is to ask the participants to complete an assessment form. Note that an external trainer will normally ask the trainee to complete such a form, but that is not usually fully appropriate for the purposes of the trainee's own organization. You must design your own form to elicit the information you want in relation to the course. The second method is to personally sit in on part of the course and observe it. It is only practical to do this in the case of major courses delivered on-site.

Competence needs are usually met by providing training, but if other action is appropriate in the circumstances this action should also be evaluated for effectiveness. The net result must be that the person now performs the tasks correctly.

See Help document 6.2.2–6.

Training records

ISO 9001 requires that you 'maintain appropriate records of education, training, skills and experience'. You are not asked to maintain copies of ancient degrees and diplomas and training course certificates. This would be nonsensical, since the knowledge and skills learned may have long since been superseded, and ISO 9000 places such emphasis on keeping necessary knowledge and skills up to date.

Nevertheless, managers and supervisors should get into the habit of recording all training, partly for audit purposes, but more importantly for reasons of effective management. The simplest form of training record is a single sheet for each employee. Each unit of training is recorded briefly on one line. When a number of people receive training at the same time it may be more convenient to make one record of the training, with the names of the trainees listed. In that case there is no need to duplicate the information by updating the individuals' training records, though it is more convenient at the time of an audit to have all information relating to an individual's training in a single record. During an audit you will be required to show the full training records for selected individuals, and you must decide which recording method makes it easiest to produce the information requested.

Training refers not only to formal training sessions, but to any coaching that is given. So, for example, if a supervisor spends some time explaining a particular aspect of a job to a person, this can be considered training. Whether you decide it is necessary to record this on the training record is your decision. The requirement is not to record all training, but to keep appropriate records.

Training records will provide one input into the identification of training needs.

See Help documents 6.2.2–1, 6.2.2–2, 6.2.2–4 and 6.2.2–5.

Awareness

Awareness in this context is the knowledge of the impact of one's actions on the ultimate quality of the output and, therefore, on customer satisfaction. A highly trained and very competent person can produce rubbish if he or she is lacking either the motivation to do the job properly or is not aware of the consequences of not doing it right. ISO 9001 does not directly address motivation, which is a complex issue, but it does insist on the simpler task of ensuring that all persons are aware of the impact that their work can have on the achievement of objectives, which include customer satisfaction. There are many ways of promoting awareness, from the regular meeting in a small company to poster campaigns and incentive schemes in larger companies. As always, you have to decide what is appropriate. Remember to keep some evidence to demonstrate that you have complied with the requirement of the standard. For example, if the managing director gives an annual address to all employees he or she should be prompted in advance to stress quality issues, and a filed copy of the notes of the speech would provide some evidence of an awareness campaign.

See Help document 5.5.2–1.

INFRASTRUCTURE (6.3)

Infrastructure refers to the supporting aspects of an operation, especially those permanent entities that affect the organization's capability to carry out its normal operations efficiently. This includes such things as buildings, equipment, computer facilities, power, water, information, transport and communication facilities.

Considering the cost of providing these facilities, it is sensible to plan and manage them carefully. Infrastructural requirements can be included in the risk assessment of the process and identified needs documented in the output of the assessment. When reviewing infrastructure consider such aspects as deficiencies that are causing bottlenecks or problems, maintenance arrangements where appropriate, the protection of the health and safety of personnel, and the impact on the external environment. The minimum that you are required to do by ISO 9001 is to provide facilities that are adequate to ensure that the product or service conforms to requirements.

MAINTENANCE

Where equipment is used in the process and its proper functioning is essential to assuring quality, it should be maintained properly. What that means in practice depends entirely on the circumstances. In some cases it may simply mean making provision for having repairs carried out speedily so that supply to customers is not adversely affected. At the other extreme a full preventive maintenance programme may be absolutely essential. In deciding what is appropriate for you there are two factors to take into consideration: the functioning of the machine and the performance of the machine. In the first case the machine is merely an aid for performing a task. When the machine functions it performs the task. Its effect on the process is primarily to affect *availability* of output. Examples are a slicing machine in a kitchen, a laser printer, a design software package, a conveyor belt or a road vehicle. For machines like this you need to have either a standby substitute or a readily available repair service in the event of breakdown.

In other cases, however, the machine may itself determine the characteristics of the output, with a consequent effect on quality. The performance of such machines needs to be kept within certain limits so that machine variability does not cause the output to drift outside specification. Examples of this type of machine include automatic control devices, measuring and recording devices (see below), heating and cooling equipment, cutting or shaping devices where dimensions are critical, and volumetric or weight dispensing machines. Where such machines are used the quality of output is dependent on the machine functioning correctly, and this probably requires some degree of regular preventive maintenance.

To set up a basic preventive maintenance programme first list each item of process equipment, define its function and identify the possible effect on quality if it were to malfunction. This task should be undertaken jointly by a technical person who is familiar with the internal mechanisms of the machine and who can describe how the malfunction will manifest itself, and a quality person who can assess what impact this may have on the quality of the eventual process output. This is basically a type of risk assessment.

When you have assessed the potential impact of all the machines, you should then identify what controls are needed to protect the process against machine failure. This may involve pre-emptive replacement of critical parts even where they have not yet failed, or regular inspection of vulnerable parts for signs of wear or other indication of impending failure. It will probably also involve frequent simple checks by the person who operates it. For example, a visual inspection of some part of the machine, which could show the first signs of oncoming problems, or listening for change in the sound of a machine, which could be an indication of parts wearing. Basic cleaning by the user may also play a role. If that is the case such cleaning should be recorded to ensure that it is carried out when specified. These controls then form the basis of a maintenance schedule, similar in nature and intent to any other quality inspection you carry out. A computerized preventive maintenance programme is merely a strictly managed system of planning and recording all aspects of maintenance, with particular emphasis on preventing failure rather than repair after failure.

See Help document 6.3–1. See also page 70.

WORK ENVIRONMENT (6.4)

ISO 9000 is universally applicable. It applies equally well to restaurants, garbage disposal operations, solicitors and babyfood manufacturers, for example. So, how can it set requirements for the work environment that apply to all? Surely the standards for the work environment are different in all these cases? Indeed they are, and this clause copes with the difference by asking you, in effect, to specify the appropriate standards for physical conditions that are needed in your situation to ensure that the product or service meets requirements. What these actual standards are will depend on the type of operation you have. In a drawing office the major concern might be provision of adequate lighting and ergonomically designed furniture, whereas in an electronics or food factory cleanliness will be particularly important.

Standards for physical conditions can very easily be incorporated into a checklist for carrying out inspections. To draw up a set of standards you should first survey the physical location of the process and define the standards that must be met to ensure that the product or service will conform to requirements. Convert those standards into a checklist and use this to carry out regular inspections to confirm that the appropriate standard for the work environment is maintained.

See Help document 6.4–1.

In addition to providing the appropriate physical conditions you should ensure that the so-called 'softer' aspects of the workplace are addressed. ISO 9001 concerns itself only with the issue of product conformity and customer satisfaction, and does not state requirements for health and safety. It is not too difficult, however, to see how the quality of the output might be adversely affected by such aspects as stress caused by concern about dangerous chemicals or bullying, poor lighting or bad ergonomics, to name just a few workplace hazards. If, in the particular circumstances, these factors could directly affect the quality of the output, then they could legitimately be considered as coming under the requirement of ISO 9001. Otherwise, health and safety issues, emphatically, do not fall within the scope of an ISO 9001 audit.

ISO 9004 touches on the issue of health and safety, mentioning safety rules and guidance, and protective equipment, and, in clause 7.1.3.2, the matter of health and safety in the context of reviewing inputs to process. Organizations have a legal requirement to manage occupational health and safety. This really means having a management system in place, equivalent to the quality management system. Identifying hazards and putting in place adequate controls against them is just one aspect of such a management system. The most effective approach to the combined requirements of quality and occupational health and safety is to integrate the efforts in these two areas under a single integrated management system. In fact, if you have any concerns for the impact of your operation on the external environment you should have a tripartite integrated management system that also includes environmental control (see page 13).

INFORMATION (6.5)

Every operation depends to some extent on information, and very often the quality of the output will be determined by the quality of the information used. To ensure that quality information is available you should manage information just as you would any other resource:

- What information is needed?
- How is this information incorporated into the decision-making process?
- Who is responsible for keeping this information up to date?
- How is the information communicated to the relevant people?
- What communication channels are there for updating information internally?
- How is information secured against theft or unauthorized use?

Where appropriate, information should be planned, managed, protected and documented just like all other resources.

Sometimes it can be beneficial to the organization to provide a library of useful texts for reference by all staff. In a large organization individuals often order textbooks, standards and codes of practice for their own purposes, and others who might use them are not aware that they are available. In such situations a central repository for those books would benefit everybody. Where such a library is set up it should be under the control of one individual, even if everybody has free access to it. Even in a small organization it can be very useful to collect relevant reference material into one place and make it generally available to all personnel.

See Help document 6.5–1.

There is another aspect to information – the information gleaned over the years by the individuals working in the organization. Very often this resource is ignored by the organization's management. There are several reasons why one should tap into this knowledge base. First, the managers are seldom the sole source of all knowledge, and much valuable information about potential problems and possibilities for improvement is known only to the people who carry out the mundane tasks. If people are not motivated to share this information for everybody's benefit, then they will not share it and the organization is the loser. Suggestion schemes can be very useful in uncovering this store of information. Progressing further, a reward for a useful suggestion for quality improvement is a very clear commitment to quality on the organization's part and is a great motivating factor for employees. If a suggestion or award scheme is adopted it is essential to respond to all suggestions received, whether used or not, since it is very demotivating when a person's suggestion appears to be totally ignored.

SUPPLIERS AND PARTNERSHIPS (6.6)

In the not too distant past most companies relied on sampling and inspecting incoming purchased materials to control quality. This involved taking a sample, presumed to be representative, and accepting or rejecting the lot based on the results of the sample and a defined acceptable level of defectives, curiously called the acceptable quality level (AQL). Sometimes this sampling was based on sound statistical principles, and sometimes not. However, even when such a scheme is soundly based there is a significant risk that you will either reject a 'good' lot or, more seriously, accept a 'bad' lot. So it is a far from ideal approach.

In recent years most organizations have begun to develop detailed quality assurance procedures for dealing with suppliers of critical materials. The benefits in this arise from the fact that the more information you have about the history of the purchased material, the less inspection you have to do and the more confidence you have in the quality of the material. The amount of testing you carry out should be based on the degree of uncertainty you have about the quality.

The level of trust between you and your supplier can range from low, where you simply have no information about the supplier, to total trust, when you allow the supplier to supply directly to the point at which you use the material, without any prior inspection on your part. The latter is known as just-in-time (JIT) supply, which can yield enormous financial savings due to the fact that the purchaser does not need to carry stocks of the materials in question.

Though most organizations would still pull back from the total commitment required for JIT, some of the principles involved can be applied in all organizations. Anything that improves your confidence in the quality of the incoming product will reduce the amount of inspection or testing you need to do, and will result in cost saving. Even without JIT you can still achieve greatly improved product quality and cost savings by building up relationships with key suppliers. In the past the relationship between supplier and purchaser was based more often on deception than trust. Now, however, most companies realize that suppliers and purchasers need each other. In fact, purchasers will often pay a premium for the confidence that the product meets specification, to the benefit of both parties.

The core elements in this relationship are reaching agreement on the specification and having effective channels of communication. A realistic specification is essential. Very often an over-enthusiastic quality manager will write a specification for the best possible material, on the basis that the better the raw material the better the product or service that can be provided ultimately. This is not necessarily so. You need to evaluate the impact that the particular material will have on the quality of your eventual output. The specification has merely to reflect what is needed in order to achieve this. Any requirement in the specification that exceeds this will simply result in higher cost without any benefit in the finished product or service. However, do not confuse this with the question of improvement. Product improvement will start with an assessment of the product. If this reveals that the product can be improved by tightening a raw material specification, then clearly you have a different situation. In that case there is a well-evaluated reason for raising the raw material requirements, and the potential benefits can be anticipated and estimated.

The nature of the communication with the supplier will depend on the circumstances. In smaller organizations, and this includes the case of a small 'cell' within a larger organization, there may be only one person dealing with suppliers, and this person will ensure that all issues are taken care of – cost, delivery time, quality, complaints and the rest. In larger organizations it is usual to have two or more people involved. The quality manager agrees the specification with his or her opposite number, monitors the quality of the delivered product by means of an inspection or testing plan, and confirms that the delivered product has conformed to specification. This person will often deal with complaints also. The logistics of the transaction are managed by a purchasing manager who agrees the price and delivery details, places the order and arranges payment on receipt of the material. In a manufacturing situation the production manager who actually uses the material will liaise directly on user issues with the person in the supplier's organization who produces the material. However, the more people involved in the communication, the more important it is to have good internal communication, so that there is no confusion, overlap or gaps.

It is in everybody's interest that these various relationships are developed to a point where the supplier has confidence that you will deal fairly with him or her, and you have confidence in the quality of the material supplied. If you are confident that the material will conform to specification without fail you may be prepared to pay a premium, financed by the reduced costs of inspecting, testing, auditing, rejection and reworking. As the relationship develops your supplier may agree to provide you with process control information, which you can evaluate as though the material supplied were the output from your own process.

Eventually you may get to the stage where the supplier will even report production problems to you, knowing that you will assess them fairly, and only reject the material where it could genuinely jeopardize your own quality. At that point your supplier's process is essentially part of your own process, carried out in a different location, but under the same control as if it were in your own premises. In practice, this will only be possible where your business represents a significant part of the supplier's output.

For the most part, purchased materials will be incorporated into your own product. This often means, as in the case of processed materials, that there is a certain dilution of the impact of any defects in the materials as supplied. However, when the material purchased is a final product that you have subcontracted you are relying totally on the process control of the supplier, and the risks involved are far greater. In this situation somebody else is manufacturing the product that will be sold under your name. You must, therefore, have absolute confidence that the supplier operates essentially the same controls and quality management system that you would operate if you were manufacturing the product.

There is an equivalent situation in the case of many services. Very often a service provider will not be able to carry out a particular order or contract due to pressure of work, but will engage a subcontractor to fulfil the order. Extreme care must be taken in selecting the subcontractor, since it is the reputation of the main service provider that will suffer if the quality of work is not adequate.

NATURAL RESOURCES (6.7)

The issue here is the protection of the organization's business rather than any particular concern for the external environment. That is not to say that you are not encouraged to look seriously at the effect your operation has on the environment. That issue is not the direct concern of ISO 9004, though it is alluded to under 'Infrastructure' in clause 6.3.

The principal natural resources most companies use are fuel and water. You may also be vulnerable to disruption of supplies of critical raw materials, such as livestock or timber.

You should examine what possibilities you have to enable you to continue operating in the event of failure of supply of any critical natural resource. Availability of these resources should be addressed in the course of your review of resources and any relevant risk assessment exercises. In practice you are usually very limited in what you can do to protect yourself against supply problems, and the best you may be able to do is to minimize the impact of such contingencies by holding economically viable levels of stock.

FINANCIAL RESOURCES (6.8)

Finance is a specialist subject that would not be possible to cover comprehensively here. However, it is useful to mention a few general points. The sourcing of finance is not something over which most managers have any control. However, all managers have an impact on how the money is spent, and particularly, on how well the money is spent. The cost of failing to achieve quality is often overlooked as a financial index in favour of overtime costs and material costs. This is probably because quality costs are usually grossly underestimated. This is analogous to the situation regarding the cost of accidents in the workplace. Safety professionals have long used the iceberg as an illustration of how the hidden costs of accidents far outweigh the visible costs (Help document 6.8–1).

The obvious visible cost is the value of the product rejected. In the case of a service organization it is the cost of repeating a job because of an error the first time. Even if a defective product can be recovered by reworking there is still a loss in time and perhaps materials. Examples of less obvious costs are the amount of management time that is spent resolving quality problems, sales staff being diverted to visit customers after a complaint has been received and lost production time when purchased materials are found to be defective. Plant breakdown can also be a serious drain on financial resources. If the process operates 24 hours per day, then lost production cannot be made up, no matter what you do, since there are only 168 hours in a week and additional time cannot be generated. Such product loss must be classed as a loss due to quality failure, since better management could have prevented it.

The overall cost of quality is influenced strongly by the manner in which quality resources are deployed. For example, end-product testing tends to be more costly than process control activities. Yet it is less effective than process control in ensuring customer satisfaction. Changing the emphasis of inspection from final product testing to process control can result in significant cost savings, and the farther upstream in the process that control is exerted, the greater the potential for cost savings.

Incentive schemes, whereby employees are rewarded for suggestions that reduce costs should be considered. Such schemes, if properly constituted, can yield very great savings and improve quality at the same time.

Whatever initiatives are taken on it is essential that there are good reporting procedures so that the information in relation to finance is conveyed to the relevant managers promptly, enabling them to take appropriate action in a timely fashion.

See Help document 6.8–1. See also page 83 – 8.2.1.4.

CHAPTER VIII

The standards: Section 7 Product realization

ISO 9004	ISO 9001
7.1 General guidance	**7.1 Planning of product realization**
7.1.1 Introduction	
7.1.2 Issues to be considered	
7.1.3 Managing processes	
7.2 Processes related to interested parties	**7.2 Customer-related processes**
	7.2.1 Determination of requirements related to the product
	7.2.2 Review of requirements related to the product
	7.2.3 Customer communication
7.3 Design and development	**7.3 Design and development**
7.3.1 General guidance	7.3.1 Design and development planning
7.3.2 Design and development input and output	7.3.2 Design and development inputs
7.3.3 Design and development review	7.3.3 Design and development outputs
	7.3.4 Design and development review
	7.3.5 Design and development verification
	7.3.6 Design and development validation
	7.3.7 Control of design and development changes
7.4 Purchasing	**7.4 Purchasing**
7.4.1 Purchasing process	7.4.1 Purchasing process
7.4.2 Supplier control process	7.4.2 Purchasing information
	7.4.3 Verification of purchased product
7.5 Production and service operations	**7.5 Production and service provision**
7.5.1 Operation and realization	7.5.1 Control of production and service provision
7.5.2 Identification and traceability	7.5.2 Validation of processes for production and service provision
7.5.3 Customer property	7.5.3 Identification and traceability
7.5.4 Preservation of product	7.5.4 Customer property
	7.5.5 Preservation of product
7.6 Control of measuring and monitoring devices	**7.6 Control of monitoring and measuring devices**

GENERAL GUIDANCE (7.1), ISO 9001: PLANNING OF PRODUCT REALIZATION

The term *product realization* refers to the day-to-day productive business of the organization, which may be manufacturing a tangible product such as computer chips, providing a service such as financial consultancy, or a combination of both, such as serving meals in a restaurant. A dictionary definition of the word *realization* is 'convert (a hope, plan, etc.) into fact; convert into money; amass (fortune, specified profit)'. So, it is an appropriate word to use here. Readers in service operations should not forget that the term *product* as used in the standards includes intangible products like services. See the comments in the Preface.

ISO 9000 is based on the concept of processes, and you should get into the habit of regarding all activities in all parts of the organization as being processes. In this chapter we are looking specifically at the various activities which together result in the delivery of a finished product or service to the customer.

Too often there is no overall view of how the organization's various activities interact, and this can result in poor communication between the personnel involved in the different processes. It is the role of senior management to ensure that everybody understands fully the interplay of the various processes.

Having defined your product realization process you must now set about planning how it can be made to produce an output that will satisfy the customer. In Chapter VI (clause 5.4.2) we looked at planning the overall achievement of quality performance. Here we are dealing with planning the specific detailed activities necessary to produce a satisfactory product or service. The basic requirements are:

- an objective, in this case a detailed specification for the product or service;
- a set of defined methods or procedures for carrying out the necessary tasks;
- personnel who are capable of doing the tasks;
- the appropriate resources (equipment, software and materials);
- an appropriate environment in which to carry out the process;
- process control activities that will ensure the process yields an output that meets requirements; and
- a means of assessing whether the output meets the requirements defined in the specification.

VALIDATION OF PROCESSES (ISO 9004: 7.1.3.3; ISO 9001: 7.5.2)

This topic is out of alignment in the two standards. In earlier draft versions of ISO 9001 and ISO 9004 this paragraph was numbered 7.5.5. The topic was moved to 7.1.3.3 in ISO 9004, but the corresponding ISO 9001 paragraph became 7.5.2. This shuffling has resulted in the anomalous numbering of sub-clauses in 7.5 of ISO 9001 compared with 7.5 of ISO 9004.

The term *validation*, as used here, needs a little explanation. To produce an output consistently and predictably within specification the process must be maintained in control. However, this is only possible if the process has the inherent capability to operate within the required limits. For example, we may need to control the level of bacteria in a food product by means of an in-line heat treatment step, pasteurization, for example. The heat treatment which the product receives, and therefore the killing effect on bacteria, will depend on a number of factors that include the viscosity and flow rate of the product, the degree of fouling of heat-exchanger plates and the initial load of bacteria. The first requirement for the process is that the process itself should be capable of delivering the required kill factor for the full working range of all these parameters. The confirmation that it has this capability is called process validation. Only when this has been confirmed do we get into the business of controlling individual *runs*, and this is called *process control*. It is important to understand that one cannot usually rely totally on testing a few samples of the final product to demonstrate process capability. It takes a substantial amount of product testing under a wide range of operating conditions to confirm that the process retains capability over the full range of conditions likely to be encountered.

Clause 7.1.3.3 of ISO 9004 covers the validation of products and processes in general, including changes, while clause 7.5.2 of ISO 9001 confines itself to the validation of what used be called *special processes*, that is, processes where the output cannot be directly verified by inspection or testing. It is not always possible and practicable to confirm absolutely that the output of a task or process meets requirements. Sometimes the only definitive test is destructive, where the item itself is destroyed or incapacitated in the test. In such situations the item is demonstrated to be satisfactory only when it is put into use. A weld is often given as the example of this. Although there are instruments to test the integrity of a weld it is usually not practical to employ them. The only test available, therefore, is to stress the joint beyond its working load, which can result in its breaking. A more striking example is the administration of a general anaesthetic to a patient. This process simply must be right or the patient may die. To some extent, computer software is another example. For very complex software packages the bugs may only come to light when the programme is put into use. In effect the testing of the programme is completed by the user after it has been delivered and put into use. For such products and processes the only way you can be assured of the quality of the output is to exercise strict control over the process at all points. That implies that the process itself is actually capable of producing a product within specification. If it is not, then no amount of tightening of the specification can improve the product.

Documenting the characteristics and standard operating conditions of the process is important to the management of the process. Once the optimum operating conditions have been established these should be translated into a process specification. This specification can then be used to check the performance of the process, and this should be done regularly. For example, in order to achieve a certain physical property in the final product you may need to control a particular process variable (temperature or pressure) within certain limits. When you have established what these limits are you must confirm these conditions can be met consistently. You then define those conditions to be the standard conditions for that step, and use them to monitor the process performance regularly.

See Help document 8.2.3–2.

Proposed changes to the standard operating conditions should be evaluated carefully, and only approved when the full potential impact is known. By including the process specification in the quality management system documentation you ensure that the process operating conditions will not be changed without due consideration (see page 36).

See Help documents 7.1.3.3–1 and 7.1.3.3–2.

Although clause 7.5.2 of ISO 9001 restricts itself to a certain category of processes it can easily and convincingly be argued that you must validate all processes. Looking at ISO 9001 clause 7.1 it is difficult to see how you could comply with it without having carried out some degree of process validation. In ISO 9001 clause 7.2.2 you are required to ensure that the organization has the ability to meet the defined requirements. So, any attempt to argue that you do not need to validate all your product realization processes is likely to fail.

PRODUCT VALIDATION (7.1.3.3)

Products should also be validated. If the product has been designed or developed in accordance with clause 7.3 then it will have been validated as part of the design process. If it has not, perhaps because it was developed prior to the installation of the quality management system, then you should carry out a validation exercise. This will involve finding out as much as possible about how the product is intended to be used, and subjecting it to conditions that are as close as possible to those it will experience during use.

PROCESSES RELATED TO INTERESTED PARTIES (7.2)

DETERMINATION OF REQUIREMENTS RELATED TO THE PRODUCT (ISO 9001: 7.2.1)

When looking at the question of customer needs there are two main considerations. The first relates to the requirements defined in the particular order or contract. This is often a specification, either your specification that the customer accepts, or the customer's which you accept. You should ensure that your working specification is sufficiently detailed to enable you to satisfy the customer. This goes beyond the characteristics of any product that may be involved, a motor car or a hamburger, for example, and can include aspects such as delivery time, integrity of packaging or cleanliness of delivery vehicle. The second consideration, additional requirements of which the customer is actually not aware, is dealt with below – 'Review of requirements related to the product'.

See Help documents 7.2–1 and 7.2–2.

LEGAL REQUIREMENTS (ISO 9001: 7.2.1c)

To define customer requirements fully you must identify what the legal requirements are for the product or service and ensure that they are adequately addressed in your processes. This is in spite of the fact that the customer may not have specifically mentioned compliance with legal requirements as a condition for purchase.

Very often the distinction between quality and safety is blurred, since much of the law relating to products deals with product safety. In the case of a food product, for example, safety is the primary quality concern among consumers and considered to be much more important than taste. Some products are strictly regulated, such as food, pharmaceuticals and electrical goods, whereas others are covered by general legislation, which states that they should be fit for intended use. Whatever your product you should acquaint yourself with the legal requirements and then take steps to ensure you comply.

An important point to emphasize here is that actual compliance with legal requirements is not necessary for compliance with ISO 9001 requirements. The expert members of the ISO working group that produced the standards were quite adamant about this. Obviously you have a legal obligation to comply with statutory requirements and you must make every effort to so comply. But if you should fail, for whatever reason, that is not in itself a breach of ISO 9001 requirements. Unfortunately, external ISO auditors sometimes think that they should act as quasi police officers. On one occasion I came across a company that had been refused certification because one of their delivery vehicles did not have a current valid road tax disc. This is clearly outside the authority of ISO 9001 external auditors. Of course, a second party audit by a customer is a different matter. It is very likely that the customer will not place the order if a legal non-compliance is discovered in an audit. But that is the customer's right. Irrespective of what ISO 9001 requires, if the customer demands something, you have no alternative but to comply if you want the business.

You probably also have legal obligations in regard to the realization process itself. The question of legal compliance in relation to processes is highly complex and you should take professional advice if you are in doubt on any matter. Your legal obligations may relate to the impact your operation has on the environment, occupational health and safety, obligations in respect of the local authorities, and social and employment legislation.

The most effective way of ensuring that you meet your legal obligations is, as always, to have a systematic, formal approach. That is, you should not be satisfied that you currently comply with the law, but should have a systematic approach for ensuring that you will always *know* that you comply. In other words, you comply because you have planned it that way, and not simply by chance. Many companies just happen to comply with their legal obligations but not because of any effort of good management on their part. Help document 7.2-3 describes a relatively simple procedure for reaching legal compliance.

You should assign to some competent person the responsibility for keeping company knowledge of legal obligations up to date. This person should be responsible for reviewing legal compliance at regular intervals.

REVIEW OF REQUIREMENTS RELATED TO THE PRODUCT (ISO 9001: 7.2.2)

The second aspect to customer requirements is that the customer very often does not know the full requirements for the product, and can only define requirements in terms of obvious performance characteristics. A client employing an architect to design a house may only define the requirements in terms of the number, type and size of rooms. But if you are the architect you will understand the unstated requirements regarding planning laws, drainage and sewerage requirements, levelling of the site, and such like. In order to ensure that all requirements, stated and implied, are met, you, the expert in this field, must identify all these aspects of the product or service and include them in your planning.

What is appropriate in determining customer requirements, as for everything else in the quality management system, depends on the circumstances. A small shop and a large manufacturing company will differ enormously in how they approach this, but the general principle is the same – do whatever is appropriate to find out what is necessary in order to satisfy the customer's expectations.

CUSTOMER COMMUNICATION (ISO 9001: 7.2.3)

Communication with your major customers is the mirror image of your communication with your suppliers. Most people like to have some specific contact person in the supplier's organization with whom they can discuss issues such as the specification, special requirements for a particular order, technical information about the product or service being purchased, and complaints about the performance of the product or the delivery of the service. These are precisely the sorts of channels of communication you should provide for your customers. The arrangements for communication should be discussed at the contract or order stage so that the parties on each side know whom to contact.

The details of such an arrangement for a large contract are fairly easy to imagine, and have been described in Chapter VII dealing with suppliers and partnerships (clause 6.6). In the case of a small company there may only be one person communicating with the customer on all aspects of the contract.

In situations where there is no direct contact with the customer, as in the case of the manufacturer of items for retail sale, the contact telephone number or e-mail address is often printed on the item itself. In the case of a service such as a railway the contact details could be posted up or printed on items such as tickets. It is particularly important to have a well-defined procedure for dealing with customer complaints.

See Help documents 8.2.1.2–3, 8.2.1.2–4 and 7.2–4.

DESIGN AND DEVELOPMENT (7.3)

The terms *design* and *development* are used interchangeably and there is no need to get too excited about the difference. Sometimes *design* is used where a new product is involved, whereas *development* refers to the establishment of a new process for the realization of the newly designed product, where this is necessary.

The clauses of the standard relating to design and development have limited application, since most companies do not carry out this activity in a manner that would require it to be classified as a separate section of their quality management systems. So, it may not be relevant to your operation. However, see below ('Design and development of processes'). The term *design and development* here does not refer to the small adjustments that are constantly made to products to improve them or to the routine adjustments to processes to keep them in control. Essentially, we are looking here at the whole process of taking a product from concept through its life cycle to consumption or scrapping at the end of its useful life, or a service project from concept stage to final commissioning and completion. The concept also applies to significant changes to the product or to its intended use, which might invalidate the original design and development process. For example, many tropical countries experience difficulties with items that were developed in moderate climates. Motor vehicles designed for temperate climates have to be *tropicalized* before they can be confidently introduced into a tropical market. While the number of changes to be made may be quite small, the entire design and development process for the vehicle has to be revisited to ensure that all aspects of the vehicle's use have been assessed for the impact of the changed climatic conditions.

To justify inclusion as a stand-alone part of your quality management system the design or development work would need to be a distinct activity carried out in a formal way at the behest of a customer. In other words, the organization undertakes to design a product or service for a clearly defined customer. This customer may be internal to the organization or external, and is the one who will ultimately decide if the final design complies with his or her requirements.

Very often the customer is not even aware that the product is new and that design or development work is involved. For example, if a client asks a training organization to deliver a training course on a particular subject, he or she may not be told that the organization has never delivered that course before. The course will simply be developed and delivered in the normal way.

Irrespective of who the customer is, the reason for including design and development in the quality management system is to build quality into the product at the earliest possible stage so that customer satisfaction is guaranteed throughout the life cycle of the product.

See Help documents 7.3–1 and 7.3–2.

DESIGN AND DEVELOPMENT OF PROCESSES

Where the development of a process is an integral part of a particular contract or order then clearly it must come under the scope of the ISO 9001 requirements, and must be developed in accordance with the requirements of clause 7.3. But what about the development of the process that routinely produces the stable range of products? Strictly speaking your normal product realization process must also be developed according to the disciplines described in these clauses. In practice, many companies are operating processes that have been developed prior to the introduction of the formal quality management system, and there are no records to indicate how they were developed. It is unreasonable for an auditor to expect to see documentation complying with the requirements of clause 7.3 for a process that was developed years previously. However, all realization processes must be assessed to confirm that they are capable of producing an output that meets the specified requirements. This is dealt with under validation (page 59). In the case of recently developed product realization processes you would be expected to have the records to show that it was developed in the prescribed manner.

DESIGN AND DEVELOPMENT PLANNING (ISO 9001: 7.3.1)

The entire development process must be planned if the final output is to satisfy the customer. Make out a flow chart for the design process, identifying all the stages, and then list the key activities for each step. It will be necessary to establish at each phase that the project is on course for successful conclusion. That will mean assessing the design output against set criteria. Later, the output will have to be checked against customer requirements. All this should be planned in advance.

Assign responsibilities to all persons involved in design and development work. Typically design is a multidisciplinary activity, usually involving personnel from such functions as marketing, production, quality and engineering. In such a situation it is very easy for confusion to arise, especially with regard to the making of decisions, if responsibilities and authority are not clearly defined.

DESIGN AND DEVELOPMENT INPUTS (ISO 9001: 7.3.2)

The design inputs are those resources, tangible and intangible, that are required for the entire design process. The first input will be the customer's requirements for the product or service. That may be a detailed specification, but sometimes is quite vague, perhaps no more than a concept. In clause 7.2.2 we mentioned the fact that the customer is not normally familiar with all aspects of the product, and this applies here also. The customer is seldom in a position to specify all the technical requirements, and certainly not those for manufacturing a product. The specification may therefore have to be supplemented by further information such as technical performance requirements, legal requirements for the product or service, codes of practice, specifications for similar products, and information from previous design projects. All the inputs are usually converted into an internal design brief or working specification for the design project.

As the designed product or service takes shape the customer may refine his or her requirements, so you must allow in your plan for the fact that the customer specification may change a number of times before the design project is finished.

DESIGN AND DEVELOPMENT OUTPUTS (ISO 9001: 7.3.3)

The term 'output' refers to the information, documentation, samples or prototypes, which come out of the design work relating to the eventual realization of a successful product. That includes a detailed specification for the product or service, with the acceptance criteria defined, and details of how to deliver the service or manufacture the product. It should also define the resources needed, such as equipment and environment, qualification of personnel, training requirements, drawings, and specifications for materials and services that must be purchased.

In other words, the design output should define everything to enable the product to be manufactured or the service to be delivered successfully. Irrespective of how simple or complex the product, the output must be comprehensive, and should address all foreseeable circumstances relating to the use and abuse of the product throughout its life cycle, to final disposal.

Since it is this output that will determine how the final product or service will perform during its life cycle, it is critical that it should be carefully assessed before being used. The design procedure should, therefore, require that the process go no further until the output is fully documented and those documents approved.

DESIGN AND DEVELOPMENT REVIEW (ISO 9001: 7.3.4)

The major worry in a complex design project is that the final design will not be available on time or will not satisfy the customer. To ensure that this does not happen, progress must be reviewed regularly to confirm that the work remains on course to give a product that meets the customer's requirements. The frequency and nature of these reviews will depend on the complexity of the project. Reviews should be scheduled at the planning stage. There may be obvious phases in the project where review should take place, or you may decide that review will be carried out at set, frequent intervals, such as regular project management meetings.

The review should involve representatives from all significant functions involved in the design or development activities. So, for example, the attendance might include personnel from the research and development function (who actually do the development work), laboratory (testing products), engineering (assessing machine performance), human resources (monitoring health and safety aspects), finance (monitoring performance against budget) and production (producing full-scale production samples). In the case of a construction project the review might be a site meeting of the architect, the engineer and the main contractor.

DESIGN AND DEVELOPMENT VERIFICATION (ISO 9001: 7.3.5)

Verification and validation are two words defined with very specific meanings in the context of ISO 9001, and not those found in a dictionary. Verification refers to an assessment of the developed product against the product brief, or internal specification, while validation refers to assessment against the stated customer requirements. The flow diagram in Help document 7.3–1 shows the relationship between them, and their relevance to the overall design process.

Where the customer provides a specification this is clearly the starting point. Usually, however, it is necessary to convert this into a detailed design brief for the design team to work on.

When the process has yielded a result that is sufficiently mature that it can be assessed for overall suitability it is first assessed against the design brief. This is the verification step. Verification may be carried out several times before the output is finally assessed against customer requirements.

See Help document 7.3.3–1.

DESIGN AND DEVELOPMENT VALIDATION (ISO 9001: 7.3.6)

When a final output has been produced, having been verified against the design brief at the appropriate stages along the way, it then remains to confirm that it meets the requirements of the customer and is fully suitable for its intended use. This is the validation step. Validation must demonstrate that the finished product, as it will be produced or delivered routinely in normal conditions, actually performs according to the requirements stated by the customer. If you have been carrying out regular reviews and have been communicating regularly with the customer, there should be no problems at this point. Failure at this point suggests a serious lack of control at some earlier point in the process.

While ISO 9000 distinguishes between review, verification and validation there is no reason why some or all of these steps cannot be carried out simultaneously, if the circumstances justify it. For example, the site meeting for a construction project would probably cover both the review and verification steps. The validation might be left until the owner takes possession and dictates the final 'snag list'. The simpler the total design or development process, the more likely it is that some of these activities can be combined. ISO 9001 merely requires that these activities are carried out. Provided you can produce the records to demonstrate that you have done this, then you comply with the requirements of the standard, even if it is the same piece of paper you submit to the auditor in answer to all three questions.

Help document 7.3.3–2 outlines a procedure for developing an in-company training course. This is an example of a service provider developing a service for a particular customer. Note that while review and verification take place during the preparation phase, validation can only take place during the actual delivery of the training course. The trainer must be prepared to make whatever changes are necessary in order to ensure the satisfaction of the course participants. A good trainer will constantly monitor the degree of satisfaction and make appropriate changes.

See Help document 7.3.3–2.

CONTROL OF DESIGN AND DEVELOPMENT CHANGES (ISO 9001: 7.3.7)

By its very nature development work involves change as the project progresses. The changes can arise as a result of the development work itself, as new ideas, methods or materials are explored. Or they may come from the customer, either as a result of a change of mind or from a refining of his or her ideas in the light of the intermediate output. Whatever the reason, it is critical to keep control of these changes and any documentation involved.

This is one situation in which revision numbers are probably essential. When discussing document control (page 35) I suggested that it is sufficient to show the date of revision alone, since this can indicate if the document is current when checked against the master list. However, in the case of design documents, which may be revised several times in a day, using a date alone may not be sufficient.

PURCHASING (7.4)

PURCHASING PROCESS (7.4.1)

Purchased materials and subcontracted services need to be given at least the same degree of attention as you give your own processes. It is amazing how often I have seen companies subject their own staff and processes to extraordinary controls, while at the same time subcontracting critical products from suppliers about whom they know virtually nothing. The relationship between purchaser and supplier is covered in clause 6.6 (Chapter VII). In this section we are looking at the routine business of purchasing.

First you must identify those items, materials and services that can have an impact on the quality of the finished product or service. Any purchased material whose quality cannot affect the quality of your output does not need to be controlled, though for purely commercial reasons this may be highly desirable. Thus, depending on the nature of your operation, you may decide to exclude, for example, stationery and fuel oil from the purchasing controls in the quality management system. Ingredients or components may be excluded if you can demonstrate that your process will correct *fully* any possible defects that might be present, but it is very rare to be in such a happy position.

All purchases identified as critical should be purchased from reliable suppliers who have been assessed for their capability to supply quality products and services. The suppliers with such capability should be listed in the approved suppliers list, and this should be included in the appropriate quality system manual. It is advisable to have a formal written procedure for the selection and approval of suppliers.

The approved suppliers must be re-evaluated at defined intervals to confirm that they continue to supply goods and services to specification. The normal frequency for this review is every 12 months, though this is not specified in ISO 9001. The correct frequency will depend on the circumstances, and senior management must decide what is appropriate.

Evaluation of suppliers usually involves a group of key personnel with the information needed for the evaluation. Help document 7.4.2–2 lists the functions usually involved. In small organizations the review may be carried out by one person working alone. The basic task is the same, however; that is, to review each supplier's performance and decide whether to renew the approval for another period.

If the necessary information is available in the right format, a non-troublesome supplier can be reviewed in as little as 60 seconds. As with all meetings it is important to prepare carefully, and not to waste time in unhelpful discussion that can be sidelined.

I am often asked, 'Does one have to audit [that is, visit] all suppliers of critical materials?' Sometimes the question is posed by a quality manager keen to visit exotic places! Clearly the answer is 'No'. Admittedly, it is easier to assess a supplier's capability if you have seen the operation, but that is not the only way, and it is possible to make a totally valid assessment of a supplier without physically visiting the premises.

For example, an initial order could be placed on the strength of the supplier's participation in an accredited quality assurance scheme, or having a local agent carry out an audit, or simply acting on the recommendation of somebody you trust. You would then use the trial material and assess the output from your process somewhat more carefully than normal. If you were satisfied, you could then make a decision on whether to place another trial order. In parallel with this you would ask for supporting information about, for example, the supplier's quality management system (see 'Purchasing information' below), controls that the supplier operates and technical details specific to the particular product. In due course you could build up the picture that would enable you to approve the supplier.

As with all other aspects of quality management, responsibilities in relation to purchasing have to be clearly defined. There are two principal responsibilities involved. The first relates to the quality or technical aspects of the material or service to be purchased and the capability of a potential supplier to meet requirements. This is normally the task of the quality manager or other person filling the technical role. The decision on whether to approve a supplier is based purely on the supplier's capability. The second responsibility relates to the actual routine purchasing activity. This involves pricing, scheduling, agreeing discounts, order size and such like. But this is confined to those suppliers already approved on quality grounds. The decision to place an order is based on purely commercial considerations, having first established that the supplier is capable of supplying a quality material consistently. In larger companies these two functions are normally carried out by different people. In a small company it might well be the same person, and there is no objection to this.

See Help documents 7.4.1–1, 7.4.1–2 and 7.4.1–3.

The word *purchasing* implies a commercial arrangement. However, there are many situations in which an organization acquires materials, legitimately, by means other than purchasing. If these materials have implications for the quality of the product or service then their supply must be controlled according to the requirements of this section.

PURCHASING INFORMATION (ISO 9001: 7.4.2)

When you receive an order from a customer you take steps to ensure that you understand fully his or her requirements, so that you can be certain of supplying precisely what is expected, thereby assuring customer satisfaction. Similarly, when you are the one placing the order you should ensure that you state your requirements clearly and unambiguously to guarantee that you receive what you expect.

When placing an order it is important to refer to the specification. If you have been ordering the same material from the same supplier for 20 years you may think that it is safe to stop quoting the precise specification. But, consider this scenario: your supplier embarks on a cost-cutting exercise and starts to produce a cheaper lower grade material. Since you have not specified what grade you require the supplier can justifiably increase his profit by supplying the lower grade material to you. Of course, you would hope that a trusted supplier would discuss this matter with you beforehand.

Where you have an agreed specification, note its reference number on the order or attach a copy to the order. That will prevent any confusion and should ensure that you get precisely what you have ordered. In many cases you will be ordering material from a catalogue. In that case the item number given in the catalogue is sufficient to identify the item fully, and should be quoted on the order.

Defining the requirements for the product may be only part of the story. Because of the impossibility of fully demonstrating product quality by means of inspection or testing you may need to lay down conditions regarding the manner in which the product is manufactured or the service delivered. What you specify depends largely on how well you know the supplier's process. Even if you know nothing about the process you may wish to set down conditions relating to the supplier's quality management system. There has been an unfortunate trend developing in recent years whereby customers insist on ISO 9001 certification for critical, or even all, suppliers. While ISO 9001 certification is highly commendable it is not an absolute guarantee of complete compliance with requirements. Equally, there are many excellent companies supplying totally reliable products, which have not gone down the road to certification, but who nonetheless have very effective quality management systems in place. There is a risk that customers will neglect the real disciplines required for effective supplier control, thinking that it is sufficient to insist on ISO 9001 certification, and that this covers all possible problems that might arise in the supply of a critical item or service. There may be instances in which it is sensible to demand ISO 9001 certification of a supplier, but do not use it as a crutch.

In certain circumstances you may need to specify particular requirements for the personnel involved in the production of the purchased product or service. An example of this is the insistence that suppliers of a food product should provide hygiene training for all personnel who have contact with a material which you will purchase, and that all such personnel are medically fit to work in a food preparation environment.

Verbal orders

Obviously, verbal orders are handled differently to written orders, but the principle is the same – you need to be sure that the supplier has recorded your order and can assure you that mistakes will not be made. Where you place verbal orders be sure to record the details of what you have ordered in some form that enables you to check the actual material when it arrives. This will help you in assessing the supplier's performance at the appropriate time. This record can be as simple as an entry in a diary, but it is probably more useful to have a dedicated place for recording it, for example, a pre-printed sheet on which you record a number of verbal orders.

See Help documents 7.4.1–1 and 7.4.1–2.

VERIFICATION OF PURCHASED PRODUCT (ISO 9001: 7.4.3)

When the material is delivered you will probably want to check that you have received what you ordered and that it meets the specification. The extent of checking that you carry out will depend on many factors, but primarily your confidence in the supplier. In the extreme case where you have no information about the supplier's capability but are forced by circumstances to use the material you may carry out 100 per cent inspection or apply a formal statistical sampling scheme. As you gather more information, and as the supplier builds up a track record you should consider reducing the level of inspection. With a lot of hard work and commitment on both sides you could get to a situation where you do no testing, as in the case of a just-in-time relationship. So, there is no clear-cut definition of what level of inspection is acceptable for incoming materials. The important thing is that you can justify what you do, and demonstrate from the known facts that it is adequate.

Ideally, a record should be kept of the receipt of all materials that have been identified as relevant to quality. Certainly, where traceability of materials through the process is an issue the lot number should be recorded. The amount of detail recorded will depend, as always, on the circumstances.

See Help documents 7.4.1–3 and 7.5.2–3.

PRODUCTION AND SERVICE OPERATIONS (7.5)

OPERATION AND REALIZATION (7.5.1)

Every organization, whether commercial, governmental or voluntary, exists to supply a service or to manufacture a tangible product. All activities in quality management are aimed at enabling the organization to carry out its primary function in the most effective and efficient manner. This clause of the standard deals with that basic aspect; other clauses are essentially ancillary to this one. People are your most valuable resource and customer satisfaction is all-important, but if you cannot put together a suitable product or deliver the basic service then the customers simply will not exist, and everything else is irrelevant. So, your primary effort must go into managing the core process of your operation.

Planning has been discussed in clause 7.1. Now we have to look at the business of producing the output for the customer.

SPECIFICATIONS (ISO 9001: 7.5.1a)

Every product manufactured and every service delivered should be documented in the form of a specification. This is a very familiar concept in larger companies, but people in many smaller companies do not see the need to have a specification for simple products. There are two main reasons why a specification is useful. First, it provides the basis for agreement between you and your customer, and can prevent many disputes over basic issues. Second, it forms the basis for your assessment of the product or service at the end of the process.

If the specification to be used has been supplied by the customer and you have agreed it then there is no need for you to rewrite this as an internal document. It should, however, be controlled just as if it were an internal quality document. If you are going to produce repeat orders for this customer over a long period there is every possibility that the specification will change from time to time as the customer identifies improvements that he or she wishes to make. If you do not control the physical copies of the specification you will, in time, discover photocopies of obsolete specifications being used. The simplest way of controlling the specifications, whether internal or external, is to assign a document control number to each and include them in an appropriate manual, or set up a manual dedicated to product specifications.

The following are some of the issues that may be appropriate to consider when drawing up a specification for a physical product:

- physical properties of the product (e.g. colour, hardness, dimensions);
- chemical properties (composition, levels of impurities, etc.);
- biological properties (enzymatic activity, permissible levels of bacterial contamination, etc.);
- components or materials to be used (grades, performance in testing);
- functional/performance properties;
- special process steps;
- packaging;

- labelling;
- instructions for use/safety instructions;
- storage conditions;
- delivery method;
- shelf life; and
- method of disposal.

In the case of a service (for example, a pest control contractor) consider the following:

- frequency of visits;
- locations to be covered;
- minimum work to be done on each visit;
- action to be taken if specified contingencies arise (for example, infestation is discovered);
- input (if any) required from the customer;
- documentation to be completed and supplied to the customer;
- response time;
- times of availability;
- materials to be used; and
- exclusions.

Notice that in the case of a service the specification looks very like some of the terms that might appear in a contract. In many cases, however, a contract with a service supplier is confined to financial or legal terms, with hardly any mention of the quality aspects of the service.

WORK INSTRUCTIONS (ISO 9001: 7.5.1b)

This has been dealt with in detail in clause 4.2 (Chapter V). The terms *work instruction* and *procedure* are used interchangeably. They both refer to written descriptions of how to perform a task. The significant point here is that the documented procedures must be available where they are required. For the most part a person who has been performing a routine task for a period will not often need to consult the procedure, if at all. However, it must be available to be consulted at all times. Thus, it must not be kept in an office that is locked at certain times, for example, a manager's office that is only open when the manager is on site. Equally, it would not be acceptable if the manual were kept on a different floor or in a different building to the workstation where the task is carried out. It is not, however, necessary to have each procedure posted up beside the workstation where it is used, though this may be appropriate or necessary in particular circumstances.

USE OF SUITABLE EQUIPMENT (ISO 9001: 7.5.1c)

Usually the manufacture of a product involves the use of equipment. Many service provision operations also require equipment. The quality management system should contain some control that ensures that suitable equipment is provided. This will involve a survey of the product realization processes. The basic requirement is that where a piece of equipment is needed in order to carry out the task, it is provided. Sometimes a task can be carried out either manually or with the help of mechanical equipment. If it can only be done reliably with equipment, then this should be provided.

As well as providing equipment you must also ensure that the equipment provided is inherently capable of operating in a way that delivers the quality required.

Note that maintenance of equipment is covered in clause 6.3 Infrastructure.

USE OF MEASURING AND MONITORING DEVICES (ISO 9001:7.5.1d)

All processes require some degree of inspection to establish whether they are operating within the acceptable limits defined for quality. In many cases this involves making a measurement using some sort of measuring device. Whatever your situation, you should review the entire process and determine if there is a need for measuring devices. Very often a small capital outlay on such a device can give much greater confidence in the quality of the output. For example, a temperature probe for measuring the internal temperature of cooked meat in a restaurant can be extremely valuable in the fight against food poisoning. Make sure that all such devices are listed in the appropriate place in your manual.

See also clause 7.6.

MONITORING AND MEASURING ACTIVITIES (ISO 9001: 7.5.1e)

The provision of suitable monitoring activities is integral to product realization, and is required by ISO 9001. As a general rule, the output from all tasks that are critical to quality should be monitored. The extent of monitoring will depend on the task involved and what impact it can have on the quality of the final product or service. Monitoring may be a simple visual check by the person performing the task or a more complex off-line inspection of a sample. These activities come under the general term of process control, which is covered in detail on page 84.

RELEASE, DELIVERY AND POST-DELIVERY ACTIVITIES (ISO 9001: 7.5.1f)

The term *release* is easier to understand for a physical product than for a service. It refers to the decision to allow the product to be delivered to the customer. It implies an assessment of the item to check that it is fit for use. In the case of a service involving a physical item release refers to the characteristics of the item at the point of handover to the customer. Examples of this type of service are window cleaning, meals in a restaurant and insurance policy documents.

For most services there is a point at which the person providing the service considers that the project has been successfully completed. For example, a quality management consultant who has advised on setting up a management system would carry out a final check to confirm that the project is indeed completed (see Help document 7.5.1–1). Such a final check could be written into the invoicing procedure; only after confirmation that everything is in order would the final invoice be sent out. Notice that in the case of a service there is often an overlap between this activity and validation (page 65). That should not cause any difficulty; it often happens that a single activity or record can satisfy more than one requirement of ISO 9001.

In all cases the issue is the formal assessment of the quality of the output to determine if it meets the customer's requirements. Usually this is most easily done using a checklist. The items on the checklist will relate closely to the original specification for the item or service.

Even a highly experienced person performing a task for which he or she is professionally qualified should consider seriously the value of such a checklist. Professionals have different ways of doing things, sometimes with different impacts on customer satisfaction. It is not always the technical aspects of the service that cause customer dissatisfaction. In any case, even the best of us forget things from time to time, and there are bound to be slight differences between the various contracts or orders for different customers, and a checklist can ensure that these minor differences are covered in the final assessment.

See Help documents 7.5.1–1 and 8.2.3–2.

IDENTIFICATION AND TRACEABILITY (ISO 9004: 7.5.2; ISO 9001: 7.5.3)

Identification and traceability are normally considered to be two aspects of the same concept, though each has its own particular features. Identification refers to the assignment of some form of tag (physical or otherwise) to items of interest so that no confusion can arise over their identity.

Most companies have experience of one or more of the following problems:

- wrong material being used resulting in a faulty product or unsatisfactory service;
- faulty product being dispatched to the customer due to failure to mark test samples correctly; and
- the wrong samples or documents being sent to a client.

There are two principal questions that must be clearly answered by the identification tag:

- What is it? Every material or item should be labelled with its identity unless it is obvious that it could not be anything else. This is particularly critical if the item can only be distinguished from others by testing or performance (for example, materials with different properties that look identical, such as chemical products or construction materials).
- To what group or lot does it belong? For example, to what project does a particular drawing refer? Or, from what batch was a particular sample taken?

The basic requirement is that it should be possible for anybody to determine the identity of the item without having to guess or to make any assumptions. Often it is not practicable for every item to have an identifying mark. Sometimes only the outer packaging for a number of items is marked. Problems of identity will arise once these items are removed from the outer packaging. You must have adequate controls in place to prevent confusion arising. Such controls could involve strict procedures forbidding the working on more than one item at a time, or physical segregation of items in well-defined areas during work in progress.

Bulk material in tanks or silos can also pose difficulties. Possible controls in this case include having marked containers at each stage of the process, and keeping records of movement of material between containers. The identity of the material contained in it may be physically written on the container, or may be recorded on computer or on paper.

Identification controls must extend to any samples taken. The decision to accept or reject product is often made on the basis of samples. If the samples are not adequately and unambiguously identified, serious errors can be made resulting in the inadvertent release for use of faulty material. Another type of identification which must be addressed is the status of an item or material in relation to any testing or inspection that has been carried out. When something has been inspected its status automatically changes, since it is now known to be either conforming or non-conforming, assuming that the inspection or test has yielded a definitive result. It is important that this information is available to any potential users or handlers of the material, particularly if it does not conform to requirements. The danger is that such material will be inadvertently used or supplied to a customer. See also page 89 for further treatment of this topic.

Traceability is the action of keeping adequate records of the usage of materials. The underlying concern here is that in the event of a subsequent problem you can establish where different materials were used and be able to identify products in which the faulty materials were incorporated, or clients whose service may have been affected by the faulty material.

There are two principal situations in which traceability records would be called upon:

1 A component, ingredient or raw material is discovered to have been faulty after it has been incorporated into a product and the product dispatched to a number of customers. All customers who received the faulty product must be traced and the faulty product recovered and replaced. The

component in question must be traced right through the process from receipt through processing, packaging, storage, dispatch and delivery.

2 A customer reports a faulty product and it is necessary to identify which component is the source of the problem. The product must now be traced back through all the process steps, and the various components that have been used in the product must be traced back to their intake and purchase. Once the full identity of the offending component has been established it may then be necessary to trace forward again, since components from that particular faulty lot may have been incorporated into other batches of product, and the customers who received those products would then have to be traced also.

The degree to which traceability is required is normally determined by the senior management of the organization, though there may be legal obligations in relation to materials such as pharmaceuticals. In deciding what is appropriate a balance must be struck between the cost of operating the traceability system and its value in the event of problems in the market. A fully comprehensive traceability system whereby everything can be accounted for can be impractical or very costly to operate, though in some cases it may be essential. In the event of a problem, however, such a system can answer all questions, and enable a product recall to be confined to precisely those customers who were definitely affected by the fault. On the other hand, if you have taken the minimalist approach you may not be able to determine the extent of the problem and may have to declare a full public product recall of a number of batches of product. For example, a fruit and vegetable shop could not possibly keep a record of every sale to every customer, and would have to exercise proportionately greater control to ensure that problems do not arise, for example, by careful selection of suppliers.

Traceability can sometimes apply to knowledge as well as physical items. In the case of a consultancy service, for example, it can be important to be able to trace a thought process through a project, and to be able to know afterwards how particular decisions or solutions were reached.

See Help documents 7.5.2–1, 7.5.2–2 and 7.5.2–3.

CUSTOMER PROPERTY (ISO 9004: 7.5.3; ISO 9001: 7.5.4)

Many organizations handle materials or items supplied by the customer which remain the property of the customer. Examples of this are a special ingredient or component to be used in the manufacture of a product, a prototype of a design for which a patent attorney is preparing a patent application, an antique fitting to be incorporated into a new building or any document that is to be returned to the customer on completion of the order or contract.

When such items are received they should be recorded. Their location should be known at all times, and in the case of materials for incorporation into a product, their use should be recorded and reconciled. They should be stored carefully and protected against damage. If any loss or damage should occur this should be recorded and notified to the customer.

Procedures should specifically cover customers' property as well as the organization's own property. It is good practice to handle all items appropriately and protect them against damage, irrespective of whether they belong to you or your customer.

PRESERVATION OF PRODUCT (ISO 9004: 7.5.4; ISO 9001: 7.5.5)

This clause deals with the post-production activities of delivery, transport and general handling of the product. These are essentially the later stages of the process and do not need to be distinguished from the earlier stages, other than to emphasize that the process is not finished when the product has been put into the warehouse. These activities should be controlled and documented as normal steps in your process.

CONTROL OF MEASURING AND MONITORING DEVICES (7.6)

Monitoring of quality is often a very simple matter – is the window clean? Is the sauce thick enough? Is the colour the same as the sample supplied? Is there any visible damage? However, monitoring often requires the use of measuring instruments to carry out checks. Such measuring instruments need to be treated with due care to ensure that they give accurate readings, and should be protected from abuse and damage.

In addition, some instruments require specific conditions for use, and you must ensure that the appropriate conditions are provided. For example, an analytical balance to weigh milligram quantities or less must be located on a very solid surface with minimum vibration.

Even given the optimum conditions, however, all measuring instruments give an error, however small. The error for each reading should be known and taken into account. Consider the following scenario: you are storing a material that is temperature-sensitive, but you do not have a practical test that will tell you if the material is still fit for use after a period of storage. Your only guarantee of fitness is to store the material below a particular temperature, 4°C, say. Otherwise the material will not behave properly in use. It might be a chemical or an adhesive, for example. If the temperature of the material is found to be above 4°C you cannot be sure that the material will perform properly. You have been checking the temperature regularly with a thermometer and finding readings of 3.8°C consistently. Since the readings have been within the specification you have been approving the material for use. Suppose you now send the thermometer to have its accuracy checked, which is called calibration, and are told that the readings are now too low by 1°C. What is your opinion now about the material currently stored at 3.8°C? You must declare it unfit for use, since you now know the true temperature to be 4.8°C. The new information about the size of the error on the thermometer has caused you to arrive at a diametrically opposite decision to your initial one. The situation is further complicated by the fact that you do not know at what point the error became sufficient to invalidate your 'accepted' decisions. See 'Calibration nonconformity', below.

Calibration is a highly technical field, and it would not be possible to deal with it comprehensively in this type of text. However, it is worth looking at some of the general principles, as it often causes confusion and argument.

CONTROL OF CALIBRATION EQUIPMENT

Any instrument or item that you use for calibration purposes should be reserved for that purpose only. For example, if you purchase a calibrated thermometer or temperature probe to carry out calibration of fixed temperature gauges on your processing equipment that instrument should not then be used for taking other routine temperature measurements. Instruments used for calibration should be put away carefully and only used under strictly controlled conditions and only for calibration. The reason for this is that all instruments develop inaccuracies with time and, the more an instrument is used, the greater the risk of inaccuracy and the shorter the validity of its current calibration. This restriction also applies to items that are used as standards. For example, a standard weight that is used to check the accuracy of a balance or weighing scales must not be used as the working counterbalance, as it is likely to suffer damage during constant use. Clearly, the degree of care to be taken must be appropriate for the significance of the measurement and its potential impact on product or service quality.

SETTING UP A CALIBRATION SYSTEM

The first important point to establish is that ISO 9001 requirements on calibration refer only to certain measuring equipment. They are the instruments that provide information that you will use in deciding whether the product or service conforms to specification. In other words, you rely on these measurements *without any confirmatory evidence from other sources* to indicate whether the product conforms or does not conform. Ideally, of course, all instruments should be calibrated, but since calibration is an expensive exercise this is not always practical.

Instruments that do not provide such information do not require calibration and are usually marked 'For indication only'. For example, in order to ensure that the final product has a particular moisture level it may be necessary to control the temperature of the process within defined limits. The temperature is therefore measured and recorded at specified times during the manufacture of the product. Subsequently, however, the product itself is tested for moisture level before being released. In that situation the temperature gauge on the process does not strictly require calibration, since you are not relying on its reading to determine the quality of the product. The critical measurement on which conformance to specification is based is the actual moisture measurement on the finished product. Product that does not conform to specification will be detected by the final test and will be rejected. Therefore, in this example, calibration is not required under ISO 9001.

Clearly, however, if the temperature gauge is sufficiently inaccurate you will end up with a non-conforming product, which the quality management system is trying to prevent. Furthermore, if there were any doubt that testing of a sample or a practical number of samples of the finished product could provide the *full* picture about the quality of the entire batch of product, then one is back to relying on controlling the temperature of the process, and in these circumstances the gauge certainly does require calibration, since in this case one cannot rely fully on the subsequent testing to confirm whether the entire batch meets specification.

SETTING THE LIMITS

Every measuring instrument gives an error. The inherent inaccuracy of each instrument must be determined and taken into account when setting the working limits for the parameter being measured. In effect, you must determine what error is acceptable for each instrument, taking into consideration the significance of the variable it is measuring. In the example of the storage of the temperature-sensitive material described on page 74 the thermometer clearly had an error of the order of 1°C. Yet the limit for the measurement was set at precisely the absolute upper limit of acceptability, that is, 4°C. It would have been more sensible to set the limit for the temperature at 3°C to allow for the error on the thermometer, and take action when the temperature approaches that value.

CALIBRATION NONCONFORMITY

Many instruments are capable of being adjusted to give the correct reading and this is a normal part of the calibration process. However, it is important to know what the reading was before any adjustment was made, the so-called *as found* reading. The reason why this is important is that the error it shows is the error that you have been working with in the period prior to calibration.

What happens when the 'as found' reading shows an error that is greater than the acceptable error? By your own definition this instrument gives you critical information on which you base your decision about conformance to requirements. The logic of the situation is that you now have a real possibility that some or all of your output since the previous calibration is outside specification. Since you do not know the point at which the error first exceeded the acceptable figure you must suspect all measurements made since the previous calibration. Therefore you must review all relevant test results since the previous calibration and identify any product that may not have conformed. In the example given earlier you could reasonably take the view that any measurements below 3.0 °C falls within specification. Any product where the reading had been above 3.0 °C is suspect, since the error of 1°C pushes the true values over 4.0 °C. In the absence of any other information about the quality of the material you must come to the conclusion that all material in the suspect range is non-conforming, and you are therefore faced with a product recall situation.

Calibration nonconformity is a serious matter!

CALIBRATION FREQUENCY

How often should an instrument be calibrated? It should be calibrated just before it develops an unacceptable error! That way you save money on unnecessary calibration and you do not have any product outside specification! Of course, it is never possible to predict when errors will develop. When you get a new instrument, or start calibrating an instrument for the first time, you set the calibration frequency at some level that seems reasonable considering all the circumstances. As the calibration history evolves you will build up a picture. If the initial interval is set at six months, and after 18 months there has been no drift, you might decide to increase the interval to nine or 12 months. If, on the other hand, at the first calibration you discover that it has already drifted outside the limits of acceptability you should decrease it, perhaps to four months. The calibration interval should be reviewed after every calibration.

CALIBRATION CERTIFICATES

There are certain basic requirements for any calibration, and you should ensure that any external calibration complies with these. Every calibration should be recorded on a certification of calibration. This certificate should show at least the following:

- the serial number of the test instrument that was used to calibrate your instrument;
- details of the calibration of that test instrument confirming that it is traceable to a recognized national or international standard. You are entitled to ask for and receive a copy of the calibration certificate for the test instrument;
- the 'as found' readings taken on your instrument *before any adjustment was made*, and the error compared with the true result. This is essential;
- the values at which the calibration was carried out, which should cover the full range over which you use the instrument;
- details of the method of calibration, if this is appropriate; and
- the readings taken with your instrument after any adjustment was made, and the error, if any, from the true values.

The term *measuring device* is broader than might at first appear. A 'go/no-go' gauge is precisely machined to identify items with dimensions not less than the acceptable minimum or not greater than the acceptable maximum. Such a gauge in constant use can suffer wear or damage, and needs to be included in the calibration programme if used for critical dimensions.

When considering each individual device you should take into account the probability that its accuracy will drift. In general, the more an item is used, the more likely it will develop an error. However, some items, by their very nature, are unlikely to develop errors. I have seen an external auditor becoming very agitated because a one-piece steel ruler used for measuring dimensions in the manufacture of kitchen furniture was not included in the calibration programme. My view on that example is that if the rule is made by a reputable manufacturer to a high standard (that is, it is demonstrated to be accurate initially) and is not abused then calibration is unnecessary, since it is difficult to see how it could develop errors.

Note, however, that a steel standard weight used for internal accuracy checks, though apparently similar to the steel ruler, is quite different, since it could easily develop errors through abuse, and would need to be included in the calibration programme.

See Help documents 7.6–1 and 7.6–2.

In some situations software programs are used as part of the measurement process, perhaps for processing measurement data and calculating results. Such programs need to be properly assessed before they are put into use to make sure that they do indeed perform as required. Furthermore, they may need to be reassessed periodically to confirm that no defects have crept in. All such periodic checks should be included in some appropriate action list to ensure that they are not forgotten. Whether this action list is the calibration plan or some other list does not matter.

The question frequently arises as to whether personnel need to be 'calibrated'. The answer, strictly speaking, is 'Yes'. However, we do not normally cover it under this section, and do not usually call it *calibration*. This issue relates to competence, covered in clause 6.2 (Chapter VII). The principle involved, however, is the same. Can you demonstrate that the error in the measurement is controlled within acceptable limits, whether that is due to the operator or the instrument? There is no need to get too excited about what label you put on your control, 'calibration' or 'competence'. The important point is that the control is in place and there is evidence that the control is effective.

One last piece of advice, beware of 'cross-checking' critical measurements. Cross-checking seems such a good thing to do but if it is not set up properly it can lead to confusion. If you identify a genuine need to cross-check, then carry out a proper calibration using a calibrated instrument. Use the less accurate instrument for day-to-day measurement and the more accurate for calibration. Too often, however, cross-checking is carried out because neither instrument is reliable – if the two readings agree we assume that they are both correct; if they do not agree we choose to believe the measurement closer to the desired reading! Instead of wasting time and running the risk of nonconformity it would be better to obtain one reliable instrument.

CHAPTER IX

The standards: Section 8 Measurement, analysis and improvement

ISO 9004	ISO 9001
8 Measurement, analysis and improvement	8 Measurement, analysis and improvement
8.1 General guidance	8.1 General
8.1.1 Introduction	
8.1.2 Issues to be considered	
8.2 Measurement and monitoring	8.2 Monitoring and measurement
8.2.1 Measurement and monitoring of system performance	8.2.1 Customer satisfaction
8.2.2 Measurement and monitoring of processes	8.2.2 Internal audit
8.2.3 Measurement and monitoring of product	8.2.3 Monitoring and measurement of processes
8.2.4 Measurement and monitoring the satisfaction of interested parties	8.2.4 Monitoring and measurement of product
8.3 Control of nonconformity	8.3 Control of non-conforming product
8.3.1 General	
8.3.2 Nonconformity review and disposition	
8.4 Analysis of data	8.4 Analysis of data
8.5 Improvement	8.5 Improvement
8.5.1 General	8.5.1 Continual improvement
8.5.2 Corrective action	8.5.2 Corrective action
8.5.3 Loss prevention	8.5.3 Preventive action
8.5.4 Continual improvement of the organization	

The sequence of topics in this chapter may be a little confusing, due to clause numbering in the standard. The text follows the ISO 9004 standard, as usual, but that means that Internal audit, for example, appears to be out of sequence, since in ISO 9004 it comes under 8.2.1 (Measurement and monitoring of system performance), whereas in ISO 9001 it is numbered 8.2.2.

GENERAL GUIDANCE (8.1), ISO 9001: GENERAL

There is an old adage in management science which states: 'If you can't measure it, you can't manage it!' Most people are familiar with the concept of taking measurements to determine if a product is fit for its intended use, but less familiar with the idea of measuring the quality of performance. Yet this is often a far better, if indirect, indicator of the overall quality of products and services.

Before you measure something you need to have two things:

- a standard against which to judge the result, and
- the possibility of taking corrective action if the result is not acceptable.

In clause 5.4.1 (Chapter VI) we covered objectives for various levels and functions in the organization. If you have drawn up a comprehensive set of objectives you will have the basis for an organization-wide standard that can be used for measuring performance.

ISO 9001 requires you to formally assess your process to determine what methods need to be employed for monitoring the performance of the process, and specifically mentions statistical techniques. Although most people shy away from statistics, they can be invaluable for extracting key information from mountains of data, and can help greatly in evaluating the effectiveness of the quality management system. They help in quantifying the contribution of various factors to risks and losses and to variation in performance. They play an important role in assuring conformity and achieving improvement.

As regards compliance with the requirements it is not sufficient to simply state in your quality manual that you do not employ any statistical techniques. You are required to determine the need for applicable methods of monitoring the continual improvement of processes. It is hard to imagine any process that could be monitored adequately without recourse to some form of statistical technique, however basic. Contrary to popular myth, not all statistics are necessarily difficult to understand and implement. The analysis does not need to be mathematically complex, and a simple plotting of a variable on a graph may be all that is needed.

See page 86 for more on statistics.

MEASUREMENT AND MONITORING (8.2)

MEASUREMENT AND MONITORING OF SYSTEM PERFORMANCE (8.2.1)

There are many different parameters that can be measured to give an indication of the performance of the system overall. Each in itself may only measure one aspect and alone would not be a sufficient index for the system as a whole, but a judicious selection of such measurements can give a good picture of the general health of the system. The following are some examples that might be appropriate:

- the number of customer orders that had to be repeated due to error;
- the cost of product that had to be rejected or reworked;
- the cost of management time spent resolving quality problems;
- employee satisfaction rating of the quality management system;
- the number of customer complaints;
- the percentage customer satisfaction rating;
- the percentage of total output within specification;
- the number of hours of unplanned *downtime* on a particular machine; and
- quantitative audit of the system using some sort of scoring scheme.

CUSTOMER SATISFACTION (ISO 9001: 8.2.1)

While ISO 9000 places great emphasis on achieving customer satisfaction, it is not a requirement that you should achieve it! What is demanded is that you should make every reasonable effort to achieve it, and to provide the resources needed to *enhance* customer satisfaction, and that you monitor the extent to which you do achieve it. Hence the somewhat convoluted wording of the standard in this clause: 'monitor information relating to customer perception as to whether the organization has met customer requirements'.

Clearly, customer complaints are an important index of customer satisfaction, or lack of it, but it would be a mistake to rely solely on that. Remember that the number of complaints may not truly reflect customer satisfaction, particularly if you manufacture a low-priced product, when the cost and inconvenience of complaining would not be worth the effort. Furthermore, it is too late when you have a complaining customer; it would have been better, if practicable, to take action to improve the situation at the 'mildly irritated' stage and prevent serious dissatisfaction.

As always, the method used to measure customer satisfaction will depend on your particular circumstances, but it will probably involve some sort of survey of a sample of customers. You are probably not in a position to get the views of every customer. This would only be practical where every sale is significant, for example, a training organization, a car sales outlet or an engineering consultancy firm. Whatever the details of your method, set up the system on a formal structured basis.

Decide what information you require and draft a suitable record sheet to facilitate the staff carrying out the survey. Do not confine the survey to the quality of the product or service itself. You want to find out about everything that annoys or irritates your customer. That can be anything from the length of time it takes you to answer the phone to the condition of your delivery vehicles or the parking habits of your drivers at the customer's premises. You will also want some information for input into your strategic planning process. This may involve asking questions about future suitability of your products or services for your current customers, and trying to get some ideas for new products or services.

Pick a sample of customers that represents your entire customer base. For example, you may need to select customers who place small, medium and large orders, or customers who have a small, medium or large impact on your turnover. You may need to take geographical variations in your market into account. Try to be objective in the selection; do not select only customers who you know are likely to give you a positive feedback.

For a small service company the entire exercise may be as simple as selecting ten clients and asking them a series of appropriate questions over the telephone. A large manufacturing company, on the other hand, might engage the services of a specialist organization to carry out an in-depth survey of customer satisfaction.

See Help documents 8.2.1.2–1 and 8.2.1.2–2.

INTERNAL AUDIT (ISO 9001: 8.2.2)

An audit is defined as a 'systematic, independent and documented process for obtaining … evidence and evaluating it objectively to determine the extent to which audit criteria are fulfilled'. Unlike the certification audit the internal audit is usually carried out by the organization's own personnel. It is also acceptable to engage an external auditor to carry it out. Senior management of the organization must lay down the objectives for the audit. The minimum objectives are to examine whether the quality management system conforms to ISO 9001 requirements and the 'planned arrangements', that is, the organization's various policies and plans, and whether the relevant procedures are being implemented.

However, this is really only part of the story. An audit with that limited objective involves little more than reading documents and checking if they are being followed. An effective audit involves much more. The auditor has to look at the effect of the procedures and methods and determine if the result is in line with the policy and plans of the organization. For example, the document control procedure may require ten signatures before a change to a document is approved. An unthinking auditor would simply check that all recent document changes had the requisite ten signatures, whereas a sharp auditor would highlight that, in the circumstances, the requirement for ten signatures was not necessary or useful. So, the objectives for the audit should include a strong element of positive improvement in addition to highlighting non-compliances. In some cases the auditor will be able to suggest improvement, and in other cases will simply recognize that the situation needs to be improved.

Managing the internal audits

You need to have a scheme for managing the audits. The elements of this scheme are:

- maintaining a panel of trained auditors;
- scheduling audits for a given period;
- assigning auditors to carry out particular audits;
- defining the scope and objectives of the audits;
- carrying out audits;
- implementing corrective and preventive action;
- reviewing the corrective and preventive action; and
- defining the frequency of future audits.

A complete audit must cover all areas of activity that are relevant to ultimate product or service quality and must specifically address all requirements of ISO 9001. In a small organization it may be possible to carry out the full audit of the entire operation in a single day. In larger organizations it is usually convenient to divide the audit into elements, and to schedule these elements over the audit cycle time – normally one year.

The frequency of internal audits is not specified. It is usually accepted that the entire system should be audited over 12 months, but some parts of the operation may need more frequent auditing. The correct frequency depends on the importance of the particular activity. The internal audit procedures should provide the flexibility to alter the frequency when necessary.

Auditing can be a time-consuming business, so you should take care that it is done not only effectively but efficiently. In a small to medium-sized manufacturing company the internal audits might take two to four half-days per year. Much depends on the complexity of the operation, the quality of the documentation, the ease of navigation through the quality management system and the skill of the auditors.

The requirements of ISO 9001 are quite complex, and it would be very easy to overlook some of the requirements, however skilled and experienced the auditor is. The standard itself is not particularly suitable to use as the primary auditing tool. Furthermore, it is obviously very general, since it has to be universally applicable. Therefore, it is much more effective to translate the requirements of the standard into a checklist of audit questions that are specific to the area and activities being audited and to the circumstances of the organization.

The auditor

The audits must be carried out by trained auditors. The nature of this training is not specified, however. There is no requirement that training must be done by external trainers, or that it has to be accredited in any way. Provided the organization has the resources and expertise, training of auditors internally is acceptable. It is not the quality of the training that is important but the quality of the auditing process. So, you need to be able to demonstrate that the training delivered has been effective, and that the auditors are able properly to carry out audits.

It is not necessary that auditors should be technically expert in the activity being audited. This would severely limit the options for the auditing panel in many organizations. I have always contended that suitability for auditing has more to do with the personal skills and characteristics of the individual than any technical knowledge he or she may have. Administration staff, especially from the financial area, often make excellent internal quality auditors, since the principal requirement for being a good auditor is the ability to ask relevant questions, assess the reply and spot inconsistencies.

Auditors should be independent as far as practicable, though the requirement for independence was deliberately removed from the standard during the drafting because of the difficulty this might pose for small companies. Ideally, auditors should not have any responsibility for the area being audited, and definitely must not audit their own work. In small companies it may not be possible to have total independence. There may be only one manager, who may also be the proprietor. In such cases it is necessary to be able to show that the audit was carried out as objectively as possible. Using an audit checklist with the appropriate level of detail can often overcome this difficulty. Another possibility is to train a family member not normally involved in the business to do the internal auditing, or to participate alongside the proprietor to give an element of objectivity.

Where practicable there should be a panel of auditors available so that there is a choice when selecting auditors to carry out particular audits. Having a panel also allows for the option of sending a team of two or more to carry out each audit. Many auditors, especially when they are new to auditing, prefer to have the support of a second person.

Where the subject matter is very technical it is advisable to include somebody in the audit team who understands the technical aspects, though this should only represent a small proportion of the audit, since the audit is essentially looking at the management of the processes rather than the technical aspects of individual products or services.

See Help document 8.2.1.3–5 for further guidance on carrying out internal audits.

Audit non-compliances

Audit non-compliances must be recorded if the corrective action is to be managed effectively. In that respect an audit non-compliance is the same as any other nonconformity. Under ISO 9001 clause 8.3 (Control of non-conforming product) or 8.5.2 (Corrective action) you will have set up some sort of reporting system for recording individual nonconformities and managing corrective action, but it could be very tedious to use this device to manage a large number of non-compliances arising from an internal audit. A simple way of overcoming this difficulty is to use the audit report itself as the record of non-compliance and corrective action. You are not obliged to record audit non-compliances in any particular way. What is important is that you implement the corrective action and can show the evidence that this has been done. What form that evidence takes is entirely up to you, and you should not be intimidated by an external auditor into using a particular record format for this or any other aspect of ISO 9001.

Help document 8.2.1.3–6 shows an example of an audit report. In this case the audit was confined to four functions – Purchasing, Product Development, Maintenance and Customer Services. The points are numbered in the first column for easy reference. Both non-compliances and suggestions (item 7) are included. Some of the points are easily corrected, for example items 4, 13, 15 and 19, and it would be very cumbersome to have to make out a nonconformity report for each of these. It would be much more practical simply to date and initial the fourth column when the corrective action has been taken. In the case of item 6, however, it is clear that a serious investigation of the circumstances must take place and this would certainly warrant a separate nonconformity report. The third column provides the facility for recording the reference to the nonconformity report, and this gives full traceability of the corrective action. Note that the scope of the activities actually audited is recorded on the audit checklist used by the auditor, which would be attached to the audit report. In that way the next person carrying out an audit in any of these areas would know what aspects had not been covered in the previous audit.

Internal audits often uncover instances of procedures not being followed. There are two possible ways of resolving this problem, either to insist on compliance with the existing procedure or to change the procedure. Sometimes the procedure is not being followed because it is impractical. In that case it is pointless to insist on compliance. Instead, the procedure should be examined to see how it could be modified to give the same degree of control in a more practical way.

When non-compliances are found during an audit it is essential to manage the implementation of corrective action. The management responsible for the area being audited must ensure that corrective action is taken. But who should follow up and monitor the implementation of the corrective action? Very often the auditor involved is expected to do this. I do not recommend this in most cases. Often, the auditor will be a junior member of the management team, chosen for his or her auditing skills, and will not be in a position to force a more senior person to act. It is much better to have a formal mechanism that takes over once the audit reports are finalized and automatically drives corrective action – a sort of unstoppable machine that continues relentlessly to the target of ensuring that all corrective action is implemented. For example, the completed audit reports could be tabled at the next weekly operations meeting and monitored from that point onwards by the appropriate group of managers.

While the primary emphasis of the internal audit is on checking compliance with ISO 9001 requirements there is no reason why the audit cannot be used for monitoring other controls that the company has implemented that do not have any direct link with ISO 9001. For example, the scope of the quality management system could be extended to include financial aspects, and internal audits could be used to check compliance with financial procedures, which do not come under the scope of ISO 9001.

It is particularly important that there is a culture of trust among the staff. The audit should be regarded as a service provided to people to help them identify deficiencies in their controls that they may have missed through being too close to the action. Everybody must be satisfied that a non-compliance will not result in any type of sanction against the person being audited. Only in those circumstances can an audit programme deliver its full potential benefits.

See Help documents 8.2.1.3–1, 8.2.1.3–2, 8.2.1.3–3, 8.2.1.3–4, 8.2.1.3–5 and 8.2.1.3–6.

FINANCIAL MEASURES (8.2.1.4)

Whatever the nature of your activities, finance is a key resource. The accountant or financial controller in the organization will certainly have a system in place for tracking income and expenditure. However, financial professionals are not usually in a position to identify what effect quality has on these figures. Indeed, in many cases even the quality experts do not realize how great an impact product or service quality can have on overall profitability. It is important for quality professionals to understand that accountants are more impressed by monetary figures than parameters such as customer satisfaction ratings, average queue length, mean time between repairs, or any of the other indices that the quality professionals use.

The most obvious parameter that should be tracked by every organization is the amount of product lost through not meeting the specification, or the number of service jobs or customer orders that have to be repeated because they were not carried out properly the first time. Amazingly, not all companies measure this index regularly, and senior managers often cannot say what percentage of output failed to meet the requirements in any recent period. In most cases even the monitoring of this fundamental index will provide a strong impetus for improvement.

Carrying out a detailed analysis of quality costs is quite a complex matter, and to set up a comprehensive system for measuring quality costs requires a significant input of management time. It involves looking at all sources of quality costs. These are often categorized under the headings of costs incurred in preventing quality problems, the cost of appraising the quality of the output and the costs arising from quality failure. By judicious quality management planning and shifting the emphasis of activities from appraisal to prevention the overall costs can be very significantly reduced.

See Help document 6.8–1.

SELF-ASSESSMENT (8.2.1.5)

Self-assessment is a very effective way of generating improvement. Self-assessment can be operated at every level, from the overall organization down to the individual, and involves measuring the performance of one's self or team against objectives set, with the aim of improving. The objectives to be achieved can be set either by the individual, the team or senior management, and can even relate to the most routine or mundane of tasks. ISO 9004 describes a methodology for self-assessment, which you can adapt to suit your own circumstances.

The ISO 9004 method works on the basis of specific questions. As an alternative, the objectives can be set in the form of a series of specific statements of how things should be, rather than simply rephrasing the guidance of ISO 9004 in the form of questions. Help document 6.4–1, though originally made out as a checklist for compliance with physical conditions standards under clause 6.4, illustrates how a set of standards can be set out that are very specific to a particular situation. Scores can be allocated to the various entries that reflect the importance of each, and performance can then be quantitatively assessed as a self-inspection exercise. To achieve and monitor improvement the individual standards to be met can be raised or new requirements introduced. In addition to physical conditions, this checklist could be broadened to include aspects of the restaurant's quality management system.

MONITORING AND MEASUREMENT OF PROCESSES (ISO 9001: 8.2.3)

Since it is not usually possible to determine the quality of the final product solely on the basis of inspection or testing, it is necessary to know that the process itself has been operating at all times under the required conditions while the output was being produced. This is called *process control.*

Process control involves identifying parameters that are important for ultimate product quality and setting limits on those parameters that will ensure that the output conforms to its specification. A programme of monitoring by means of testing or inspecting can then be put in place. Traditionally, this monitoring has been the role of an independent quality control function. The main disadvantage in this approach is that the people responsible for the quantity of the output very often do not feel that they have any responsibility for its quality, since somebody else appears to be attending to that. Indeed, people manufacturing a product who are under pressure to maintain output at all costs sometimes are tempted to conceal information from the quality inspectors in order to maximize output, with little concern for the fact that the product may not conform to specification.

Responsibility for product quality

It is very important that one person should be totally responsible for ensuring that the appropriate operating procedures are implemented and that an output is produced that meets the defined requirements. In a manufacturing situation the person who should be held responsible is the line manager who takes the credit for meeting the production targets. Unfortunately, it is the quality manager who is often considered responsible for ensuring that output meets specification. If the quality manager does not have full control and authority over the process, then he or she cannot be held fully or solely liable for faulty product. The role of the quality manager should be to set standards that are adequate to ensure quality, and to have an effective quality management system in place that will facilitate the achievement of quality. If the product fails to meet requirements due to a deficiency in any of these aspects, then the quality manager must take the responsibility. If failure is due to avoidable operational factors then the line manager must take responsibility. If a faulty product is delivered to the customer because it was not picked up by final inspection procedures then both the line manager and the quality manager are responsible, but for different reasons. The line manager must be held accountable for not having adequate process controls in place to prevent faulty product from being made, and the quality manager for not having reliable controls in place for detecting the faults. Considering the difficulty in detecting faults by testing, one could argue that the sin of the former is the greater. Responsibility must be clearly defined, and matched with the appropriate authority. For an illustration of how responsibilities might be defined see QM-11 in the sample quality manual (page 124).

Process control testing

A process control programme must have the flexibility to respond to changing needs. It takes a little skill to document a programme that is sufficiently definitive, yet flexible enough not to be too restrictive. One way of coping with an inspection plan that needs frequently to change is to allow for a periodic revision of the plan. The relevant manual would contain a description of how this revision procedure operates and a copy of blank inspection forms, but the actual details would be decided by the manager or supervisor on each occasion, and this changing information would not appear in the manual. In such situations make sure that the personnel involved have documented authority to define and change the testing plan.

See Help document 8.2.2–1.

When a process control parameter is found to be drifting outside the limits set, corrective action should be taken immediately. Should this fact be recorded? The answer depends on what significance you attach to the drift, but such corrective actions would not usually be recorded, being considered to be part of the normal adjustment of the process to maintain it within control. If, however, the same parameter frequently drifts outside the limits, for no obvious reason, then a nonconformity report would probably be appropriate, since this is clearly a chronic problem, as opposed to a single, non-significant occurrence. Help document 8.2.3–2 shows a simple record form that combines the basic information about a production process, including the process control testing and the testing carried out on the final product, and provides the opportunity to record any other relevant information about incidents that might have affected the quality of the product. Under 'Comments/Incidents' the production personnel would record any unusual incident, for example, plant breakdown, problems with raw materials or abnormalities of plant performance. This type of information can be invaluable in later investigations into the cause of complaints or other nonconformities. If a nonconformity report has been raised it is sufficient to refer to that report, and the person assessing the quality of the final product can search it out and see the details of the incident. It is not usual to be able to record all the information necessary for final assessment of the product on a single sheet. More usually, the production information alone fills one or more sheets and final product testing a similar number of sheets. The principal remains the same, however – capture all the information that may be useful either for product release or for subsequent investigation into quality failure.

In the case of a service provider, records may be essential for knowing the current state of a project and what tasks have been completed. This is particularly important where different people may be involved in the same project, and each person must be able to resume activity precisely where the previous person left off, with no risk of gaps or duplication. The point is obvious if you consider a medical practice, where a number of different practitioners may be dealing with one patient on different occasions.

See Help document 4.2–5.

MONITORING AND MEASUREMENT OF PRODUCT (ISO 9001: 8.2.4)

The extent to which the end product needs to be tested depends on the level of control you have exercised over the process, that is, it is related to the risk of the product not conforming to specification. End product testing is carried out because you are not entirely sure about its quality. So, where you have minimal confidence in your process you may have to carry out a 100 per cent inspection, and we saw at the beginning of the book that even this is no guarantee that the product sent to the customer will conform to requirements. If, however, you have exercised sufficient control at all points throughout the process then your confidence in the quality of the end product will be high, and a much reduced amount of product testing can be performed, essentially just to confirm this. ISO 9001 is not prescriptive as to what you must do. You are simply required to verify by monitoring the characteristics of the product at appropriate stages of the product realization process that the requirements for the product are met.

To make the management of testing easier you should draw up a testing plan or plans. It can be very useful to draw these up in tabular form, showing the testing at each step and the specification to be achieved, with references to the test methods. It can also include other useful information such as the person or function responsible for the test, and the action to be taken in the event of nonconformity, though this information can equally well be documented in the test method itself.

Statistical techniques are often used in assessing product quality. For example, a sample is taken from a batch of end product and a decision to accept or reject is made on the basis of the result on that sample. It is important that such sampling schemes are based on sound mathematical principles so that the conclusions drawn are valid. I have seen many examples of pseudo-statistical methods that are invented primarily on the basis of convenience. The number of samples to be tested is often chosen to coincide with the number of samples the testers can handle. Sometimes the sample size is couched in terms such as 'half the square root of the number of pallets plus one', giving it a very authentic sound, but with no statistical basis whatever. Furthermore, the accept/reject criteria are often chosen so that nothing will be rejected! Do not try to invent statistical methods. There are sufficient well-proven sampling schemes that have been drawn up to suit all purposes, which contain clear instructions on how to reach valid decisions based on the results of samples.

A word about 'Retesting Syndrome', a debilitating condition that is very prevalent. What is the normal reaction when testing shows that a product is outside specification? Most people will repeat the test. Then what? If the result pleases them they release the product on the basis that the first result was incorrect. If not, they may retest a second time. When this result is within specification this confirms what they wanted to believe, that is, that the product conforms to specification. If the repeat test result is outside specification they may repeat again. Only when a number of retests fail to yield a result within specification do they finally and reluctantly admit that the product does not conform. This approach is based on the Principle of Selective Test Perversity, which states that a result within specification is never false, whereas a result outside specification is always false! Not surprisingly this 'principle' is disproved time and again. Unfortunately it is usually only when the customer returns the faulty product that the correctness of the original non-conforming result is established. But by that time it is too late, and the damage has been done. The original result, even if contradicted by a number of subsequent results, should be regarded as correct and should be included in the overall result. It may be, for example, that *all* the results are correct and that there is a low level of nonconformity that is not distributed homogeneously throughout the product, and which only shows up in a small number of samples.

There are very few circumstances in which a test result may safely be discarded. A result should only be discarded if there is a specific reason to believe that there was an error in the way the test was carried out. Examples of such circumstances are:

- the sample itself was subsequently found to be faulty, damaged or contaminated in some way;
- an instrument used in the test was subsequently found to be faulty;
- the test was carried out by an inadequately trained person.

The unpleasantness of the result is not in itself sufficient reason to believe that there was an error.

Product release

Have a very clear procedure for release of a product, or signing off a service project as complete. Identify the persons or functions that have authority to release a product. Define what discretion with regard to nonconformity, if any, is allowed to the person releasing the product.

In most cases certain information must be assessed or reviewed prior to release. Specify what this information is. For example, since you will not rely totally on end-product testing you will probably need to review process control results before you make a final decision on whether to release the product. If you provide a service, there may be certain documents that need to be reviewed before you decide that the contract has been successfully completed.

Finally, keep an adequate record of the release process, showing the identity of the person who performed the release, and the identity of the material involved.

See Help documents 7.5.1–1, 8.2.3–1 and 8.2.3–2.

MEASUREMENT AND MONITORING THE SATISFACTION OF INTERESTED PARTIES (ISO 9004: 8.2.4)

The question of customer satisfaction has been dealt with on page 79. This clause deals with other interested parties, in particular, the people who work in the organization, the owners, suppliers and society in general.

Staff

The people who work for the organization will have many and varied expectations. Since every organization depends heavily on its people for ultimate success it follows that senior managers should take steps to satisfy these needs as far as practical. Certain basic expectations are universal. For example:

- safe and reasonably pleasant working conditions, considering the particular circumstances;
- adequate monetary reward;
- adequate training for the job;
- recognition for work well done; and
- absence of unjustified stress, for example, unfair criticism, bullying or undue pressure to produce output.

These factors should be addressed not only for reasons of social concern, but also because they can affect the quality of output. See also clause 6.4 (Chapter VII).

Owners

The owners are interested in seeing that the objectives they have set for the organization are achieved. These objectives are usually expressed in financial terms. Other owner requirements may relate to public perception of the organization with regard to ethical behaviour, treatment of personnel and concern for the environment. These objectives need to be converted into working versions that can be used to measure performance at operational level. Usually the senior managers are sufficiently motivated by self-interest considerations to ensure that the interests of the owners are adequately reflected in working goals at various levels of the organization.

Suppliers and partners

The partners referred to in this clause are those suppliers with whom you may have built up a close supply relationship, as in the case of just-in-time suppliers. With regard to the interests of suppliers and partners ISO 9004 confines itself mainly to addressing the purchasing process, though it does make a passing reference to 'mutual benefits derived from the relationship'.

Of course, the relationship between supplier and customer may be much deeper than just satisfaction with the purchasing process. Suppliers and customers depend on each other. The success of the customer company is often reflected in increased business for the supplier company, and conversely the closing of a large company can have devastating impact on small companies supplying it. It should be part of the strategic planning to assess the effect your operations have on your suppliers, and you should take all reasonable steps to maintain the good relationship and protect the interests of the supplier, in as far as those interests do not conflict with your own organization's interests. Showing concern for a supplier can result in benefits such as security of supply, preferential pricing structures and increased attention to quality on the part of the supplier.

Society

Ethics and business do mix. In recent years companies have come to realize that public perception of their concern for society and the environment can have real impact on their operations and profitability. As each succeeding generation becomes more concerned with ethical behaviour, companies will find it more difficult to attract the brightest and best if they do not show adequate care about the impact of their operations on society. In addition to the impact of your operation on the environment consider how the following factors could or should be taken into account in your management approach:

- the exploitation of cheap labour by your suppliers or subcontractors;
- human rights issues in countries from which you purchase materials;
- supplying materials to companies that are seen to be acting not in the best interest of society; and
- employment of people from minority groups.

At a very practical level you should look at the immediate society in which your organization operates and see how you can best interact with it to the benefit of the organization and the community. For example, do you try to employ local people at all levels in the organization assuming they meet the qualification requirements? Do you interact with local schools and explain to them the nature of the organization's operation? Do you give them any form of sponsorship or allow them to use your social facilities when this is practical?

Your quality policy, or mission statement, should reflect your concern for the interests of these various parties.

CONTROL OF NONCONFORMITY (8.3)

When the result of a test or an inspection indicates that the item or material inspected does not meet requirements, action must be taken immediately to prevent the faulty material being used inadvertently. It is surprising how often such faulty product is dispatched to the customer in spite of its known defects. A procedure must be in place whereby all such materials are clearly identified as non-conforming. For example, the offending material can be physically moved to a clearly marked quarantine area. Extreme care must be taken if this is the only control, since the material appears to lose its non-conforming status the moment it is moved from the quarantine area.

Also quite common is the use of labels or tags. Thus a yellow label with the words 'Under test' might be placed on the item immediately it is produced, to be covered later by a green ('Accepted') or a red ('Reject') label. One difficulty with this type of system is that it can often be difficult to gain access to all items in a large warehouse to relabel them when test results become available, which may happen some time after the materials have been stacked away.

The most effective system that I have seen in operation is one that uses bar-coding throughout the production and distribution process. A bar code is assigned at the moment the finished item is created and a test status of 'Not yet tested' is automatically assigned to it on computer. At the point of dispatch all items have their bar codes checked and only those whose status has been changed to 'Approved' can be dispatched. Authority to change test status is confined to authorized personnel, and the process of changing the status is password controlled. This system eliminates any necessity to physically segregate non-conforming product or to change labels or tags.

Whatever system is chosen must be operable in all circumstances. It is pointless to demand that red labels be put on all non-conforming pallets if many of them are inaccessible. Equally, physical segregation of the non-conforming materials is not possible if they can only be accessed at time of dispatch.

This clause does not just apply to manufacturing operations, and often has an application in service organizations, since it applies to any item or material that is faulty. That includes drawings or documents that contain an error, and faults listed on a 'snag list' drawn up on completion of a job. In the case of documents, the non-conforming status can be simply shown by a single stroke through each page or an 'X' at a certain defined point. The method used should be written into the procedure for nonconformity or documented in some other appropriate place.

See Help documents 8.3.1–1, 7.5.2–1 and 7.5.2–2.

NONCONFORMITY REVIEW AND DISPOSITION (8.3.2)

Once the problem has been identified and the material removed from possible use, a decision must be taken on what to do with it. There are several possibilities that are acceptable:

1 It may be possible completely to correct the nonconformity by repairing or reworking the material. It may be possible to incorporate it into another batch of the same product. It may be possible to dismantle it and reuse the components in other products. If any of these options are adopted the repaired or reworked item must be rechecked to make sure that the nonconformity has been fully corrected.
2 There may be another customer whose specification is not so tight, and who will accept the material. This is known as regrading. The material is no longer non-conforming because it meets specification, even if it is a different one to that against which it was manufactured.
3 You may decide that the problem is not serious enough to warrant rejection. This is called a product waiver or concession. This should be approached with great care. Before you approve a waiver you

should check your contract with the customer. If the material is outside the conditions of the contract you may not consider a waiver without the approval of your customer. If you have a good relationship with your customer and have built up trust there is a good chance that the customer will accept the material in spite of the nonconformity. When drawing up a purchasing specification a buyer often makes it a little tighter than necessary to allow for some error on the part of the supplier. Thus, the nonconforming material may be acceptable to your customer even though it is outside the specification that has been given to you.

Perhaps you do not have a contract, but the customer buys a standard product that you produce, for example, a motor car or a bar of chocolate. The bar of chocolate might not be quite the precise colour that your specification requires, or the car might have an imperfection in the paintwork on the underside of a door. You have then to decide whether the material is sufficiently close to the specification that the customer will not notice it and that the nonconformity will not affect performance in normal use during the life cycle of the product.

4 If none of the first three options is appropriate the material must be discarded or destroyed.

In the case of non-conforming materials related to a service project there may be no other option but to discard the item, since they may not be relevant to any other project.

See Help document 8.3.2–1.

When a non-conforming product is released for use this fact is often concealed or denied. Many people think that reject products must be destroyed, even though, for commercial reasons, they have no intention of doing so unless there is absolutely no alternative. Concealing this or denying that it is happening is a big mistake for two main reasons. First, the facts are likely to come to light in an audit by a customer or the certification body. This will cause far more problems since there is no defined procedure for dealing with the situation. Second, if the fact of the nonconformity is not debated openly within the organization and subjected to the rigours of the corrective action procedure, it is likely that the root causes will not be addressed and corrected and the problem will continue to recur.

Remember, there is nothing shameful in having something go wrong. The shame would arise from a failure to deal correctly with the problem. Everybody knows that *all* organizations have problems. What distinguishes the good from the mediocre is how they investigate the causes and implement true corrective action.

While the term *nonconformity* is normally associated with a faulty product or a service task that has not been carried out properly, it also applies to the processes of the quality management system. So, for example, the discovery that a person is carrying out a quality-significant task for which he or she has not been adequately trained should result in the same sort of investigation and corrective action as would happen in the case of faulty product. Incidentally, note that the corrective action in such a case would have to involve more than simply training the person! (See 'Corrective action', page 92.)

ANALYSIS OF DATA (8.4)

In most organizations information and data is constantly collected. All this data should be analysed to see what information it contains. Unfortunately, in many cases the task is considered finished when the data is collected. But thick files of data are of little use in themselves and are only valuable if they are examined closely to see what underlying information they contain.

In relation to gathering information remember the following rules:

● No inspection without recording.

- No recording without analysis.
- No analysis without action.

The purpose of data analysis is to extract the core information. This analysis is often aimed at identifying the causes of problems, for example, where data is sorted into different categories that help identify which of a number of possible causes is the significant one. Analysis can also indicate trends and permit preventive action to be taken before nonconformities arise.

ISO 9001 requires you to analyse appropriate data to evaluate the effectiveness of the quality system in relation to customers, suppliers, processes and products, for the purpose of identifying opportunities for improvement.

Detailed analysis of nonconformities can help pinpoint where losses are occurring and where improvements can be made. For example, within the overall figure for rejection, it may be useful to identify individual causes. A food product may be rejected for such reasons as:

- Clostridia, which might point to a contaminated raw material;
- Enterobacteriaceae, caused perhaps by bad post-processing hygiene;
- E. coli, caused by poor personal hygiene;
- burnt particles, due to lack of control of the process temperature; and
- flavour and odour abnormalities, caused by holding intermediate product too long due to plant breakdown.

In a service operation failure may be broken down into categories such as:

- job done to the wrong specification (computer order input error, inadequate review of requirements);
- wrong materials delivered (inadequate identification of materials, disorganized storage of materials); and
- service carried out late (inadequate maintenance of vehicles, too many service jobs scheduled for the time available).

When the information has been gathered and analysed it should be communicated to everybody with an interest in the subject. Graphical representation of data is a very effective way of communicating this type of information. The level of reject product should be of universal interest in a manufacturing environment, and this can easily be shown as a percentage of total output. A refinement of this is to show also the cumulative figure to date. The advantage of this is that people can see the performance of the entire year to date. If the figures show great variation from period to period, perhaps because the numbers involved are very small, it may be more appropriate to plot a moving average for a number of periods. Thus, the graph might show the average figure for the previous four weeks and this figure would be updated every week. That may help to even out the 'bumps' and make it easier to see trends.

See Help document 8.4–1.

When presenting any information in this way the objective or the target value to be achieved should also be shown, so that everybody can see how performance rates against the target.

See also 'Monitoring and measurement of product' (page 86).

IMPROVEMENT (8.5)

Improvement is the key to survival and growth. An organization that does not improve continually will not be able to keep pace with its competitors and certainly not get ahead of them. The adage 'if it's not broken don't fix it' is probably the fallacy that has achieved widest respectability. If we had adopted it as a principle we would still be happily living in the Stone Age, content with our primitive lot.

CONTINUAL IMPROVEMENT (ISO 9001: 8.5.1)

The quality management system itself must improve continually and ISO 9001 requires that you facilitate this. While corrective action in relation to existing problems, the prevention of foreseeable problems and internal auditing will all lead to improvement, you are expected to take a more strategic approach that involves the regular evaluation and review of the quality policy and objectives. ISO 9001 concerns itself purely with the improvement of the quality management system, but ISO 9004 recommends that improvement be sought in all areas, including product quality. In fact, you should take a broad view of the possibilities for improvement. Improvement can be made in all areas, even those not directly related to the quality of product or service, and even when no obvious problems are apparent.

CORRECTIVE ACTION (8.5.2)

The term 'corrective action' is used in relation to a problem that has already occurred. 'Preventive action' refers to potential nonconformities that have not yet occurred. This is arguably the most critical clause in the two standards. The essential points involved in a corrective action procedure are:

- correctly identifying the root causes of the nonconformity;
- investigating the causes of the problem fully; and
- ensuring that effective and permanent action is taken to minimize the risk of it happening again.

Corrective action is only effective if it addresses the root causes of the problem, and very often the obvious corrective action does not. Identification of the root causes is not as simple as it might seem. For example, sometimes the corrective action recorded consists of delivering a warning to somebody to do the job properly in future. It may be, however, that the root cause is not carelessness by the individual, but a failure by supervisors to enforce rules consistently or, perhaps, inadequate training. There is a theory used in risk management known as the domino theory of loss causation. This states that you can trace back from the loss through the superficial causes (actions and short-term conditions) and underlying causes (human factors and work factors) to the root causes of the problem. It further states that there are only three basic root causes for any loss. In the case of a quality problem we can state them as follows:

- the issue that caused the nonconformity was not addressed at all in the quality management system; or
- the issue may have been addressed, but the standards for performance that were set were inadequate to achieve quality consistently; or
- the issue was addressed and adequate standards were set, but there was a failure to achieve full compliance.

Note that all three root causes lie within the scope of action by the managers, not operators. In other words, the root cause of all problems can be traced to a failure of management!

Of course, it is not always possible readily to identify the root causes of a problem. But a genuine effort must be made. Beware of being satisfied with the first half-plausible cause, especially where it does not call for any significant effort on the part of the manager involved. The question to ask is not just 'How did this happen?' but to follow up with 'Why did it happen?' For example:

- 'How did the problem happen?' – a widget broke. Corrective action in such a situation usually amounts to nothing more than replacing the widget.
- But – 'Why did the widget break?' A little probing might reveal that there were inadequate maintenance arrangements. Perhaps the consequences of a broken widget were not foreseen. There may be inadequate inspection by operators or supervision by supervisors. Perhaps people were not properly trained to be aware and pick up signs of impending problems. So, what might at first seem to have been an 'accident' for which nobody is responsible, is in fact due to failure to manage the situation properly. No wonder some managers are reluctant to carry out thorough investigation of nonconformities!

When is corrective action necessary? Managers often have a very selective approach to the application of corrective action, without any clear criteria as to when to apply it. ISO 9001 is quite clear – action must be taken to prevent recurrence of nonconformities. That means that *every* nonconformity must result in corrective action! After all, every loss of product, and every service job that has to be repeated, is a loss of profit, and prevention of a repeat of that loss will result in improved profit if a cost-effective corrective action can be identified and undertaken.

In fact, the term 'nonconformity' should be taken to refer to any occurrence, including customer complaints, that has resulted in difficulty to the operation of the organization, since any difficulty results in some loss of management time at the very least.

Corrective action should address all possible variants of the current case and prevent it *or anything like it* happening again. For example, suppose it is discovered that a product is faulty because it has been made to an obsolete specification. The traditional corrective action is to update the specification, and nothing more. A serious attempt to implement corrective action would immediately look at the bigger picture. Are other obsolete specifications in use? Since there is clearly a problem with document control, what other documents apart from specifications might be obsolete? Who was supposed to keep the documents up to date, and are there other tasks that this person has not performed? This line of questioning is designed to extract the maximum benefit from the incident.

There should be some means of tracking corrective action to ensure that nothing slips between the cracks in the normal work routine. A good method is to operate the nonconformity reporting system in conjunction with a routine daily or weekly operations meeting. This can ensure that nonconformities are kept 'live' until they are resolved to the satisfaction of the group, and corrective action completed.

Every incident should be investigated to some degree. In many cases the investigation will be carried out by the supervisor or line manager responsible for the activity. More significant cases may justify setting up a team to investigate the circumstances. It may be useful to have some written guidance on how to decide whether formal investigation should be carried out.

Follow-up monitoring is critical to the success of corrective action. This means checking some time later that the corrective action taken is permanent. This can be done simply by requiring the corrective action record to be signed off a specified period after it is completed.

See Help documents 8.5.2–1 and 8.5.2–2.

LOSS PREVENTION (8.5.3), ISO 9001: PREVENTIVE ACTION

Corrective action is much easier to identify than preventive action, since it relates to problems that have already arisen. It is more difficult to identify problems that have never actually occurred – yet. Under clause 4.1 the process will have been defined in terms of its individual steps. This exercise can now be revisited with a view to identifying preventive action. Check at each step for any potential quality problems that could realistically arise, and this should indicate where preventive action may be appropriate.

In the food industry a technique known as HACCP (pronounced 'hassip') – hazard analysis and critical control points – nicely illustrates the concept. This technique involves a detailed analysis of each step of the entire process by a multidisciplinary team to identify any food safety hazards that could arise and the appropriate control measures to prevent them. The remarkably similar-sounding HAZOP (hazard and operability) technique serves the same purpose for chemical processes, and is based on the 'What if …?' line of questioning. Other techniques such as failure mode and effect analysis (FMEA) and fault tree analysis (FTA) serve a similar purpose, and would be more than adequate to comply with the requirements of this clause.

In addition to occasional formal review of your process, you can use the data analysed under clause 8.4, for example, graphs showing trends, to identify preventive action.

The effort put into preventive and corrective action should be commensurate with the benefits that can be achieved. In other words, you would not be expected to invest a great deal of resources into preventing a minor problem.

The quality manual should contain a description of the various initiatives that are used for identifying preventive action, and these should be supported by a written procedure describing how preventive action is identified and implemented.

See Help documents 8.5.3–1, 8.5.3–2, 8.5.3–3, 5.4.2–2 and 5.4.2–3.

CONTINUAL IMPROVEMENT OF THE ORGANIZATION (8.5.4)

The emphasis in the quality management system must be on making things happen rather than hoping that things will turn out all right. Thus, you should actively plan at several levels to generate improvement. Small improvement can be made in all areas, often without significant capital investment. If you hold a frequent (daily or weekly) operations meeting (see page 45), which I strongly recommend, this incremental improvement can become a routine feature. The possibilities for major improvement projects can be considered at the less frequent but regular management meetings and at the management review. It is important to remember that the managers of the organization are not the sole source of ideas for improvement, and you should ensure that all personnel are encouraged to contribute to the improvement process and that managers facilitate this input from other personnel. See also clause 6.5 (Chapter VII) for comments on suggestion schemes.

Since improvement is to be an organization-wide activity it is useful to have a uniform approach to it throughout the organization. The well-known Plan–Do–Check–Act formula is very effective for this:

- *Plan*: assess the current situation and incorporate objectives into the work plan to improve it.
- *Do*: carry out the planned activities and attempt to reach the objectives.
- *Check*: assess whether the objectives have been met.
- *Act*: identify what action needs to be taken to close any gap between performance and objectives.
  This information is now used as an input to the new cycle at the next planning stage.

The Plan–Do–Check–Act approach can be used at any level. At the highest level it can be used for improvement of the organization. At the level of the individual it can be used either to direct the individual's overall performance or to improve the way in which a single task is performed. The result of this cycle is inevitable improvement.

PESSIMISM RULES – OK?

For a brief but glorious period of a few hours in Kyoto on 5 July 2000 the final draft of the ISO 9004 contained the following clause:

> *8.5.5 Improving the world*
>
> Management should not restrict improvement to organization performance but should actively seek opportunities to improve the whole world in order to satisfy everyone all the time about everything.

Unfortunately we will never know what effect this splendid aspiration would have had on the future of humanity, as the cynics succeeded in having it removed.

Now that we have looked at all the elements of ISO 9004 we can start to list the actual component parts of a management system, the documents, records and activities that are needed in order to comply will the requirements of ISO 9001.

Quality management systems: practical aspects

CHAPTER X

The elements of the ISO 9001 quality management system – service operations

The following is a list of documents and activities that are generally required in a service organization in order to comply with ISO 9001 requirements. In treating services it is very difficult to give general advice that will be relevant to all services. With manufacturing operations there is a certain basic sameness about them all – in most cases components are collected and put through some sort of machinery, a physical product comes out the other side, which is tested, released and dispatched to the customer. Some services involve the handling of a physical product, and such organizations may have testing equipment that requires calibration. They may undertake testing of product or transport of materials, but they may not have any design aspects. Other services, such as consultancy, may not involve a physical product, but will be heavily involved in designing solutions for clients. So, each service provider must examine the list, select those elements that are applicable and ignore those that are not.

The actual requirements will depend on the nature of the service supplied and the circumstances of the organization, including its size.

In order to understand the full detail of what is needed it is essential to consult ISO 9001 directly. Some of the items listed are strong recommendations rather than strict requirements of ISO 9001.

Note that many of the items listed below are normally included in the quality manual and may only be a few sentences long.

ISO 9001, SECTIONS 1 TO 3

There are no specific requirements stated in ISO 9001, Sections 1 to 3.

ISO 9001, SECTION 4

DOCUMENTATION
- One or more manuals containing the procedures of the quality management system (QMS).
- A flow chart showing the service delivery process and other related processes of the organization and how all the processes interact with each other.
- A description of any information that is necessary for the proper operation of the processes:
  - quality manual, including any permitted exclusions claimed;
  - procedure for control of quality documents; and
  - procedure for control of quality records.
- A description of any services or production activity that are subcontracted ('outsourced') and the controls that are in place to ensure quality.

RECORDS TO BE KEPT

- Disposal of critical quality records.

ACTIVITIES

- Control quality documents.
- Control quality records.
- Control all subcontracted products and services with equivalent control to own activities.

ISO 9001, SECTION 5

DOCUMENTATION

- Quality policy.
- Quality objectives for all relevant levels of management and functions.
- Defined authorities and responsibilities for all persons whose duties can affect service quality.
- Nomination of a management representative.
- Description of internal communication channels.
- Procedure for management review.

RECORDS TO BE KEPT

- Evidence that planning for quality is routinely done.
- Evidence of effective internal communication.
- Records of management reviews.

ACTIVITIES

- Top management must be involved in:
  - communicating the importance of meeting customer requirements;
  - complying with legal obligations;
  - setting quality policy and objectives; and
  - management reviews.
- Communicate effectively between management levels and functions.

ISO 9001, SECTION 6

DOCUMENTATION

- List of any specific requirements regarding qualifications or competence of personnel.
- Procedure for identifying training needs.
- List/description of any special facilities that are essential for delivering a quality service.
- Definition of physical standards in the workplace necessary for delivering a quality service.
- Specifications (incorporating customer and legal requirements) for any products or materials that could affect service quality, whether used in providing the service or supplied to the customer.
- Description of the arrangements for communication with the customer.

RECORDS TO BE KEPT

- Evidence of evaluation of resource needs.
- A current training plan.
- Appropriate records of relevant training.
- Assessment of training.

ACTIVITIES

- Provide adequate resources for the quality management system and the processes.
- Assign competent personnel to all tasks relevant to quality.
- Provide adequate training.
- Assess the effectiveness of training.
- Ensure that people's working conditions are conducive to quality output.

ISO 9001, SECTION 7

DOCUMENTATION

- A quality plan for each contract or project, or a set of documents showing how quality has been planned into the service delivery process.
- A method for establishing and recording customer requirements.
- Specifications for any physical manufactured or assembled product.
- Service specification.
- Procedure for validating any process where the output cannot be directly assessed.
- Review of customer requirements for every contract, project or order.
- Procedure for design/development work.
- List of items, materials and services purchased which could impact on service quality.
- List of suppliers of these items. (This and the previous list can be combined.)
- Specifications for purchased materials.
- Procedure for selection and approval of suppliers.
- Procedure for review of suppliers.
- Description of the inspection to be carried out on incoming purchases.
- Procedures or work instructions for tasks that can impact on quality, where necessary.
- Description of arrangements for maintenance of any critical equipment used in providing the service.
- Plans for inspecting and testing the processes and products.
- Description of how any materials used in providing the service are identified and how they can be traced from purchase to use.
- Description of how the test status of items or materials are shown.
- Procedures or rules for handling materials, including customer property.
- Calibration plan, incorporating the list of instruments that require calibration.
- Procedure for managing calibration activities.
- Procedures for any calibrations carried out internally.

RECORDS TO BE KEPT

- A record of what the customer ordered or what you undertook to provide, for each order or project.
- Design reviews.
- Design verification results.
- Design validation results.
- Supplier review.
- Records of items purchased.
- Inspection of incoming materials.
- Validation reports for processes where the output cannot be directly assessed for conformity.
- Appropriate record of service delivery activities.

- Traceability of materials used in the service or provided to the customer.
- Damage or loss of any materials or items supplied by a customer.
- Appropriate stock control records for any physical material handled, if appropriate.
- Calibration certificates for calibrations carried out externally.
- Calibration records for calibrations carried out internally.
- Corrective action for instances of where instruments were found to be out of calibration.

ACTIVITIES

- Carry out reviews, verification and validation for all design/development projects.
- Physically mark or otherwise identify all items and materials adequately.
- Take adequate precautions in relation to any material supplied by a customer.
- Handle all items and materials in a way that protects them from damage and deterioration until the moment they are used or delivered to the customer.
- Carry out measurements in the proper manner.
- Protect measuring instruments against damage and unauthorized adjustment.

ISO 9001, SECTION 8

DOCUMENTATION

- Document describing measurement and monitoring activities aimed at improving the processes, service conformity with customer requirements and the quality management system.
- Descriptions of any statistical techniques used.
- Method for monitoring customer satisfaction.
- Procedure for internal audits.
- Checklists for internal audits.
- Current schedule for internal audits.
- Method of monitoring the processes to confirm that they remain capable of performing as required.
- Inspection plan or checklist for completed contract or project.
- Procedure for deciding that the service has been delivered fully and to the customer's satisfaction.
- Procedure for dealing with faulty items or materials which prevents them being used inadvertently.
- Procedure for recalling or replacing any faulty items supplied to the customer.
- A description of the approach to analysis of data for improvement of the processes.
- Procedure for corrective action.
- Procedure for preventive action.

RECORDS TO BE KEPT

- Customer satisfaction level.
- Improvement activities.
- Evidence that the need for statistical techniques was reviewed.
- Internal audit reports.
- Results of any monitoring of the actual process of delivering the service.
- Results of any product testing carried out.
- Results of any evaluation of the service output on completion of a project.
- Corrective action from internal audits.
- Action taken in respect of non-conforming materials.
- Evidence of activities designed to generate continual improvement.

- Corrective action.
- Risk assessment.
- Preventive action.

ACTIVITIES

- Improve the quality management system continually.
- Assess the need for statistical techniques as part of the monitoring activities.
- Provide training for internal auditors.
- Prevent inadvertent use of non-conforming materials.
- Take action to prevent recurrence of nonconformity.
- Carry out a risk assessment to identify potential causes of nonconformity.
- Analyse data, as appropriate, to identify opportunities for improvement.

CHAPTER XI

The elements of the ISO 9001 quality management system – manufacturing operations

The following is a list of documents, records and activities that are generally required in a manufacturing operation in order to comply with ISO 9001 requirements. However, the actual requirements will depend on the circumstances of the organization. In order to understand the full detail of what is needed it is essential to consult ISO 9001. Some of the items listed are strong recommendations rather than strict requirements of ISO 9001.

Note that many of the items listed below are normally included in the quality manual and may only be a few sentences long.

ISO 9001, SECTIONS 1 TO 3

There are no specific requirements stated in ISO 9001, Sections 1 to 3.

ISO 9001, SECTION 4

DOCUMENTATION
- One or more manuals containing the procedures of the quality management system.
- A flow chart showing the processes of the organization and how those processes interact with each other.
- A description of any information that is necessary for the proper operation of the processes.
- Quality manual, including any permitted exclusions claimed.
- Procedure for control of quality documents.
- Procedure for control of quality records.
- A description of any services or production activity that are subcontracted ('outsourced') and the controls that are in place to ensure quality.

RECORDS TO BE KEPT
- Disposal of critical quality records.

ACTIVITIES TO PERFORM
- Control quality documents.
- Control quality records.
- Control all subcontracted products and services with equivalent control to own activities.

ISO 9001, SECTION 5

DOCUMENTATION
- Quality policy.

- Quality objectives for all relevant levels of management and functions.
- Defined authorities and responsibilities for all persons whose duties can affect quality.
- Nomination of a management representative.
- Description of internal communication channels.
- Procedure for management review.

RECORDS TO BE KEPT

- Evidence that planning for quality is routinely done.
- Evidence of effective internal communication.
- Records of management reviews.

ACTIVITIES TO PERFORM

- Top management must be involved in:
  - communicating the importance of meeting customer requirements;
  - complying with legal obligations;
  - setting quality policy and objectives; and
  - management reviews.
- Communicate effectively between management levels and functions.

ISO 9001, SECTION 6

DOCUMENTATION

- List of any specific requirements regarding qualifications or competence of personnel.
- Procedure for identifying training needs.
- List/description of any special facilities required.
- Definition of physical standards in the workplace necessary for quality.
- Specifications (incorporating customer and legal requirements) for all products.
- Description of the arrangements for communication with the customer.

RECORDS TO BE KEPT

- Evidence of evaluation of resource needs.
- A current training plan.
- Appropriate records of relevant training.
- Assessment of training.

ACTIVITIES TO PERFORM

- Provide adequate resources for the quality management system and the processes.
- Assign competent personnel to all tasks relevant to quality.
- Provide adequate training.
- Assess the effectiveness of training.
- Ensure that people's working conditions are conducive to quality output.

ISO 9001, SECTION 7

DOCUMENTATION

- A quality plan for each contract, or a set of documents showing how quality has been planned into the production process.
- A method for establishing and recording customer requirements.

- Specifications for finished products.
- Procedure for validating processes where the output cannot be directly assessed.
- Review of customer requirements for every contract or order.
- Procedures for design/development work.
- List of items, materials and services that impact on quality.
- List of suppliers of these items. (This and the previous list can be combined.)
- Procedure for selection and approval of suppliers.
- Specifications for purchased materials.
- Procedure for review of suppliers.
- Description of the inspection to be carried out on incoming purchases.
- Procedures or work instructions for tasks that can impact on quality, where necessary.
- Description of arrangements for maintenance of critical equipment.
- Plans for inspecting and testing the processes and products.
- Description of how materials are identified and how they can be traced through the process.
- Description of how the test status of items or materials are shown.
- Procedures or rules for handling materials, including customer property.
- Calibration plan, incorporating the list of instruments that require calibration.
- Procedure for managing calibration activities.
- Procedures for any calibrations carried out internally.

RECORDS TO BE KEPT

- Record of what the customer ordered or what you undertook to do or supply, for each contract or order.
- Design reviews.
- Design verification results.
- Design validation results.
- Supplier review.
- Records of items purchased.
- Inspection of incoming materials.
- Validation reports for processes where the output cannot be directly assessed for conformity.
- Appropriate record of the production history.
- Traceability of materials through the process.
- Damage or loss of any materials or items supplied by a customer.
- Appropriate stock control records.
- Calibration certificates for calibrations carried out externally.
- Calibration records for calibrations carried out internally.
- Corrective action for instances of where instruments were found to be out of calibration.

ACTIVITIES TO PERFORM

- Carry out reviews, verification and validation for all design/development projects.
- Physically mark or otherwise identify all items and materials adequately.
- Take adequate precautions in relation to any material supplied by a customer.
- Handle all materials in a way that protects them from damage and deterioration until the moment they are used or delivered to the customer.
- Carry out measurements in the proper manner.
- Protect measuring instruments against damage and unauthorized adjustment.

ISO 9001, SECTION 8

DOCUMENTATION

- Document describing measurement and monitoring activities aimed at improving processes, product conformity and the quality management system.
- Descriptions of any statistical techniques used.
- Method for monitoring customer satisfaction.
- Procedure for internal audits.
- Checklists for internal audits.
- Current schedule for internal audits.
- Method of monitoring the processes to confirm that they remain capable of performing as required.
- Inspection plan for finished product.
- Procedure for release of product.
- Procedure for dealing with non-conforming product.
- Product recall procedure.
- Procedure for dealing with faulty items or materials which prevents them being used inadvertently.
- A description of the approach to analysis of data for improvement of the processes.
- Procedure for corrective action.
- Procedure for preventive action.

RECORDS TO BE KEPT

- Customer satisfaction level.
- Improvement activities.
- Evidence that the need for statistical techniques was reviewed.
- Internal audit reports.
- Corrective action from internal audits.
- Process monitoring results.
- Product testing results.
- Release of product.
- Identity of person who released the product.
- Action taken in respect of non-conforming product.
- Evidence of activities designed to generate continual improvement.
- Corrective action.
- Risk assessment.
- Preventive action.

ACTIVITIES TO PERFORM

- Improve the quality management system continually.
- Assess the need for statistical techniques as part of the monitoring activities.
- Provide training for internal auditors.
- Prevent inadvertent use of non-conforming product.
- Take action to prevent recurrence of nonconformity.
- Carry out a risk assessment to identify potential causes of nonconformity.
- Analyse data, as appropriate, to identify opportunities for improvement.

CHAPTER XII

Sample quality manual

The quality manual on the following pages is intended to show how one particular company set out the description of its quality management system. Every ISO 9000 organization is expected to produce a document resembling this. However, do not confuse this example with a template for producing your own quality manual. In the manual you will read about many things that this company does which may not be appropriate, or even helpful, for your organization. You should, therefore, look on this strictly as a guide to the overall approach to producing the manual.

The quality manual is the place where the policy and strategy for quality are described. It is the sort of document you could give to prospective clients or customers to demonstrate how seriously you take quality and customer satisfaction. It should contain an accurate and reasonably specific description of your quality management system. It does not, however, contain the detailed information on operating the quality management system. Each section of the manual contains references to specific procedures that are part of this particular company's system. By using references, the quality manual does not need to be changed every time one of the procedures referred to therein is changed.

It would not be possible, or even helpful, to give examples of all such procedures in a book like this, since many of them will be procedures for specialist tasks that might only apply in a particular company. Where examples are given they relate to tasks that are carried out either because the standard expects it or because they are regarded generally as beneficial.

For convenience in this book the Help documents referred to in the main commentary on the standards and those referred to in the sample quality manual are combined in one set at the back of the book. All Help documents have reference codes derived from the clause numbers of the ISO 9004 standard. Obviously, the references contained in your own quality manual will be to your own internal procedures, which will be coded in some unique way that you consider appropriate.

The manual contains some references to safety to demonstrate how quality and safety could be integrated into a single system, but the main safety reference is to a separate manual for the occupational health and safety management system. See QM–04 and QM–18. The safety manual would be exactly equivalent to this quality manual. Note that occupational health and safety does not come under the scope of ISO 9000, and may therefore be omitted from the quality manual. The only exception is where an occupational health and safety issue could affect product or service quality or customer satisfaction, for example, bad lighting or un-ergonomic workstations for quality inspection work. The whole issue of occupational health and safety needs to be addressed, however, either as part of an integrated management system or as a separate management system with its own manual and documentation.

The circulation list for this particular company contains 13 names. Since this is a fairly large company this is not unreasonable. In a smaller organization the list would be much shorter.

The management system described in the manual addresses primarily those elements for which ISO 9001 lays down requirements, since that is what forms the basis of the external audit. All standard references on the page titles, therefore, are to ISO 9001.

To facilitate changes to the manual it has been subdivided into separate sections. The sections are coded QM–01 to QM–35. In that way the whole manual does not need to be revised and reissued when a single change is made. There is no need to divide it in this way if you do not wish to.

Note that all the documents in the quality manual have been signed by the Managing Director. (Help document 5.6.1–3 shows that M. Smith is the Managing Director.) This is appropriate in the case of the quality manual, since this manual defines responsibilities and sets the policy and strategy for quality, as well as defining the structure of the quality management system.

ABC Ltd
Quality System Document

Reference QM–00	Approved for use by *Mark Smith*	Date of issue/revision 25.1.2001	Page 1 of 2
Title: Contents			

Document title	Reference	Date of current version
Contents	QM–00	25.1.2001
Circulation list	QM–01	15.1.2001
Scope of the quality management system	QM–02	20.1.2001
Company background	QM–03	15.1.2001
Quality management system	QM–04	20.1.2001
Quality documentation	QM–05	20.1.2001
Records	QM–06	20.1.2001
Management commitment	QM–07	15.1.2001
Customer focus	QM–08	15.1.2001
Quality policy	QM–09	25.1.2001
Quality objectives and quality planning	QM–10	20.1.2001
Management responsibility and authority	QM–11	20.1.2001
Management representative	QM–12	20.1.2001
Internal communication	QM–13	25.1.2001
Review of the management system	QM–14	20.1.2001
Resource management	QM–15	20.1.2001
Human resources	QM–16	25.1.2001
Infrastructure	QM–17	15.1.2001
Work environment	QM–18	15.1.2001
Production planning	QM–19	20.1.2001
Customer-related processes	QM–20	20.1.2001
Control of development work on products and processes	QM–21	20.1.2001
Purchasing	QM–22	25.1.2001
Product specifications	QM–23	15.1.2001
Procedures/work instructions	QM–24	15.1.2001
Servicing	QM–25	15.1.2001
Identification and traceability	QM–26	15.1.2001
Preservation of product	QM–27	15.1.2001
Measuring and monitoring devices	QM–28	15.1.2001
Measurement of conformity and improvement	QM–29	15.1.2001
Monitoring customer satisfaction	QM–30	15.1.2001
Internal audit of the quality system	QM–31	15.1.2001

Reference QM–00	Approved for use by *Mark Smith*	Date of issue/revision 25.1.2001	Page 2 of 2

Document title	Reference	Date of current version
In-process and final product testing	QM–32	15.1.2001
Control of non-conforming product	QM–33	15.1.2001
Analysis of data	QM–34	15.1.2001
Improvement	QM–35	15.1.2001

ABC Ltd
Quality System Document

Reference QM–01	Approved for use by *Mark Smith*	Date of issue/revision 15.1.2001	Page 1 of 1
Title: Circulation list			

Copy	Authorized holder
Master	Quality Manager
1	Managing Director
2	Financial Controller
3	Personnel Director
4	Production Director
5	Customer Services Manager
6	Training Manager
7	Information Services Manager
8	Product Development Manager
9	Production Manager
10	Engineering Manager
11	Laboratory Manager
12	Materials Manager

ABC Ltd
Quality System Document

Reference	Approved for use by	Date of issue/revision	Page 1 of 1
QM–02	*Mark Smith*	20.1.2001	

Title: Scope of the quality management system (1.2)

ISO 9001 excluded clause:

7.5.4. Customer property

The company does not handle any materials supplied by the customer.

In the event of this arising at any stage the protection of customer property is adequately addressed in the existing procedures.

ABC LTD
QUALITY SYSTEM DOCUMENT

Reference QM–03	Approved for use by *Mark Smith*	Date of issue/revision 15.1.2001	Page 1 of 1
Title: Company background			

ABC Ltd commenced manufacture of food products in Upper Gumtry in the mid-1970s and its output has grown approximately fourfold since then.

In 1981 the company became a wholly owned subsidiary of the multinational company Galactic Nutrition plc and became part of one of Europe's biggest food producers.

ABC Ltd employs approximately 250 people in Upper Gumtry, including 13 management, 25 other administrative staff and 12 supervisory staff.

ABC sources materials from suppliers around the world. However, where possible materials are purchased locally.

The production process continues 24 hours per day, seven days a week throughout the year. The output of the factory is exported to 15 countries in Europe and Asia.

The facility at Upper Gumtry comprises eight main departments, as follows:

- Product Development
- Bulk Production
- Packing
- Laboratory
- Quality
- Engineering
- Materials Handling
- Finance (incorporating Customer Services).

The Product Development function develops new products for the company's product range and carries out contract development for food retailing groups.

Packed product is sold in consumer packs through retail outlets.

Bulk material is supplied to packing factories within the Galactic Nutrition group.

The company supplies and services a range of food dispensers under licence from XYZ Dispensers plc.

In 1992 Upper Gumtry became the first factory within the group to gain certification to ISO 9001.

ABC LTD
QUALITY SYSTEM DOCUMENT

Reference QM–04	Approved for use by *Mark Smith*	Date of issue/revision 20.1.2001	Page 1 of 3
Title: Quality management system (4.1)			

ABC Ltd operates an integrated management system whereby the management of quality and safety is achieved by optimum utilization of management resources.

The quality element of the management system of ABC Ltd is based on ISO 9001. The safety element is based on ISA 2000 (a health and safety system developed by the author and also available from Gower: *ISA 2000: The System for Occupational Health and Safety Management*, Volumes 1 and 2 (2000)). The systems are documented in a set of manuals containing the process flow charts and describing how the processes interact.

This **Quality Manual** is the document that identifies and describes the processes of the quality management system. The quality management system is based on the guidance of ISO 9004 and the requirements of both ISO 9001 and the Galactic Nutrition corporate Quality Manual. It takes precedence over all other operations documentation.

All quality documents in the management systems belong to one of the manuals in the system. Each manual is assigned to the head of a department who is totally responsible for its control. As far as possible 'loose' documents are not part of the system. Where they are necessary, the existence and location of each one is recorded and the document is controlled.

The **General Procedures Manual** gives detailed operational procedures in relation to safety and quality. It is used as a vehicle to inform managers of:

- procedures and requirements that cross departmental lines; and
- universal requirements applicable in all departments.

Each department has a copy of the manual.

The **Product Development Manual** contains a description of product development activities of the company. It contains the flow chart for product development and the detailed procedures.

The **Product Manual** defines the products that are made by the company, and contains the detailed product specifications.

The **Purchasing Manual** contains:

- the specifications for critical purchases outlining the quality and safety requirements; and
- the detailed purchasing procedures.

The **Laboratory Manual** contains:

- the official laboratory test methods;
- the laboratory and quality control procedures;
- product sampling and testing plans; and
- the safety procedures that relate specifically to the laboratory.

Reference QM–04	Approved for use by *Mark Smith*	Date of issue/revision 20.1.2001	Page 2 of 3

The **Production Manual** contains:

- a flowchart of the production operation with critical control points for quality identified;
- details of process controls carried out by production personnel; and
- operating procedures (work instructions) for the Production operation. Documented procedures include details relating to quality and safety aspects of the tasks involved.

The **Customer Services Manual** contains:

- specific procedures for dealing with customers;
- procedures relating to surveys of customer satisfaction; and
- procedures for handling customer complaints and analysis of complaint statistics.

The **Engineering Manual** contains:

- the preventive maintenance programme;
- details of those elements of the calibration programme for which the Engineering Department is responsible;
- any specific safety or quality requirements in relation to the significant items of plant in the factory; and
- details of all disperser-servicing contracts.

The **Materials Handling Manual** ('Stores Manual') contains the procedures relating to the handling and control of goods during intake, storage and dispatch, and addresses the safety of personnel and the protection of the materials against damage.

The **Information Systems Manual** contains details of the controls over electronic data, including procedures for security of data and programs.

The **Personnel Manual** contains:

- details of the general safety and quality regulations in force in the company;
- details of induction and general training programmes;
- any specific qualification requirement in respect of individual functions (e.g., certificates of competency, licences, etc.); and
- details of company procedures in relation to commendation and disciplinary procedures.

Individual department manuals contain (in addition to the items listed above):

- the standards for physical conditions within the area;
- procedures for tasks carried out within the department;
- the details of the safety hazards that have been identified, risk assessment of these hazards, and the safeguards and controls that are in place, in accordance with Health and Safety legislation; and
- specific safety rules relating to tasks performed in or under the control of the particular department (specialized safety rules).

Where appropriate, detailed safety and environmental aspects of individual tasks have been incorporated into the Standard Operating Procedures (work instructions).

Reference QM–04	Approved for use by *Mark Smith*	Date of issue/revision 20.1.2001	Page 3 of 3

Reference information

The Quality Manager maintains a library of relevant reference information, including copies of relevant legislation. These documents are controlled.

References: 4.1–1 Interaction of processes.
         6.5–1 Reference library.

ABC LTD
QUALITY SYSTEM DOCUMENT

Reference QM–05	Approved for use by *Mark Smith*	Date of issue/revision 20.1.2001	Page 1 of 1

Title: Quality documentation (4.2.2 and 4.2.3)

Quality manual (4.2.2)

This quality manual is the primary document defining the quality management system. It takes precedence over all other procedures.

Control of documentation (4.2.3)

All documents included in any of the manuals listed below are subject to documentation control. The essential elements of this control are unique identification of documents, approval of the content and issue of documents, control of circulation and control of obsolete documents.

Responsibilities for producing and controlling the manuals, including the final authorization of the documents is as follows:

Manual	Authorizing Manager
Quality	Managing Director
General Procedures	Quality Manager
Product Development	Product Development Manager
Product	Quality Manager
Purchasing	Quality Manager
Laboratory	Laboratory Manager
Production	Production Manager
Engineering	Engineering Manager
Customer Services	Customer Services Manager
Materials Handling	Materials Manager
Information Systems	Information Systems Manager
Personnel	Personnel Director

Two other sets of documentation are controlled under the ISO 9001 document control procedure:

Material safety data sheets	Laboratory Manager
Hazardous substances risk assessment	Laboratory Manager

Reference: 4.2–2 Procedure for control of documentation.

ABC LTD
QUALITY SYSTEM DOCUMENT

Reference	Approved for use by	Date of issue/revision	Page 1 of 1
QM–06	*Mark Smith*	20.1.2001	

Title: Records (4.2.4)

Records are kept in relation to all activities covered by ISO 9001.

A batch history is recorded for every batch of product, showing the identification details of all materials used, the critical processing conditions, the personnel involved and dispatch details.

Quality records are required to be written in clearly legible form, dated and kept in an orderly manner. Records are kept filed in chronological order, except where this is clearly not appropriate.

Significant records relating to quality have been defined and listed in the Procedure for Control of Records in the General Procedures Manual. These records are retained for specified periods and may not be destroyed except with the approval of the Quality Manager.

Reference: 4.2–4 Procedure for control of quality records.

ABC LTD
QUALITY SYSTEM DOCUMENT

Reference QM–07	Approved for use by *Mark Smith*	Date of issue/revision 15.1.2001	Page 1 of 1

Title: Management commitment (5.1)

Top management demonstrates its commitment to the improvement of the quality management system by the following:

a) During the annual management review of the quality management system by the senior management team quality objectives are set for each function and management level in the company and the quality policy is reviewed.

b) The Production Director attends the two-monthly interim review of the quality management system for the purpose of motivating middle management and stressing the importance of complying with customer and legal requirements.

c) During the interim management review the management team assesses the availability of resources necessary for effective operation of the system.

d) The Quality Manager ensures that every issue of the company newsletter contains some quality-related issue.

e) A programme of 'management tours' is in operation whereby all managers visit all areas under their control at appropriate intervals.

References: 5.6.1–2 Procedure for interim management review.
5.6.1–1 Procedure for annual management review.
5.1–2 Guidance on management tours.
5.5.2–1 Promoting quality awareness.

ABC LTD
QUALITY SYSTEM DOCUMENT

Reference QM–08	Approved for use by *Mark Smith*	Date of issue/revision 15.1.2001	Page 1 of 1
Title: Customer focus (5.2)			

The company bases all its quality initiatives on the target of total customer satisfaction.

Packed product is manufactured to company specifications. Regular surveys of customer reaction are carried out and the results fed back to production and product development departments.

Bulk product is manufactured for customers to their specification. Close communication is maintained with the customer by several functions to ensure that full satisfaction is guaranteed.

All employees are regularly reminded of the importance of customer satisfaction by means of presentations by the Quality Manager and line managers and supervisors.

The company carries out regular surveys of customers to establish current customer requirements.

References: 5.2–1 Guidance: customer focus.

8.2.1.2–1 Procedure for customer surveys.

ABC LTD
QUALITY SYSTEM DOCUMENT

Reference	Approved for use by	Date of issue/revision	Page 1 of 1
QM–09	*Mark Smith*	25.1.2001	

Title: Quality policy (5.3)

ABC Ltd is committed to:

- producing a quality product which satisfies, and if possible exceeds, customer expectations;
- providing employees with all relevant information and appropriate training in relation to quality;
- facilitating employees to develop their skills and knowledge to the benefit of both the employees and the company;
- complying with all relevant statutory requirements;
- maintaining a management system that meets the requirements of ISO 9001 and facilitates the production of quality products;
- providing a safe environment for its employees;
- setting measurable quality objectives; and
- striving continually to improve performance in relation to quality.

The company regards quality as the responsibility of all persons working in the company, and expects all employees to act at all times to maintain safe working conditions and to report all nonconformities promptly.

This Policy Statement has been endorsed by all departmental managers.

Responsibilities

Authorizing the quality policy: Managing Director.
Making the quality policy known to all personnel: Quality Manager.
Ensuring the quality policy is reviewed annually: Managing Director.

ABC Ltd
Quality System Document

Reference	Approved for use by	Date of issue/revision	Page 1 of 1
QM–10	*Mark Smith*	20.1.2001	

Title: Quality objectives and quality planning (5.4)

Quality objectives (5.4.1)

Quality objectives are set for all functions in the company and all levels of management. Objectives are stated in quantitative terms so that performance can be measured. Where appropriate objectives are set higher each time to facilitate improvement. Progress towards objectives is reviewed during interim management reviews to ensure that they facilitate improvement.

For all relevant departments, objectives include the achievement of product conformance to specification.

Quality management system planning (5.4.2)

The quality objectives can only be achieved if the quality management system facilitates this. Emphasis is placed on the planning of the processes that form the overall system. Planning is achieved by means of regular review of the system, with particular emphasis on the provision of resources and the improvement of both the system and overall performance.

The interim management review addresses the need for changes arising from any current difficulties or planned changes so that control of the quality management system is maintained at all times.

Risk assessment is carried out formally in all departments. For risk assessment of the process (HACCP) see QM–19.

ABC Ltd
Quality System Document

Reference QM–11	Approved for use by *Mark Smith*	Date of issue/revision 20.1.2001	Page 1 of 6

Title: Management responsibility and authority (5.5.1)

The management structure of the company is shown below:

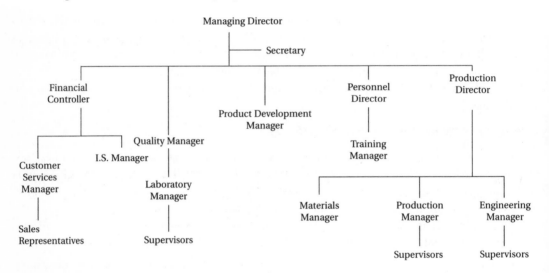

Responsibilities and authority in relation to quality

The Managing Director reports to the main Board of Galactic Nutrition and is responsible for all activities of ABC Ltd. This includes ultimate responsibility for:

a) the quality of product released to the market;
b) ensuring that corporate policy in relation to quality and safety is understood by all personnel;
c) ensuring that there is an adequate local policy in relation to quality and safety;
d) ensuring that the policy is fully implemented by means of an effective management system;
e) ensuring that adequate resources are made available for the proper implementation of the management system; and
f) declaring a product recall situation when necessary.

The task of ensuring quality in operational matters is delegated to the Production Director.

The Financial Controller is responsible for:

a) ensuring that the financial control system facilitates the smooth operation of all other departments;

Reference	Approved for use by	Date of issue/revision	Page 2 of 6
QM–11	*Mark Smith*	20.1.2001	

b) carrying out quality cost analysis, and reporting this to the senior management team at specified intervals; and

c) directing the information systems department.

The Personnel Director is responsible for:

a) ensuring that there is an adequate system in place for training of personnel in all aspects of their work, particularly with respect to quality;

b) ensuring that this system meets the requirements of managers and complies with ISO 9001 requirements;

c) approving the annual training plan; and

d) promoting a management approach to personnel that is mindful of the welfare and personal development of all employees.

The Production Director is responsible for :

a) all activities within the factory related to production;

b) ensuring the safety of all operations carried out on site through periodic reviews;

c) ensuring that the company policy in relation to quality is understood by all personnel, and that it is fully implemented;

d) ensuring that the production methods employed are effective, and give an adequate level of confidence to the company that the specified quality standards are being achieved; and

e) implementing the product recall procedure when necessary.

The Quality Manager is responsible for:

a) maintaining, developing, monitoring, and reporting on the quality elements of the Management System as required by ISO 9001, and any other company directives in relation to quality management;

b) decisions on the release of all product. This includes ensuring through adequate consultation that the correct decision is taken in relation to non-conforming product;

c) advising management on the disposal of non-conforming product;

d) ensuring that the company has adequate knowledge of developments in relation to food safety, quality management and relevant legislation;

e) the approval and monitoring of all raw material suppliers;

f) communication of complaint information to the factory management team;

g) co-ordinating the investigation of quality nonconformity and monitoring the effectiveness of corrective action; and

h) document control.

The Quality Manager has the right of appeal to the Corporate Director of Quality at Galactic Nutrition on all matters relating to quality.

Reference	Approved for use by	Date of issue/revision	Page 3 of 6
QM–11	*Mark Smith*	20.1.2001	

The Quality Manager is the 'management representative' referred to in ISO 9001. In his or her absence the Laboratory Manager deputizes, except in the case of decision on non-conforming product, which is taken by the Managing Director.

The Product Development Manager is responsible for:

a) translating the requirements of the customer into a design specification;
b) developing a product which meets the design specification and customer requirements; and
c) ensuring that quality aspects are incorporated into the product at all stages of development.

The Training Manager is responsible for:

a) monitoring the implementation of the annual training plan;
b) delivering general (company) induction to all new employees;
c) sourcing authorized training required by managers for themselves or their staff;
d) ensuring that there is an adequate system in place for monitoring the quality of training delivered;
e) maintaining training records for all external training carried out; and
f) drawing up the annual training plan.

The Customer Services Manager is responsible for:

a) ensuring that customer orders are fulfilled promptly and fully;
b) promoting the sale of products;
c) carrying out adequate surveys of representative customers to establish accurate customer requirements and levels of satisfaction;
d) ensuring that there is an effective system in place for handling customer complaints;
e) carrying out appropriate statistical analysis of customer complaints; and
f) ensuring that there are adequate and appropriate channels of communication with customers.

The Information Systems Manager is responsible for:

a) ensuring that all electronic information systems comply with the relevant requirements of ISO 9001 in relation to the control of data and computer programs;
b) maintaining records of all development in relation to company computer software;
c) ensuring that all critical computer records are adequately secured against loss;
d) ensuring that there is adequate protection (software and procedures) against computer viruses; and
e) ensuring that all computer hardware is maintained operational, and that adequate back-up facilities are available at all times.

The Laboratory Manager is responsible for:

a) day-to-day management of the laboratory;
b) carrying out all testing schedules given in the Laboratory Manual;
c) release of raw materials and packaging materials;

Reference	Approved for use by	Date of issue/revision	Page 4 of 6
QM–11	*Mark Smith*	20.1.2001	

d) release of product within specification; and

e) implementation of the calibration programme in respect of laboratory testing equipment.

The Materials Manager is responsible for:

a) ensuring that raw materials of approved quality are available for the production process in good time and in sufficient quantity to meet the needs of the production schedule;

b) planning the production schedule in a manner which ensures customers receive product when required;

c) maintaining a file of approved suppliers, from whom all purchases of specified materials are made;

d) identifying potential suppliers;

e) ensuring that handling of stored materials is adequate to maintain the quality of the product up to the moment of final delivery;

f) ensuring that materials are stored in a safe manner; and

g) ensuring that there is an adequate system in operation for stock control and stock rotation.

The Production Manager is responsible for:

a) ensuring that product is manufactured to specification;

b) ensuring that all relevant information in relation to quality is given to the Quality department, so that accept/reject decisions can be made on the basis of accurate information; and

c) ensuring that the production process is halted if he or she is satisfied that the product is likely to be defective, or that unacceptable safety risks exist.

The Engineering Manager is responsible for:

a) ensuring that all equipment is maintained in an appropriate state of repair, and subjected to statutory and other necessary checks. As far as possible this is to be achieved by preventive maintenance;

b) ensuring that other managers are acquainted with the likely safety and quality implications of equipment in use or proposed for use;

c) ensuring that service work for customers with dispenser service contracts is carried out on time and properly;

d) ensuring that all maintenance work done in the factory, whether by company personnel or outside contractors, is carried out in a proper manner, without jeopardizing product quality or safety of personnel; and

e) implementing the calibration programme in respect of all measuring equipment with the exception of laboratory testing equipment.

Reference QM–11	Approved for use by *Mark Smith*	Date of issue/revision 20.1.2001	Page 5 of 6

All department heads are responsible for:

a) ensuring that all activities are adequately documented in the form of controlled procedures, that these documents adequately address quality, and that they are reviewed and maintained up to date;

b) ensuring that all documented procedures, plans and schedules are carried out as specified;

c) ensuring that all specified records are made and kept securely for the specified period;

d) ensuring that all personnel are adequately trained for their tasks;

e) maintaining records of all internal training delivered;

f) ensuring that the processes of the department are assessed periodically for risks to quality and customer satisfaction, and appropriate preventive action taken; and

g) ensuring that adequate corrective action is taken in relation to all nonconformities of product or the quality management system.

Supervisors (all departments) are responsible for:

a) supervising all activities for which they have responsibility;

b) ensuring that documented procedures are followed, and the necessary records kept;

c) being aware of all activities in the particular area at all times;

d) ensuring that no unauthorized activity is carried out;

e) carrying out the regular inspections specified in the various manuals and procedures;

f) informing the department manager of any quality nonconformities;

g) identifying training needs, and maintaining records for internal training;

h) encouraging compliance with the quality policies and procedures; and

i) being aware of any personnel-related issues that could affect the team's performance, and reporting these to the department manager.

Sales staff are responsible for:

a) ensuring that customer orders are taken accurately and entered on the computer promptly;

b) communicating effectively and courteously with customers;

c) reporting promptly all useful feedback in relation to product or service quality to the Customer Services Manager.

Employees

All employees are required to comply with their legal obligations in relation to food safety and hygiene and occupational health and safety.

All employees are required to carry out all tasks in accordance with the training they received and written procedures.

All employees are required to report any process abnormality that could affect product quality adversely.

All employees should consider themselves responsible for the quality of the product to the extent that their work impacts on quality.

Reference	Approved for use by	Date of issue/revision	Page 6 of 6
QM–11	*Mark Smith*	20.1.2001	

The Document Controller is responsible for:

a) making controlled copies of documents that have been properly authorized by the owner of a manual;
b) circulating the controlled copies to the persons on the documented circulation list;
c) issuing instructions regarding the destruction of old documents; and
d) maintaining a file of obsolete originals, properly marked.

Other detailed responsibilities are given in the relevant individual procedures.

Deputies
Unless specifically documented, a person's immediate superior deputizes in his or her absence.

ABC LTD
QUALITY SYSTEM DOCUMENT

Reference	Approved for use by	Date of issue/revision	Page 1 of 1
QM–12	*Mark Smith*	20.1.2001	

Title: Management representative (5.5.2)

The Quality Manager has been nominated as the management representative required by ISO 9001. He or she is responsible for ensuring that there is an appropriate quality management system in place and that it is maintained. He or she also reports formally to management reviews (verbally to the interim two-monthly review and by written report to the annual review).

The management representative promotes awareness of customer requirements by means of a noticeboard, by putting regular entries in the company newsletter and by making presentations to management and operators.

The management representative's principal function is to monitor the performance of the quality management system and ensure that any deficiencies or opportunities for improvement are reported promptly to the Managing Director.

Reference: 5.5.2–1 Promoting quality awareness.

ABC Ltd
Quality System Document

Reference QM–13	Approved for use by *Mark Smith*	Date of issue/revision 25.1.2001	Page 1 of 1

Title: Internal communication (5.5.3)

Communication is recognized as an important part of ensuring product quality.

Operations meetings are held daily involving production, quality, engineering and logistics personnel. This meeting is the basic means of communication between the functions involved in operational control.

The company issues a newsletter, approximately two-monthly, and this is used to communicate appropriate quality information among all company personnel.

Noticeboards are located in the canteen and main corridor. Part of these are sectioned off for exclusive use by the Quality Manager for matters of quality and safety.

All supervisors and managers are encouraged to hold team meetings at least monthly, partly for quality awareness purposes but also to communicate information.

References: 5.5.3–1 Procedure for daily operations meetings.

5.5.2–1 Promoting quality awareness.

ABC Ltd
QUALITY SYSTEM DOCUMENT

Reference	Approved for use by	Date of issue/revision	Page 1 of 1
QM–14	*Mark Smith*	20.1.2001	

Title: Review of the management system (5.6)

The quality management system is assessed regularly to confirm its continuing suitability and effectiveness.

Two-monthly interim review

At two-monthly intervals a short interim review of the quality system is conducted. The review is chaired by the Quality Manager and is attended by representatives from all departments.

Minutes of the meeting are kept. Items requiring action are noted, and responsibilities for corrective action are assigned. The department manager is responsible in every case for ensuring that agreed corrective action is taken.

Reference: 5.6.1–2 Procedure for interim management review.

Annual review

An annual review of the entire Management System is carried out by the senior management team. The purpose of this review is to assess the overall performance of the system against the defined objectives, and to identify any modifications that are necessary. The review takes account of the findings of the internal and external audits carried out since the previous annual review.

A full report of this review is prepared. Items requiring action are noted and responsibility for corrective action is assigned. Follow-up action is monitored to ensure that all items are satisfactorily completed.

Reference: 5.6.1–1 Procedure for annual management review.

ABC Ltd
Quality System Document

Reference	Approved for use by	Date of issue/revision	Page 1 of 1
QM–15	*Mark Smith*	20.1.2001	

Title: Resource management (6.1)

Provision of resources

The company ensures that resources are provided for all the processes of the quality management system by reviewing resources at each two-monthly management review.

The Managing Director is responsible for ensuring that adequate resources are provided.

Reference: 5.6.1–2 Procedure for interim management review.

ABC Ltd
Quality System Document

Reference	Approved for use by	Date of issue/revision	Page 1 of 2
QM–16	*Mark Smith*	25.1.2001	

Title: Human resources (6.2)

Recruitment and competency

Specific requirements for individual jobs are defined, where appropriate, by the manager for the area. These requirements can include formal qualification and experience, as well as demonstrable ability to perform specific tasks competently. Candidates are selected on their suitability for carrying out the tasks involved.

Placement

Before being assigned any new tasks a person's suitability is assessed by the manager of the area and the appropriate personnel record updated.

Reference: The Personnel Manual contains the procedures relating to personnel matters, including details of system for managing training activities within the company.

Induction and training

All personnel receive both induction and refresher training. Staff who handle product are all trained in basic food hygiene.

Ongoing training needs are formally identified annually, and converted into an annual training plan.

All training is recorded as it is carried out. Individual training records are kept for each person, and these are reviewed annually by the person's manager.

All formal training is evaluated for effectiveness primarily by monitoring trainee performance after training.

References: 6.2.2–3 Procedure for identification of training needs.
6.2.2–1 and 6.2.2–2 Training records.
6.2.2–6 Training evaluation sheet.

Awareness

The company operates several schemes to promote quality awareness, including use of the company noticeboards and newsletter, and posters and signs. The management representative (see 5.5.3) is responsible for promoting quality awareness.

Reference: 5.5.2–1 Promoting quality awareness.

Reference QM–16	Approved for use by *Mark Smith*	Date of issue/revision 25.1.2001	Page 2 of 2

Supervision

All tasks are carried out under supervision. Supervisors are present on all shifts and in each department.

ABC Ltd
Quality System Document

Reference QM–17	Approved for use by *Mark Smith*	Date of issue/revision 15.1.2001	Page 1 of 1

Title: Infrastructure (6.3)

Infrastructure

Infrastructural requirements are reviewed at the interim management review as part of the review of resources.

Production plans and procedures specify standards for equipment, workspace, facilities, hardware, software and supporting services. Monitoring and maintenance activities are documented and carried out regularly.

References: Production Manual.
             Engineering Manual.

Preventive Maintenance

A review of maintenance requirements has been carried out under both the HACCP study and the safety Hazard Identification and Risk Assessment analysis. A preventive maintenance system is in operation, designed to prevent breakdown of plant and to identify potential quality and safety hazards before they occur.

Plant maintenance procedures are in place. The details of plant maintenance procedures are documented in the Engineering Manual. Those items of plant critical to quality or safety have been identified and a system of checking of this equipment is in operation.

Weekly, monthly and annual inspection checklists are in operation to help identify problems before they arise.

Reference: Maintenance procedures, schedules and plans are detailed in the Engineering Manual.

ABC LTD
QUALITY SYSTEM DOCUMENT

Reference	Approved for use by	Date of issue/revision	Page 1 of 1
QM–18	*Mark Smith*	15.1.2001	

Title: Work environment (6.4)

Maintaining the work environment in a suitable state is essential for producing a quality product. The HACCP Plan describes all the controls required to maintain the work environment in a suitable condition. These controls have been incorporated into the documented procedures under ISO 9000.

Particular attention is paid to hygiene control. Regular housekeeping inspections are carried out in each department. Back-up hygiene audits are carried out by the QA department, according to documented schedules. Plant hygiene is monitored by swabbing according to documented schedules.

References: 8.5.3–2 HACCP Plan.

Cleaning schedules and procedures are contained in department manuals.

Standards for physical conditions and inspection checklists are contained in department manuals.

Occupational health and safety is managed under the ISA 2000 management system (Seaver, M. and O'Mahony, L. (2000), *ISA 2000: The System for Occupational Health and Safety Management*, Volumes 1 and 2, Gower: Aldershot). This addresses all issues and physical conditions that could cause distress to staff and thereby affect the quality of their work.

Reference: The Safety Management System Manual contains the description of the occupational health and safety management system.

ABC LTD
QUALITY SYSTEM DOCUMENT

Reference	Approved for use by	Date of issue/revision	Page 1 of 2
QM–19	*Mark Smith*	20.1.2001	

Title: Production planning (7.1)

Planning

The company places great emphasis on the quality planning process. Customer requirements for the product are defined in detailed specifications, and each process is planned so that the specification is achieved consistently. Objectives are set for each process and performance against these objectives is monitored regularly. Each new product is planned as a specific project. See the section on product development (QM–21). Before a product goes into full production the entire system needed to guarantee customer satisfaction is documented. This includes all production and quality control methods, resources, inspection and testing activities and records.

Both the two-monthly interim review and the annual review of the system include a review of resources to confirm that they are adequate.

Reference: 5.4.2–1 Guidance on planning.

Risk assessment

A detailed HACCP (hazard analysis and critical control points) analysis of the entire process has been undertaken from raw material receipt right through to the point at which the customer takes responsibility for the product to identify any potential hazards and assess the risk to product quality. Critical control points identified in this analysis are controlled to minimize the risk of nonconformity. The controls have been integrated into procedures, process control inspection and testing schedules, cleaning schedules and physical inspections. The risk assessment has been fully documented, and is reviewed annually.

References: 5.4.2–2 and 5.4.2–3 Risk assessment.
　　　　　　　　8.5.3–2 HACCP Plan.
　　　　　　　　Process control inspection and testing schedules are contained in the Laboratory and Production manuals.

Validation of processes (7.5.2)

The heat treatment and spray-drying steps are the most critical points in the entire production process. While the effectiveness of the heat treatment can be assessed by subsequent sampling and testing of the resultant bulk batch, the spray-drying process is susceptible to sporadic microbiological contamination if the spray dryer and its associated fittings are not maintained in a hygienic condition. Such contamination cannot be reliably detected by testing of the finished product, and therefore this step must be strictly controlled to prevent microbiological problems. The drying and

Reference	Approved for use by	Date of issue/revision	Page 2 of 2
QM–19	*Mark Smith*	20.1.2001	

post-drying steps are evaluated at daily management meetings to ensure continuing suitability. It is assessed in depth during the annual HACCP review.

Any change to the operating conditions must be evaluated according to a defined procedure.

Only staff who have been adequately trained are permitted to carry out these process steps.

References: 7.1.3.3–1 and 7.1.3.3–2 Introducing process changes.

8.5.3–2 HACCP Plan.

ABC LTD
QUALITY SYSTEM DOCUMENT

Reference	Approved for use by	Date of issue/revision	Page 1 of 1
QM–20	*Mark Smith*	20.1.2001	

Title: Customer-related processes (7.2)

The company produces a range of products to its own specification. The Customer Services department ensures that the product continues to satisfy customers' needs by carrying out regular surveys of customers. The specifications are comprehensive and address both the stated requirements and all others necessary for the product, including legal requirements. All relevant information from customer surveys is fed back into the product development and/or product realization processes, and any necessary improvements made.

Reference: 8.2.1.2–1 and 8.2.1.2–2 Customer surveys.

On receipt of every order from a customer or production contract from an associate company the requirements of the order or contract are formally reviewed to ensure that it can be fulfilled to specification and on time.

Reference: 7.2–1 and 7.2–2 Procedures for handling customer orders.

Communication channels have been set up to enable customers to communicate easily with the company. This refers particularly to feedback in relation to complaints, provision of technical information about the products, any difficulties in relation to orders or deliveries, and changes to requirements that the customer communicates after the initial agreement has been made.

Reference: 7.2–4 Procedure for customer communication.

ABC LTD
QUALITY SYSTEM DOCUMENT

Reference	Approved for use by	Date of issue/revision	Page 1 of 1
QM–21	*Mark Smith*	20.1.2001	

Title: Control of development work on products and processes (7.3)

Product development

The company has an active product development function. It is the policy of the company that quality is designed into all products throughout the development process.

Product development is carried out according to documented procedures detailed in the Product Development Manual. A product brief is produced for every product development project. The brief includes quality requirements (especially statutory requirements) and indicates performance test criteria.

At each stage of the development process quality requirements are reviewed to ensure that the product meets the requirements of the product brief. In the case of internal development projects the Customer Services Manager is regarded as the customer.

Finished product samples are tested in accordance with the acceptance criteria laid down in the product brief.

Production scale samples are approved by the customer before full production can begin.

Full records are kept of all development work. Each trial is individually identified by code.

For each developed product a comprehensive product file is produced containing all relevant documents and methods relating to the manufacture, testing and shelf life of the product.

Reference: The Product Development Manual contains the detailed procedures for product development control.

Process development

All changes to processes must be carried out according to the written procedure. Where the change involves a capital investment of £5000 or more a Process Change Brief must be produced. This brief includes quality and safety requirements of the modified process. The change must be approved by the Managing Director, and only after all the requirements specified in the brief have been implemented and verified, or resolved in some other satisfactory way. Other changes do not require a formal brief to be produced, but the change must be approved by the Quality Manager. The procedure for requesting changes to the process specifies that quality and safety consequences of the change be evaluated. The procedure requires that all changes be fully documented.

Reference: 7.1.3.3–1 and 7.1.3.3–2 Introducing process changes.

ABC LTD
QUALITY SYSTEM DOCUMENT

Reference	Approved for use by	Date of issue/revision	Page 1 of 2
QM–22	*Mark Smith*	25.1.2001	

Title: Purchasing (7.4)

Items and services that can have a direct impact on the quality of the product are subject to purchasing control. They may only be purchased from suppliers that have been assessed and deemed capable of supplying to specification consistently. A list of approved suppliers is maintained.

Quality and safety requirements for purchased goods are detailed in individual specifications. Only goods that comply with these requirements are ordered.

Suppliers are continuously assessed and their performance against requirements evaluated. Records are kept of supplier performance. Suppliers are reviewed at least annually and may be delisted for failure to supply quality materials.

All purchases are made by the purchasing officer in the Materials department, with the exception of laboratory materials, which are made directly by the Laboratory Manager.

Purchase orders are sent out for all purchases defining precisely what is being ordered. Where necessary additional quality requirements are attached to the purchase order.

Two-way communication is maintained between ABC Ltd and suppliers. Each supplier is kept informed about the performance of the product supplied. ABC Ltd has a policy of building long-term relationships with suppliers where appropriate.

A procedure exists to control emergency purchases from non-approved suppliers.

Stock control of raw materials is a computer-based system.

Verification of incoming materials (7.4.3)

Where required by the inspection and testing plan, specific testing is carried out to ensure conformance to specified quality or safety requirements. In the case of quality, the level of inspection of incoming goods depends on the level of confidence in the supplier, the experience with the particular material and its potential impact on the final product.

Certificates of conformity or test may be accepted as evidence of conformance with regard to quality, at the discretion of the Quality Manager. Where stipulated by written instruction the goods inwards inspector carries out inspection and testing to ensure goods and services conform to specified requirements. All verification is carried out against company specifications.

The company has a small number of key suppliers who supply directly to stock on the basis of performance over a long period and frequent close communication at various levels between the company and the suppliers. The agreement on this is documented in specific contracts with these suppliers.

References: 7.4.2–1 Procedure for approval of suppliers.
            7.4.2–2 Procedure for review of suppliers.

Reference	Approved for use by	Date of issue/revision	Page 2 of 2
QM–22	*Mark Smith*	25.1.2001	

7.4.2–3 List of approved suppliers.

7.4.1–1 Purchasing procedure.

7.4.1–2 Verbal orders.

ABC Lᴛᴅ
Qᴜᴀʟɪᴛʏ Sʏsᴛᴇᴍ Dᴏᴄᴜᴍᴇɴᴛ

Reference	Approved for use by	Date of issue/revision	Page 1 of 1
QM–23	*Mark Smith*	15.1.2001	

Title: Product specifications (7.5.1)

All products are made to detailed company specifications. These specifications cover all relevant physical, chemical, nutritional, organoleptic and microbiological characteristics of the product, and ensure that the product meets legal requirement and gives customer satisfaction.

References: Product specifications are contained in a dedicated section of the Product Manual.
        7.2–3 Guidance on legal compliance.

ABC Ltd
Quality System Document

Reference	Approved for use by	Date of issue/revision	Page 1 of 1
QM–24	*Mark Smith*	15.1.2001	

Title: Procedures/work instructions (7.5.1)

The process is documented in a series of manuals containing all the procedures for carrying out the process properly, and all operators have been instructed in the correct methods of working. The documented procedures are available close to all workstations.

The manager of each department is responsible for maintaining the procedures up to date, and for ensuring that the processes are adequately described in the procedures.

Reference: See QM–04 for a description of the manuals in the quality management system.

ABC LTD
QUALITY SYSTEM DOCUMENT

Reference	Approved for use by	Date of issue/revision	Page 1 of 1
QM–25	*Mark Smith*	15.1.2001	

Title: Servicing (7.5.1)

The company supplies and services a range of food dispensers under licence from XYZ Dispensers plc.

Work carried out by employees off-site is subject to the same quality and safety controls and procedures as on-site work.

Servicing activities are carried out according to documented procedures drawn up from the manufacturer's manuals.

A register is kept up to date of all customers holding dispensers with service contracts. The list includes the details of the equipment held, serial numbers and details of the particular service contract.

A complete manual for each item of equipment is provided in each service van.

Records are kept of all servicing activities carried out.

Reference: Servicing procedures are detailed in the Engineering Manual.

ABC Ltd
Quality System Document

Reference QM–26	Approved for use by *Mark Smith*	Date of issue/revision 15.1.2001	Page 1 of 1
Title: Identification and traceability (7.5.3)			

Product

Product identification is maintained at all stages from first use of raw materials to dispatch of finished product. Each batch of product is given a unique batch identification number in the Materials department, and this forms the basis for product traceability. All product is identified by bar-code label. Movement of product through the process is recorded on computer.

The company has a product recall procedure in place to facilitate the recall of non-conforming product if necessary. All dispatches are recorded in sufficient detail to allow traceability outwards to the retail outlet. Internally there is traceability that allows product to be traced to the supplier's lot number of the materials used.

Reference: 7.5.2–2 Product Recall Procedure.

Identification of status in respect of quality inspection and testing

Procedures are in place to ensure that the inspection and test status of product (including raw materials) at all stages of the process is easily known. This is achieved by means of a centralized computer-based bar-coding system. Four possibilities for status exist: Passed all tests, Not yet tested, Reject and Rework. Reading the bar code or manually entering the batch number and pallet number quickly establishes the status.

There are automatic blocks (computer controlled) in the materials-handling system that alert operators if an attempt is made to use unapproved materials.

Incoming production materials are given a status on arrival.

Authority to change test status is restricted to the Laboratory Manager.

Physical labelling

Where practicable, non-conforming product is clearly identified by a red label and is moved to a quarantine area, in addition to its electronic non-conforming status.

References: 7.5.2–1 Procedure for inspection and test status.
8.3.1–1 Procedure for non-conforming product.

ABC LTD
QUALITY SYSTEM DOCUMENT

Reference	Approved for use by	Date of issue/revision	Page 1 of 1
QM–27	*Mark Smith*	15.1.2001	

Title: Preservation of product (7.5.5)

Controls are in operation to ensure that materials are handled with proper care at all stages from the moment goods are received all the way through to formally handing over the finished product to the customer.

Personnel are trained in the methods to be used in specific tasks. Handling methods are designed to protect the product and the handlers against damage and injury.

Suitable storage facilities are provided, which protect the product against deterioration during its full storage period.

Stock is inspected regularly to ensure that product is not deteriorating or damaged, and that storage conditions are safe. Incompatible materials are stored apart.

All movements of stock and raw materials in and out of storage are recorded. A strict stock rotation system of first in – first out (FIFO) operates in both the raw material and finished goods warehouses.

Transport

The company employs external hauliers to transport its product. Every vehicle is inspected before loading to ensure that it is suitable. Records are kept of all dispatches (vehicle identification, date and product batch numbers) to aid traceability.

References: Handling and packing procedures are documented in the Production Manual.
Storage and transport procedures are documented in the Materials Manual.

ABC Ltd
QUALITY SYSTEM DOCUMENT

Reference QM–28	Approved for use by *Mark Smith*	Date of issue/revision 15.1.2001	Page 1 of 1
Title: Measuring and monitoring devices (7.6)			

Each department's manual contains the list of any items of equipment that give measurements used to assess product quality, and the calibration requirements for each.

Maintenance of measuring equipment

Each instrument is uniquely identified either by a number or by its location.

All equipment is regularly maintained or inspected, and kept in good working order.

Calibration

All equipment used to assess product quality is calibrated to a written schedule. Calibration procedures include identification of suitable test equipment, identification of accuracy and precision required, the method and frequency of calibration and the accuracy required for each measurement. Action when instruments are found to be out of calibration is also specified.

Where possible standards for calibration are traceable to a national standard. In all other cases, there is documented evidence of the justification for the standard used.

Calibration is carried out both by company personnel and by accredited external calibration agencies.

Records of all calibrations are retained for reference.

The current calibration schedule is filed in the Engineering Manual.

Reference: 7.6–1 Procedure for control of measuring instruments.

ABC LTD
QUALITY SYSTEM DOCUMENT

Reference	Approved for use by	Date of issue/revision	Page 1 of 1
QM–29	*Mark Smith*	15.1.2001	

Title: Measurement of conformity and improvement (8.1)

The company has a management policy of setting measurable objectives in all areas of activity and measuring the degree to which the objectives are met. Improvement is generated by means of raising the standards to be achieved when this is appropriate.

Statistical objectives in relation to product conformity are set at the annual management review and these are modified, as appropriate, at interim management reviews.

Performance objectives that reflect the effectiveness of the quality management system are also set. These relate, among other things, to customer complaints and customer satisfaction rating.

References: 5.6.1–1 Procedure for annual management review.

5.6.1–2 Procedure for interim management review.

8.2.1.2–1 and 8.2.1.2–2 Customer surveys.

8.2.1.2–3 and 8.2.1.2–4 Customer complaints.

Risk assessment of all quality management system processes is carried out at least annually by department managers with a view to minimizing risks and identifying opportunities for improvement.

Reference: 5.4.2–2 and 5.4.2–3 Risk assessment.

Statistical techniques (8.1)

A review of the need for statistical techniques in relation to quality has been included in the HACCP programme. A number of control points have been identified as requiring control charts to facilitate process control, and these have been put in place.

Where relevant, acceptance sampling of incoming materials is carried out in accordance with a recognized statistical sampling plan authorized by the Quality Manager.

Pareto analysis of non-conforming product is used to prioritize corrective action.

The methods used are fully described in the General Procedures Manual.

ABC Ltd
Quality System Document

Reference	Approved for use by	Date of issue/revision	Page 1 of 1
QM–30	*Mark Smith*	15.1.2001	

Title: Monitoring customer satisfaction (8.2.1)

The Customer Services department carries out monthly surveys of customer satisfaction by personal interview at selected retail outlets.

The results are analysed and form one input into the following interim management review.

References: 8.2.1.2–1 Procedure for customer surveys.
8.2.1.2–2 Customer survey form.

ABC LTD
QUALITY SYSTEM DOCUMENT

Reference	Approved for use by	Date of issue/revision	Page 1 of 1
QM–31	*Mark Smith*	15.1.2001	

Title: Internal audit of the quality system (8.2.2)

Internal audits are carried out systematically to ensure that the quality system conforms to ISO 9001 and is being implemented properly and fully. Audits are carried out according to a documented schedule, at a frequency that ensures that the entire system is assessed at least every 12 months.

Audits are carried out using the appropriate checklist by trained auditors nominated by the Quality Manager. Where possible auditors are not assigned to audit the department where they normally work. Results of audits are recorded and reviewed, and the appropriate corrective or preventive action implemented permanently.

The current internal audit schedule is filed in the General Procedures Manual.

References: 8.2.1.3–1 Procedure for internal quality audits.
8.2.1.3–2 ISO 9001 internal audits checklist.
8.2.1.3–3 Internal audit plan.
8.2.1.3–5 Notes on internal auditing of quality systems.

ABC Ltd
QUALITY SYSTEM DOCUMENT

Reference	Approved for use by	Date of issue/revision	Page 1 of 1
QM–32	*Mark Smith*	15.1.2001	

Title: In-process and final product testing (8.2.3 and 8.2.4)

Process control is achieved by production personnel carrying out in-process inspection according to documented inspection plans that specify what checks are to be made, the frequency, the standard to be achieved and the action to be taken if anything is found to be non-conforming.

Sampling and testing is carried out at various stages of manufacture to ensure that the product meets specification.

The laboratory provides a service of verifying 'first off' samples, laboratory testing and additional in-process checks to the Production Department.

Immediate corrective action is taken when any result is out of specification.

Appropriate process parameters are controlled within defined tolerances optimal for product quality.

Inspection prior to use (8.2.3)

Specified equipment is inspected before use. Sometimes this is for reasons of health and safety (for example forklift trucks) and sometimes for quality reasons (hygienic condition of product tanks).

Reference: These checks are detailed in the procedures for the individual tasks involved.

Monitoring and measurement of final product (8.2.4)

Final product is sampled and tested according to defined written schedules, and assessed against the appropriate specification.

References: 8.2.3–1 Product release procedure.

The Production and Laboratory manuals contain the detailed inspection and testing plans.

All testing is carried out in accordance with written procedures and results of all testing are recorded. These records are reviewed by the manager or supervisor, and this review forms part of the eventual product release procedure.

ABC LTD
QUALITY SYSTEM DOCUMENT

Reference QM–33	Approved for use by *Mark Smith*	Date of issue/revision 15.1.2001	Page 1 of 1

Title: Control of non-conforming product (8.3)

Non-conforming product is defined as any instance of product outside its specification in any respect.

Written procedures require that immediate steps be taken to neutralize the nonconformity. Initial action must be either to correct the problem or to remove the item from use. This requires that non-conforming product be clearly marked, and the associated records updated.

The manager in charge of a process has the authority to shut down that process until the nonconformity is eliminated, if necessary.

Operators are encouraged to report all instances of nonconformity as part of the hazard reporting programme, even 'near misses' where no loss was incurred.

All non-conforming product remain in quarantine until the Quality Manager has made a decision about it.

There is a written procedure covering the control of non-conforming product. This procedure deals with all stages, right up to the disposal of the product.

Reference: 8.3.1–1 Procedure for non-conforming product.

Product recall

There is a written recall procedure in place for recalling product from the market, should it be necessary to do so. Product recalls are ordered by the Managing Director, and the Production Director is responsible for implementing the procedure and liasing with official agencies.

References: 7.5.2–2 Procedure for product recall.
               Corporate Crisis Management Manual.

Reporting nonconformities

All instances of product nonconformity are recorded and reported to the daily operations meeting. All personnel are required to report any information relevant to product quality so that decisions can be based on accurate information.

References: 5.5.3–1 Procedure for daily operations meeting.
               8.5.2–2 Nonconformity/corrective action report.

ABC LTD
QUALITY SYSTEM DOCUMENT

Reference	Approved for use by	Date of issue/revision	Page 1 of 1
QM–34	*Mark Smith*	15.1.2001	

Title: Analysis of data (8.4)

All data collected is analysed to extract information in relation to performance and improvement.

Specific parameters are measured and traced to help identify trends. All department heads are required to analyse relevant data to provide information relating to customer satisfaction, conformance to customer requirements or internal specification, the performance of the processes and product, and the quality of purchased materials and suppliers' performance.

The resultant analysis is presented to the appropriate management meeting for review and action.

References: 8.4–1 Guidance on analysis of data.

5.6.1–2 Procedure for interim management review.

ABC Ltd
Quality System Document

Reference	Approved for use by	Date of issue/revision	Page 1 of 2
QM–35	*Mark Smith*	15.1.2001	

Title: Improvement (8.5)

Continual improvement of the quality management system is achieved by regular review of data at the appropriate management level within the company. The frequency of review is appropriate for the activity and information being reviewed, ranging from daily review of corrective action to annual review of quality policy.

At each interim management review the possibilities for improvement are examined, and where possibilities are identified action to implement the improvement is planned.

Reference: 5.6.1–2 Procedure for interim management review.

Corrective action (8.5.2)

There is a written procedure for corrective action that will reduce the possibility of the defect, error or failure recurring. The procedure covers all aspects of the company's activities. Particular emphasis is placed on identifying the true root cause of the nonconformity rather than superficial causes.

Corrective action is taken in respect of both product and quality management system nonconformity.

There are procedures in place which monitor the effectiveness of the corrective action, and which ensure that the action taken is permanent.

Reference: 8.5.2–1 Procedure for corrective action.

Preventive action (8.5.3)

Specified data in relation to quality is reviewed at the two-monthly interim management review meetings in order to identify trends that would indicate a need for preventive action.

All departments carry out regular risk assessment exercises to identify potential quality problems and possibilities for improvement.

A formal preventive action analysis in relation to product has been carried out in the form of HACCP. The entire operation has been analysed to identify points at which product nonconformity could arise. Controls have been put in place at these points, and regular monitoring has been incorporated into inspection plans.

The HACCP analysis is reviewed every 12 months, and more often if a need is identified.

Preventive action in relation to the quality management system is discussed and planned at the two-monthly interim management review.

Where preventive action is required it is carried out under the corrective action procedure to ensure permanent implementation.

Reference	Approved for use by	Date of issue/revision	Page 2 of 2
QM–35	*Mark Smith*	15.1.2001	

References: 8.5.3–1 Procedure for preventive action.

8.5.3–2 HACCP Plan.

5.4.2–2 and 5.4.2–3 Risk assessment.

THE LAST WORD

There are aspects of quality that have not been addressed in this book, and that was quite deliberate. Such topics as benchmarking and the evaluation of the level of maturity of the system are very beneficial activities to undertake. However, they come after you have the basics right. If you implement the advice given in the book you will have in place effective mechanisms for preventing problems and generating improvement, and the majority of companies would be quite satisfied to reach that situation.

One last piece of advice: beware of rushing to embrace every latest management theory fad. Make sure that you are not adopting it because you are reluctant to get involved in the basics and want to do something more fashionable and exciting. I have heard quality managers enthusing about total quality management without even being aware of the simple problems all around them that could be solved by very basic procedures.

All of the fads are simply based on common sense. And remember, there is only so much you can say about quality before you start to repeat yourself. It has all been said before!

PART D

Practical help

CHAPTER XIII

List of Help documents

The reference given is shown at the top of the first page of the document.

Interaction of processes – manufacturing	4.1–1
Interaction of processes – service	4.1–2
Guidance on ISO 9000 procedures	4.2–1
Procedure for control of documentation	4.2–2
Document change request form	4.2–3
Procedure for control of records	4.2–4
Guidance on records	4.2–5
Operations manual – service operation	4.2–6
Message of support from top management (example)	5.1–1
Guidance on management tours	5.1–2
Guidance: customer focus	5.2–1
Quality policy	5.3–1
Quality objectives for laboratory (example)	5.4.1–1
Guidance on planning	5.4.2–1
Procedure for risk assessment	5.4.2–2
Guidance on risk assessment	5.4.2–3
Promoting quality awareness	5.5.2–1
Procedure for daily operations meeting	5.5.3–1
Procedure for annual management review	5.6.1–1
Procedure for interim management review	5.6.1–2
Minutes of ISO 9001 annual management review meeting, 2000 (example)	5.6.1–3
Department induction record (production personnel)	6.2.2–1
Training record	6.2.2–2
Procedure for identification of training needs	6.2.2–3
Versatility chart	6.2.2–4
Versatility chart (completed example)	6.2.2–5
Training evaluation sheet	6.2.2–6
Notes on an ISO 9000 maintenance system	6.3–1
Physical conditions checklist – restaurant	6.4–1
Procedure: reference library	6.5–1
Quality failure costs – the iceberg model	6.8–1
Procedure for introducing process changes	7.1.3.3–1
Process change request form	7.1.3.3–2
Procedure for handling customer orders (packed product)	7.2–1
Handling orders for bulk product (customer contract review)	7.2–2
Guidance on legal compliance	7.2–3
Procedure for customer communication	7.2–4

CHAPTER XIV

Help documents

4.1–1 INTERACTION OF PROCESSES – MANUFACTURING

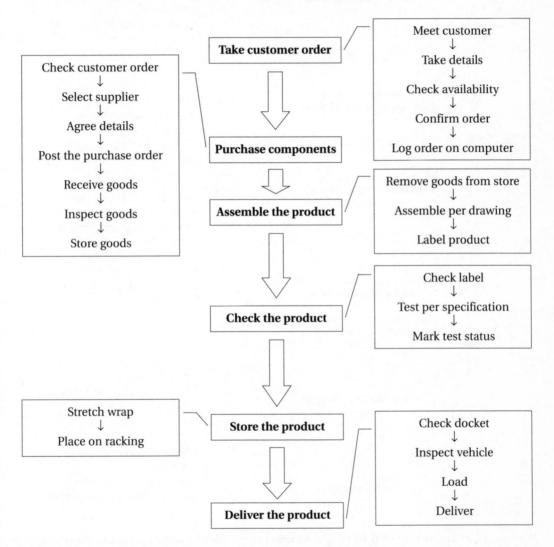

The flow chart is not intended to be a comprehensive representation of a set of processes. It is intended purely to show how the various sub-processes interact, and how they may be represented in diagrammatic form suitable for inclusion in the quality manual.

Note that the flow chart represents only the main product realization process (see Section 7). There are other processes which are not shown here, for example, training, risk assessment, corrective action and improvement.

4.1–2 INTERACTION OF PROCESSES – SERVICE

It would be impossible to present a flow chart that describes a generic service delivery process that would apply to all services. This one illustrates the process steps that might apply to services such as a management consultancy project or an architectural design project.

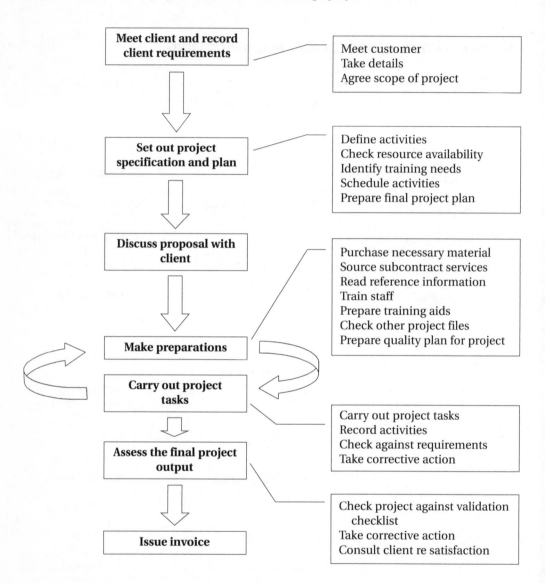

The flow chart is not intended to be a comprehensive representation of a set of processes. It is intended purely to show how the various sub-processes interact, and how they may be represented in diagrammatic form suitable for inclusion in the quality manual.

Note that the flow chart represents only the main service process. There are other processes that are not shown here, for example, training, risk assessment, corrective action and improvement. For simplicity, the purchasing sub-process is not shown, but can be seen on the manufacturing flow chart (Help document 4.1–1).

4.2–1 GUIDANCE ON ISO 9000 PROCEDURES

There are certain issues that must be addressed when preparing ISO 9000 procedures.

DOCUMENT IDENTITY

Every document must have a unique identification, which is usually a code number. This number may or may not bear any relation to the numbering of ISO 9001 clauses, and is usually chosen on the basis of the subsections of the organization itself. Thus, all purchasing documents might have a prefix 'P' and service-related documents a prefix 'S', for example.

NUMBER OF PAGES

Each page should be marked with the page number and the document should display the total number of pages it contains. This is to prevent a document being used, from which pages, perhaps an attachment, are missing.

RELEASE FOR USE

It should be clear that the document has been released for use. That usually means displaying the name and/or signature of somebody who has been given the authority to release, or approve, the document in question.

OBJECTIVE

It is very useful to state what the objective of the procedure is. Exactly what is the procedure trying to achieve? What problems will be prevented by its implementation?

SCOPE

To what, precisely, does the procedure apply? Does it apply universally? Or only in certain circumstances? Or only to certain products or processes?

METHOD

The method for performing the task in question should constitute the major part of the procedure. A documented procedure is required where the absence of a procedure could put quality in jeopardy. That fact will determine the level of detail that is appropriate. Beware of writing unnecessary detail in procedures. This can cause problems later, since whatever is stated in the procedure must be implemented. After all, procedures are provided on the basis that what they contain is important for quality, and since you have included it in the procedure, you obviously consider it important for quality. An auditor is therefore quite entitled to fault you for not implementing your procedures fully.

The description of the method should answer the questions:

- What is to be done?
- How is it done?
- When and where is it to be done?
- How does one know that it has been done properly (for example, by testing, inspecting or measuring)?
- What is to be done if there are problems (for example, failure)?

RECORDS

It should specify what record, if any, is to be kept.

RESPONSIBILITIES

It should be clearly stated who is to carry out the task described. This is particularly important if several people are involved, or if it is not obvious who is to do it.

KEEP IT SHORT AND SIMPLE

Procedures should not be long or complex. They should be worded in the same way as simple verbal instructions:

1 Check the delivery docket against the purchase order.
2 Inspect the outer packaging for damage.
3 If damaged, affix red label and place the material into quarantine.
4 If satisfactory sign the delivery docket and put the material into the next available bay.
5 Send the purchase order to the Accounts office, copy to Quality Control.

For a more complex task it may be better to break it down into a number of short procedures to facilitate document control.

PROBLEMS OF DOCUMENT CONTROL

A problem arises when a single change is to be made to a long document of many pages. Suppose you have a 20-page document, with a single document code and date of issue, and perhaps a revision number. A little thought will reveal that altering a single page while ensuring that the revised document is fully distinguishable from the original is not a simple task, though it is not impossible. It is much more convenient to have a number of individual shorter documents.

USE SIMPLE LANGUAGE

Since the purpose of a procedure is to clarify and prevent confusion it is important that it should state *exactly* what is intended to prevent misinterpretation. Imprecise words should be avoided. A statement such as 'The operator measures the temperature *regularly*' and '*Most* records need to be retained' are open to different interpretations, and are not precise enough to ensure that everybody does the task the same way.

Avoid the passive voice as far as possible. A statement like 'The problem is reported to the manager' leaves the possibility open that nobody will actually take it upon themselves to inform the manager. Better is, 'When this happens the *operator must inform* the manager'.

OPERATING CONDITIONS

Usually it is not necessary to describe in detail how a machine or instrument should be operated, since this information is usually available in the supplier's manual, and the person will have been trained in its use. But it may be important to specify the operating conditions for your particular circumstances, since these will be unique to your operation.

Where a process is controlled by maintaining some parameter at a target level the procedure should specify the range within which the parameter must be controlled, rather than simply the target. Thus, it is more instructive to the operator to state that the temperature of the process is to be maintained between 148°C and 152°C than to state that it should be maintained at 150°C.

TESTING AND INSPECTIONS

The procedure must include any quality checks to be carried out and any samples that must be taken. The inspection method should be described. Alternatively the inspection can be described in a separate procedure and a cross-reference made to it.

DUPLICATION

Usually it is not a good idea to duplicate information in different procedures. The risk is that the information may be changed in one source and not in the other, resulting in one of them containing inaccurate information. It is better to use cross-references instead.

4.2–2 PROCEDURE FOR CONTROL OF DOCUMENTATION *Page 1 of 1*

Objective To ensure that all documents critical to product quality or implementation of the quality system are maintained up to date.

Scope All documents in any of the quality system manuals. See quality manual, Section QM–05.

DOCUMENT CHANGE PROCEDURE

All controlled documents are issued by the Document Controller, nominated by the Quality Manager.

Person suggesting or requesting the change

1 Photocopy the original document and mark it 'DRAFT' very clearly.
2 Mark in the changes on this sheet.
3 Pass it to the manual 'owner' for technical evaluation.

Manual 'owner'

4 Evaluate the change, with particular reference to the effect the change could have on product quality, or its impact on other company activities or departments.
5 If you are satisfied that the change is beneficial sign the approval of the change on the draft. (If you are not absolutely certain about this then you are strongly advised to consult other persons, particularly the Quality Manager).
6 Pass the draft to the Document Controller.

Document Controller

7 Check that the change has been properly authorized.
8 Revise the date on the document.
9 Revise the issue date on the index of the appropriate manual.
10 Print the revised document.
11 Get the manual 'owner' to sign the original.
12 Make the appropriate number of controlled copies.
13 Stamp each one 'Controlled copy' in red ink on page 1.
14 Distribute the copies and remove the obsolete copies.
15 Destroy all obsolete copies, except the original.
16 Mark the original of the obsolete document 'Withdrawn' and file it in the obsolete documents file.

Note: The manuals are held on computer to facilitate changes to documents. However, this is not an official copy of the manuals, and has no status under document control.

RESPONSIBILITIES

Ensuring that document control procedures are observed – Document Controller.

Approval of the content of a document – the 'owner' of the manual involved. The manual 'owners' are defined in the quality manual.

4.2–3 DOCUMENT CHANGE REQUEST FORM   *Page 1 of 1*

Document Reference: _____   **Source:** _____   Manual

Reason for Change

Signed _____   Date _____
        (Person requesting the change)

Please attach an uncontrolled copy with the proposed changes clearly marked in, and pass to the Manager who approved the original document ('Authorizing Manager').

Approval by Authorizing Manager

The changes proposed are approved and may be implemented immediately.

Other Comments

Signed _____   Date _____
        (Authorizing Manager)
Please pass this Form to the Quality Manager after signing.

Issued and circulated per document control procedure on _____
                                            (date)

Signed _____
        (Quality Manager)

4.2–4 PROCEDURE FOR CONTROL OF RECORDS

Objective To ensure that all records relating to critical quality matters are made in a proper manner, and are readily available when required.

Scope Those records listed below.

PROCEDURE

1 Records should be clearly written in permanent ink.

2 Errors should be corrected by striking through and writing the correction above or to one side. Initial and date the correction.

3 Each separate sheet should be dated.

4 Records should be signed (or initialled) by the supervisor (or manager) when completed.

5 The person making the record should highlight any abnormality at the time (for example, by putting a ring around the relevant entry) and then take the appropriate action. Appropriate action depends on the circumstances, but may be to:

   a) notify the supervisor or manager;

   b) correct a defect;

   c) quarantine product; and

   d) institute the corrective action procedure.

6 Records should be placed in the appropriate file as soon as practicable.

7 Records should be retained as follows:

Record	Minimum retention time
Production records	3 years
Cleaning records	3 years
Product test results	3 years
Complaint reports	3 years
Product development records	20 years
Nonconformity records	2 years
Corrective action records	10 years
Any other record mentioned in a procedure	Until after the next external surveillance audit.

DISPOSAL OF RECORDS

1 None of the records listed above may be disposed of without the approval of the Quality Manager.

2 Record the details of all records destroyed – record title, first date/last date, date of disposal and signature.

NOTE TO THE READER

The above retention times are what this particular company considered appropriate in its circumstances. They should not be taken as recommendations.

4.2–5 GUIDANCE ON RECORDS   *Page 1 of 2*

The purpose of a record is to provide a written history of some event. Here it is any record that relates to matters covered by the quality system. This includes such things as test results, log sheets, training records and nonconformity reports. Since not all records are quality records the system should contain a list of the records.

A comprehensive record will include the following:

- a title describing the activity involved, for example, 'Customer satisfaction survey';
- the title of the specific information recorded, for example, 'Thickness';
- the details necessary to pinpoint the precise circumstances, for example, date, time and location;
- the actual result or observation;
- the identity of the person who made the observation;
- any additional comments that are relevant; and
- the signature of an authorized person, for example a supervisor, indicating that the results have been assessed and accepted.

GENERAL

Ideally records should not contain blanks. If a test or inspection is not carried out for some reason, a brief explanation should be written on the record, for example, 'test equipment broken'. The record should show that the significance of the missing result was assessed and a decision taken as to follow up action, if any.

If part of a record form is no longer used the form should be amended if this is practical. If it is not practical, it should be clearly stated in the appropriate place that the particular test or inspection is no longer required.

Records should be permanent. It is usually not acceptable to make records in pencil.

Errors in records should not be obliterated by correcting fluid. Make corrections by means of a single stroke through and put the corrected data above or to the side. The correction should be initialled and, if appropriate, dated.

Blank record forms should be subjected to document control just as if they were procedures. That will ensure that any changes to the form will be implemented permanently, and the obsolete form will not reappear in the system at a later stage.

While records are usually made on specially designed forms there is no absolute requirement in ISO 9001 that this should be so. Recording information in a diary can be quite acceptable, provided it is properly controlled and protected against loss or damage, as required by the standard. But it does not have to be pretty!

Very often the amount of paper moving around can be minimized by combining records on one record sheet. It may be appropriate for the record sheet to accompany a material or product, with different persons filling in different information at each location, rather than having separate record sheets for the different locations.

TEST SPECIFICATIONS

The person carrying out an inspection or test should know what the acceptable limits are for that variable. Where possible this specification should be printed on the results sheet for easy reference. When a result outside those limits is recorded this should be highlighted, for example, by putting a ring around the offending result so that it is brought to the attention of the person who reviews the sheet. Every non-conforming result needs an explanation and a very brief comment about its subsequent disposition. For example, the operator or supervisor might write alongside the non-conforming result 'Supplementary test OK', where this indicates that the situation was investigated further and everything was determined to be satisfactory. If no comment is made about a non-conforming result and the record sheet is filed away, it appears as if the nonconformity was not noticed by anybody, or else that it was spotted but nobody cared about it. Either way you project yourself in a bad light. An auditor automatically checks a number of record sheets, having first asked what the specifications are. Any non-conforming result is likely to be found and commented upon negatively.

COMPUTER-BASED RECORDS
Where records are held on computer, or backed up on to disk or tape, they should be subjected to equivalent or identical controls as hard-copy records.

RECORD STORAGE
Records must be stored in an orderly manner, so that they can be retrieved in a reasonable time when required. They should also be secured against accidental loss or deliberate damage. In a large organization it may be useful or necessary to keep a log of all records showing where they are stored. Access to records should be restricted to those who need to view them.

RETENTION TIMES
The length of time that important records are required to be kept should be documented. There may be legal implications, and this should be taken into account when defining retention times.

DISPOSAL OF RECORDS
Records should only be disposed of under authority from a designated person. There should be a defined method for disposing of critical records. A record should be kept of the disposal showing the identity of the records destroyed.

4.2–6 OPERATIONS MANUAL – SERVICE OPERATION

Contents

Document	Code	Date
Section 1: General management procedures		
Guidelines on planning and improvement	101	15 Jan 2001
Procedure for approval of changes to the process	102	15 Jan 2001
Control of documentation	103	10 Jan 2001
Control of records	104	10 Jan 2001
Procedure for management review	105	10 Jan 2001
Procedure for internal quality auditing	106	10 Jan 2001
Checklist for internal quality audits	107	10 Jan 2001
Guidance on dealing with customers	108	10 Jan 2001
Procedure for customer surveys	109	10 Jan 2001
Procedure for customer complaints	110	10 Jan 2001
Procedure for corrective action	111	10 Jan 2001
Procedure for risk assessment and preventive action	112	15 Jan 2001
Procedure for product recall	113	10 Jan 2001
Quality awareness	114	10 Jan 2001
Section 2: Purchasing		
Purchasing process flow chart	200	10 Jan 2001
Procedure for selection and approval of suppliers	201	10 Jan 2001
Procedure for review of suppliers	202	10 Jan 2001
Procedure for purchasing and receipt of materials	203	10 Jan 2001
List of approved suppliers and materials	204	15 Jan 2001
Section 3: Service control procedures		
Process flow chart	300	10 Jan 2001
Typical daily schedule for operators	301	15 Jan 2001
Procedure for handling customer orders/contracts	302	10 Jan 2001
Procedure for task A	303	25 Jan 2001
Procedure for task B	304	10 Jan 2001
Procedure for task C	305	10 Jan 2001
Procedure for task D	306	10 Jan 2001
Procedure for task E	307	10 Jan 2001
Procedure for task F	308	10 Jan 2001
Procedure for storage/stock-rotation	309	15 Jan 2001
Procedure for controlling non-conforming product	310	10 Jan 2001
Maintenance and calibration of equipment	311	15 Jan 2001
Procedure for release of product	312	15 Jan 2001
Identification codes	313	10 Jan 2001
Section 4: Materials handling		
Procedure for control of cold stores	400	10 Jan 2001
Control of storage temperature	401	15 Jan 2001
Procedure for intake of product	402	10 Jan 2001
Procedure for order preparation and dispatch	403	10 Jan 2001
Procedure for identification and traceability	404	10 Jan 2001

Section 5: Inspection and testing

Quality inspection plan	500	10 Jan 2001
Procedure for physical conditions inspection	501	15 Jan 2001

Section 6: Cleaning

General cleaning rules	600	10 Jan 2001
Cleaning schedule	601	15 Jan 2001
Standard cleaning procedure	602	10 Jan 2001
Cleaning procedure – chills	603	10 Jan 2001
Cleaning of dry storage areas	604	10 Jan 2001
Cleaning procedure – miscellaneous items	605	10 Jan 2001
Pest control	606	10 Jan 2001

Section 7: Personnel

Procedure for identification of training needs	700	10 Jan 2001
Induction programme	701	10 Jan 2001
Company rules for quality	702	10 Jan 2001
Protective clothing requirements	703	10 Jan 2001

Section 8: Record sheets

Training record form	801	10 Jan 2001
Cleaning record sheet	802	10 Jan 2001
Temperature log sheet	803	10 Jan 2001
Inspection record sheet (stored product)	804	15 Jan 2001
Incoming materials/dispatch record	805	15 Jan 2001
Nonconformity and corrective action sheet	806	15 Jan 2001
Complaint form	807	15 Jan 2001

Controlled copies

Controlled copies of the various sections of this manual are circulated as follows:

Section 1: General Manager; Stores Controller; Office Manager.
Section 2: General Manager; Office Manager.
Section 3: General Manager; Stores Controller.
Section 4: General Manager; Quality Inspector.
Section 5: General Manager; Stores Controller.
Section 6: General Manager; Stores Controller.
Section 7: General Manager; Office Manager.

NOTE TO THE READER

The above example shows the contents page from the operations manual of a company providing a cold storage service, with a management team of three.

This company has decided that all quality system documentation can be most usefully contained in one manual. It has been divided into sections representing the main areas of activity. The different sections are circulated to the relevant people.

Note that the numbering system for individual documents does not bear any relation to the ISO 9001 standard headings. That is because this company found this a more convenient way of managing the documentation. The quality manual would contain the cross-references under each clause of the ISO 9001 standard.

Many of the procedures mentioned in the sample quality manual do not appear in the system of this particular company. For example, there is nothing documented about how quality awareness is promoted. There is no requirement to have a procedure for this – you simply have to be able to show that you do it.

Detailed tasks are identified by the letters A to F. In a larger company there might be so many such tasks that a separate manual would be justified.

5.1–1 MESSAGE OF SUPPORT FROM TOP MANAGEMENT (EXAMPLE) *Page 1 of 1*

TO ALL STAFF

Congratulations to everybody! Winning the award for Most Progressive Company in the country was very gratifying, and will do no harm in our customers' eyes.

Six months ago we embarked on the 'Keep Kustomers Koming Kampaign' and recent results all round indicate that it will be highly successful. Already we have recorded a 20% drop in customer complaints. There is still a long way to go, but we are on the way!

We have recently begun an exercise to make our products even more reliable (the FMEA project), and most of you will be asked to make an input at some point. Be aware that this type of exercise is critical to our long-term success, so please help out in any way you can.

I intend to continue my regular tours of the factory, and will be happy to talk to anybody about quality issues that concern them (or anything else). Any urgent item however, should be referred immediately to your front-line manager, or you can use the Suggestion Form.

Everybody will have read of the problems which Bloggtronics had, and will have seen the Product Recall notices in the paper. That could happen to us if we let our standards slip. We mustn't get complacent.

Thanks to everybody for the excellent performance this year to date.

Jonathan Black

J. Black (MD)

5.1–2 GUIDANCE ON MANAGEMENT TOURS

Objectives   To demonstrate commitment to quality.

               To keep informed of local developments.

Scope   All areas under the control of a manager.

Frequency   Chief Executive: 6-monthly.

               Department Managers: monthly.

Important   A management tour complements, but does not replace, routine quality inspections or audits, which should be carried out by front-line managers and trained auditors, respectively.

               Tours should be planned according to the above frequency.

THE TOUR

1 Prepare by informing yourself in advance of relevant issues.

2 Notify the front-line manager in the area of your intention to do a tour.

3 Ensure the front-line manager keeps a (brief) record of the tour.

4 Do not be critical. Leave that for the front-line manager.

ITEMS FOR CONSIDERATION DURING THE TOUR

1 Difficulties individual operators may be experiencing.

2 Problems arising in quality inspections.

3 Customer complaints relating to the area.

4 Agreed corrective action from previous tours, inspections, and corrective action requests.

5 Recent decisions in relation to quality.

6 Importance of quality to the customer and the company's profitability.

5.2–1 GUIDANCE: CUSTOMER FOCUS

Acme Ltd directs all its quality initiatives towards ensuring customer satisfaction.

All managers are required to include the following topics in induction for new employees, where appropriate:

- customer specifications – control and filing, absolute need to meet the requirements;
- dealing directly with customers; and
- possible impact of the job on customer satisfaction.

When carrying out a risk assessment of a process, managers should define hazards in terms of the potential to compromise customer satisfaction.

The Sales department carries out regular surveys of customer satisfaction and feeds this back into the quality system via the regular operations meetings. All managers are required to implement whatever action is recommended or appropriate in response to the customer feedback.

Any employee receiving formal feedback from a customer is required to report this to the Customer Services Manager in the first instance. Employees are encouraged to report also any informal or unofficial comments, provided this does not compromise the customer or the company.

All employees should give the impression at all times that the customer is right. This should be done without prejudice to any action that the company may need to take in the future. In other words, employees should always be conciliatory towards the customer and show sympathy towards the customer's viewpoint without compromising the company's scope for action.

Managers authorized to make commercial decisions in relation to the customer should weigh carefully the possible consequences of opposing a customer on any issue, and the likely knock-on effect.

RESPONSIBILITIES

Ensuring that the company is kept informed about customer requirement for all products – Customer Services Manager.

Ensuring that all employees are aware of the importance of the customer – department managers.

Ensuring that customer requirements are adequately addressed and incorporated into the product specifications – Quality Manager.

Ensuring that quality plans are adequate to ensure that the product meets customer requirements – Quality Manager.

5.3–1 QUALITY POLICY

ABC Ltd is committed to:

- producing a quality product which satisfies, and if possible exceeds, customer expectations;
- providing employees with all relevant information and appropriate training in relation to quality;
- facilitating employees to develop their skills and knowledge to the benefit of both the employees and the company;
- complying with all relevant statutory requirements;
- maintaining a management system that meets the requirements of ISO 9001 and facilitates the production of quality products;
- providing a safe environment for its employees;
- setting measurable quality objectives; and
- striving continually to improve performance in relation to quality.

The company regards quality as the responsibility of all persons working in the company, and expects all employees to act at all times to maintain safe working conditions and to report all nonconformities promptly.

This quality policy has been endorsed by all departmental managers.

RESPONSIBILITIES

Authorizing the quality policy – Managing Director.

Making the quality policy known to all personnel – Quality Manager.

Ensuring the quality policy is reviewed annually – Managing Director.

The text of the quality policy above is a direct copy of the text of QM–09 in the sample quality manual and should not be altered independently of that document

5.4.1–1 QUALITY OBJECTIVES FOR LABORATORY (EXAMPLE)

2001

Date   *12 / 12 / 2000*

Laboratory manager:
- 10% of total lab cost (based on 2000) to be transferred from final product testing to process control testing and/or supplier control.
- One technician to be working full time on supplier control by the end of the year.

Supervisor:
- Absentee level to be reduced to 3% by means of motivation and training initiatives, and moving technicians to different tests regularly.
- Versatility chart to be 50% shaded by the end of the year.

Laboratory technicians (individual):
- Average assay of external standard sample over the year to be within 0.25% of 'true' result.

Laboratory technicians (team):
- Autoclave down-time to be reduced to maximum 20 hours by means of better care when operating it.

Signed: *Liz Jones*

          Laboratory Manager

5.4.2–1 GUIDANCE ON PLANNING

Objective To ensure a consistent approach to planning throughout the company.

Scope Routine activities.

Improvement activities.

Specific projects.

GUIDANCE

The purpose of planning is to ensure that a particular target is met by design rather than by accident or good fortune. Planning occurs at several different points in the quality management system. All planning, however, has certain basic features:

1 Define the scope and overall objectives that must result from the plan.
2 If appropriate, involve other people who have a contribution to make or who are stakeholders in the outcome of the planning.
3 Decide what has to be done in order to achieve the desired outcome.
4 Schedule the necessary activities and assign them to individuals. Set dates for interim reviews to monitor progress.
5 Set measurable targets so that you will know objectively if the planning has been successful.
6 Ensure that there are effective channels of communication between the people involved.
7 Identify any additional resources that may be needed for a successful outcome.
8 Identify what information needs to be collected either as an input to or as an output from the project.
9 If appropriate, identify how the tasks are to be carried out.
10 Keep a record of the plan and targets, and any other information that may be useful afterwards.
11 Include a final review in the plan to verify that the original objectives have been met.

This list is intended as guidance. In many cases planning is carried out by individuals working alone. The same principles apply, however.

5.4.2–2 PROCEDURE FOR RISK ASSESSMENT

Objective   To provide a consistent approach within the company to identifying:
- potential problems for quality of product or service or customer satisfaction; and
- opportunities for improvement to products or service and the quality management system.

Scope   All departments.

All processes (activities) within a department.

Note: All department managers must undertake this exercise at least once a year, even if the department has no apparent direct link with the product or customer satisfaction.

PROCEDURE

1 List all steps in the process.
2 Identify all possible hazards to quality associated with each step.
3 Describe the consequences for quality of each hazard.
4 State the likely severity of these consequences.
5 Identify *all* the possible causes of each hazard.
6 Assess the probability of each cause actually happening and causing the consequences identified in 3.
7 Determine the level of concern (the risk) in relation to each cause.
8 Prioritize the causes for preventive action (control).
9 Identify a suitable control for each cause, commensurate with the level of concern expressed.
10 Set targets for each control, so that you can check that the cause of the hazard is being controlled.
11 Set up a routine of monitoring each control at defined intervals.

ANALYSIS OF DATA

When trying to identify the causes (immediate, underlying and root) of the potential hazards, and to estimate the probability make use of all relevant data.

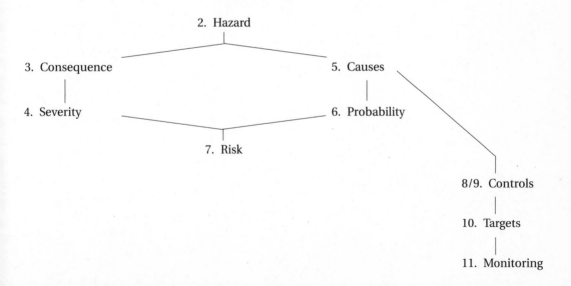

Summary of risk assessment and control

Hazards are prevented from causing nonconformity by placing controls on the factors that cause the hazards to arise. This leads to effective, long-term corrective action by addressing the root causes of potential problems.

Note that step 4 implicitly addresses the extent of the problem, such as the number of people or items affected, while step 6 implicitly addresses the likelihood of the hazard being detected, both of which have a bearing on the overall risk.

5.4.2–3 GUIDANCE ON RISK ASSESSMENT

In determining how serious a potential hazard is you need to consider two aspects:

- *Severity:* how severe would the consequences be if the hazard were to occur?
- *Probability (or frequency):* what are the chances that they will happen, or how often are these hazards likely to occur *and* to cause the consequences you identified?

It is not sufficient to ask how severe the damage is likely to be. Consider the potential injury caused by an employee going insane and putting poison into a food product – fatal for the consumer. Should you, therefore, put in place a programme of psychological examination of all employees who might come in contact with the product? Is it really necessary to go to those lengths, for a problem that is extremely unlikely to arise?

In fact, it is the combination of *severity* and *probability* that gives an indication of the true *risk* (level of *concern*), or the probability that you will have a serious problem. This determines the priority that should be given to controlling the hazard.

In determining the probability, work on the basis that there are no controls in place currently. The outcome of this whole exercise is a structured preventive action system implemented throughout the organization. It will form a central part of the quality management system, and everybody will depend on it to define the controls essential for quality. All critical quality controls should, therefore, be shown in it. Otherwise there is a risk that a control will be dropped at some future point because it has not been listed as having any role in prevention. Imagine the situation where the financial controller queries the cost of the contract for monitoring temperature alarms on a cold store. When the risk assessment is examined it turns out that temperature alarms are not listed as a critical control. 'It has not been identified as a useful control for quality, so drop it and save money!' In fact, the reason it does not feature in the risk assessment is because everybody knew that there could not be a problem with temperature control *because* it was constantly monitored and alarmed! By including existing controls in the risk assessment you will establish the justification for them. That will ensure that in the future new personnel with no knowledge of the history of the process will be able to see the reasons for the various controls that are in place.

RISK MEASUREMENT

Use the matrix to make a rough estimate of the risk:

1. Rate the severity of the hazard in question as High, Medium, or Low.
2. Rate the possible frequency of the hazard as High, Medium, or Low.
3. For each hazard read off the risk rating (1 to 5) from the point where the Severity line crosses the Frequency line. For example, a hazard with a Medium severity and a Low frequency gives a risk rating of 2. See matrix.

Hazards can be rated from 1 (very low risk) to 5 (very high risk) using this method.

		Severity		
		High	Medium	Low
Frequency	High	5	4	3
	Medium	4	3	2
	Low	3	2	1

5.5.2–1 PROMOTING QUALITY AWARENESS

Objective To promote awareness of quality throughout the company.

Scope All company employees.

All departments.

NOTICEBOARD AND NEWSLETTER

The Quality Manager places notes and information relating to quality in the company newsletter and on the noticeboard. Any person wishing to contribute should contact the Quality Manager. Topics that would be relevant include:

- new problems that have been encountered;
- new solutions to existing problems;
- comments from customers;
- letters received from customers; and
- improvement ideas.

The ISO 9000 section of the noticeboard is restricted to those notices that relate to quality. Nobody other than the Quality Manager may post or remove notices.

All notices display a posting date and are removed as soon as their usefulness is past.

POSTERS

From time to time the Quality Manager will put up posters relating to quality. These generally reflect a particular theme. They should not be defaced.

DEPARTMENTAL ACTIVITIES

All managers are required to promote quality awareness in their departments. The manner in which they do this is left to individual managers. Options include:

- team talks ('toolbox talks') by supervisors;
- one-to-one talks with individuals;
- incentive schemes (with the approval of the Managing Director);
- presentations by individuals; and
- handouts.

CONTENT

Quality awareness activities should address the following issues:

- the importance of achieving customer satisfaction;
- reporting nonconformity;
- accurate record-keeping;
- following procedures;
- reporting problems with existing procedures;
- accurate labelling of materials;
- possibilities for improvement; and
- information coming through from complaints.

5.5.3–1 PROCEDURE FOR DAILY OPERATIONS MEETING   *Page 1 of 1*

Objectives   To provide a means of internal communication.

To ensure that key management and supervisory personnel communicate effectively on operational issues.

Scope   All issues that relate to the day-to-day operation of the factory.

PROCEDURE

The following functions are represented:

- production (manager or supervisor);
- quality assurance (manager);
- engineering (maintenance supervisor);
- stores (supervisor);
- materials (manager or planner); and
- laboratory (manager or supervisor).

The meeting is chaired as the meeting decides, but ideally by each function in turn.

The meeting is held every day irrespective of availability of the usual participants. All functions should be represented if possible, even if the above persons are not available.

TARGET AGENDA AND SCHEDULE

10.00	Production plan for next 24 hours
10.10	Review of previous day's production (process control, output, safety, incidents)
10.20	Maintenance
10.30	Review of latest product quality data
10.40	Review of nonconformity reports and complaints received
10.55	Follow-up action
11.00	Finish

Participants are free to attend only those points on the agenda for which they are required, if they so wish. Each participant should communicate back to his or her department all points that are relevant.

The meeting should be used for reviewing and planning. Detailed discussion on specific points should be set up as sub-items to be resolved outside the meeting.

NOTE TO READER

The above procedure relates to the traditional management structure and an environment where personnel from different departments are involved in the routine product realization process and where confusion could arise due to communication difficulties. Clearly, for a multidisciplinary team or cell, working as a unit and carrying out all the functions described above, the procedure will be somewhat different.

However, the basic principle is the same – the meeting covers the *Plan* element of the Plan–Do–Check–Act cycle, as well as some aspects of the *Check* and *Do* elements.

5.6.1–1 PROCEDURE FOR ANNUAL MANAGEMENT REVIEW   *Page 1 of 2*

Objective   To ensure that the quality system is assessed by senior management to confirm that it continues to be effective.

Scope   All activities documented in the company's quality system manuals.
All relevant requirements of ISO 9001.

PROCEDURE

1 The review is carried out 12-monthly.

2 Attendance: Managing Director, Production Director, Quality Manager, Financial Controller, Personnel Director, Customer Services Manager, Product Development Manager.

3 The agenda is as shown in the table.

Agenda item		By
Review of corrective action	Reports on the effect of corrective action taken after previous review.	All
Quality policy	Review of the suitability and implementation of quality policy.	All
Quality objectives	Review of performance against departmental quality objectives. Setting of new objectives.	All
Customer satisfaction and complaints	Current assessment of customer satisfaction levels, including complaints. A review of the summary of complaints received since the previous management review, including an appraisal of the overall performance on complaints, whether improving or not.	Customer Services Manager
Product quality	Review of product data to confirm that quality is maintained and to identify any improvements that can be made or preventive action that can be taken.	Quality Manager
Process performance	Confirmation that the process continues to perform satisfactorily and yield output conforming to specification.	Production Manager
Internal audits	A review of the internal audits carried out. The group should decide whether any significant changes need to be made to the quality system as a result of the findings.	Quality Manager
External quality audits	Any quality audits carried out by external agencies are reviewed. In particular, do the results broadly agree with the internal audits? Is any action required?	Quality Manager
Quality improvements and preventive action	Are there any other measures that could be taken to improve the company's performance in quality, or the quality of the product? Have any appropriate preventive actions been identified?	All

Continued

Agenda item		By
Resources	Are resources currently provided adequate for the proper functioning of the quality management system? And to guarantee customer satisfaction?	Financial Controller
Overall system performance	Formal report by the Quality Manager.	Quality Manager
System changes	Planned changes to the operation. Discussion on whether they could impact on the effectiveness of the quality management system.	Managing Director
Any other business		All

Concluded

4 All participants are required to bring to the review a summary of relevant data relating to their own areas.
5 The outcome of this review is documented, including:
  ● the overall assessment of the performance of the quality system; and
  ● corrective action, the name of the person assigned to carry it out, and the target completion dates.
6 The Quality Manager monitors the implementation of the corrective action until the action has been completed, and reports on progress at each management meeting.

RESPONSIBILITY

The Managing Director is responsible for carrying out the management review and ensuring that any resulting corrective action is taken.

5.6.1–2 PROCEDURE FOR INTERIM MANAGEMENT REVIEW   *Page 1 of 1*

Objectives   To ensure that the quality system is assessed frequently.

To ensure that objectives are being met.

Scope   Objectives set at the annual management review.

PROCEDURE

1 The review is carried out two-monthly.
2 Attendance: Quality Manager, Materials Manager, Customer Services Manager, Engineering Manager, Training Manager, Production Manager.
3 The agenda is shown in the table.

Agenda item		By
Review	Review of action from previous management review.	All
Quality objectives	Review of performance against departmental quality objectives.	All
Customer satisfaction and complaints	Current assessment of customer satisfaction levels, including complaints.	Customer Services Manager
Product quality	Summary of product classification figures to date.	Quality Manager
Process performance	Confirmation that the process continues to perform satisfactorily and yield output conforming to specification.	Production Manager
Internal audits	Progress on implementing schedule.	Quality Manager
External quality audits	Action required for forthcoming external audits.	Quality Manager
Quality improvements and preventive action	Analysis of current data. Possibilities for improvement.	All
Resources	Requirements for additional resources.	All
Current assessment of system performance	Brief presentation.	Quality Manager
Quality management system planning	Discussion on any changes that may be necessary to maintain the quality management system arising from current difficulties or planned changes in any area.	All

4 All participants are required to bring to the review a summary of relevant data relating to their own areas.
5 The Quality Manager takes minutes of the meeting and notes any follow-up action.

RESPONSIBILITY

The Quality Manager is responsible for carrying out the interim management review and monitoring the implementation of corrective action.

Individual department managers are responsible for ensuring that the agreed corrective action is taken promptly.

5.6.1–3 MINUTES OF ISO 9001 ANNUAL MANAGEMENT REVIEW MEETING, 2000 (EXAMPLE)

Present:

M. Smith	Managing Director	**Date:** 22.12.2000
B. Yu	Quality Manager	
C. Neil	Customer Services Manager	
J. Macken	Financial Controller	
A. Kanda	Product Development Manager	
P. Michaels	Production Director	
L. Martinez	Personnel Director	

Agenda item		Action	By
Review of corrective action	All actions arising out of last year's management review have been implemented. All managers report that they have been effective.		
Quality policy	The policy was discussed. It was decided that we need to strengthen what it says about legal aspects of the product. MS will draft up a new version and circulate it for comment. Otherwise satisfactory.	MS	Jan 10
Quality objectives	Objectives for all departments reviewed. All departments easily met their targets. Proposed objectives for next year were considered briefly, but we agreed we were setting them too low. Objectives need to be set higher for next year. All will re-submit objectives.	All	Jan 10
	We agreed to look at the possibility of setting targets for maximum amount of product lost for the different reasons. BY and PM will look into this to see what is practicable.	BY/PM	End Jan
Customer satisfaction and complaints	Customer satisfaction rating is now at 85%. This is still below the level of last spring before the burnt product problem. By current trends we should be up to 90% by February. MS, BY and CN will review in February.	MS/BY/CN	16 Feb
	Complaint levels for the year were 17% down on last year. They would have been lower were it not for the burnt batch. That problem is now sorted out. Targets for next year will be broken down into categories and tie in with reject level objectives. See quality objectives above.		

Continued

Agenda item		Action	By
Product quality	Product quality has improved. Average total bacterial count has reduced from 1500 per gram to less than 1000 per gram for the year. Solubility is a little better than last year. No specification item is worse than last year, apart from the burnt product problem.	AK/PM	End Jan
	Total quantity rejected was down by 15% on last year. Target of further reduction of 15% was set for this year. Principal reason for rejection was burnt product. AK and PM will investigate what else can be done to minimize the problem and improve the product.		
Process performance	All processes performed well with exception of purchasing. The problem of confusion over specifications (March) will not arise again. Entire purchasing system has been overhauled.		
Internal audits	These were carried out between July and November. Problems were found in all departments and are currently being addressed. There is a general problem in all departments with corrective action. Corrective action is being taken in most instances but people are still not operating the formal procedure. All managers must tighten up on this.	All	Now
	In some cases corrective action is not addressing root causes, and managers are relying on disciplinary action to prevent recurrence. LM to present a strategy to help managers at next interim review.	LM	End Jan
	HACCP system was audited and reviewed in September. No major non-compliances. No significant modifications were needed.		
External quality audits	ISO 9001:2000 certification audit is due in mid-February.		
	Best Buy Ltd audit: we scored A1, up from A2. Nothing significant noted.		
	Eurobean Products Ltd audit: auditor found several instances of document control problems. Our internal audits did not pick this up. Audit rated us at 93%, up from 87% last time.		

Continued

Agenda item		Action	By
	All department heads to review document control immediately.	All	Now
	LM and BY to review internal auditor training and take corrective action if necessary.	LM/BY	15 Jan
Quality improvements and preventive action	New floor in the production area has made a huge difference. The next major item to address is the relocation of raw material unpacking away from the mixing area. PM will submit a proposal.	PM	End Feb
Resources	Since RR left there is a weakness in the area of hygiene audits. At least two people need to be trained up to give cover here. LM to organize a.s.a.p.	LM	Now
	Testing facilities are too stretched even now. If we get the ADP contract we will not be able to cope. BY to investigate and report back in 5 weeks.	BY	End Jan
	Elsewhere resources are adequate.		
Overall system performance	BY reported that the system is satisfactory, considering it is relatively new. Most managers agree that it is helping to prevent errors. Some managers have not completed the introduction of all staff to the quality manual, but this is due for completion in March. BY will monitor progress and report separately to MS.	BY/MS	16 Mar
System changes	Tenders submitted for several new markets. Potential for large increase in output. Will need to review resources nearer the time.	BY/MS	April
Any other business	None.		
Next review	Next full review is scheduled for December 2001. BY will agree date in November and circulate details.	BY	Nov

Concluded

Signed   *Mark Smith*   Date   *22/12/2000*

         Managing Director

6.2.2–1 DEPARTMENT INDUCTION RECORD (PRODUCTION PERSONNEL)

Employee's Name _____ Date of Commencement _____ Date of Induction _____

Training topic	Trainer	Duration	Date of Training	Evaluation	Manager's Sign.
Production processes					
Quality manual and procedures					
Basic hygiene					
Personal hygiene					
Temperature control					
Hygiene rules					
Cleaning					
Record-keeping					
HACCP					

To be completed by manager 2–4 weeks after induction

Date	Assessment of trainee's competence/awareness/performance	Signed

194

6.2.2–2 TRAINING RECORD

Name: _____   Job Title: _____

Date	Training			Evaluation		
	Material covered	Duration	Trainer	Comments	Signed	Date

6.2.2–3 PROCEDURE FOR IDENTIFICATION OF TRAINING NEEDS   *Page 1 of 1*

Objective   To ensure that all staff continue to have adequate training to enable them to carry out their tasks properly.

Scope   All company employees.

PROCEDURE

Department managers

Before 15 November each year carry out a review of training requirements for all persons in your department. Consult each individual during this process.

Use the following list as a guide to possible sources of training needs:

- tasks carried out by the individual;
- personal development;
- quality management system;
- customer satisfaction survey results;
- complaints;
- technological developments in relation to products, service or information technology;
- planned changes to the company's activities or scale of operation;
- new products;
- health and safety;
- redeployment; and
- any other relevant factors.

Record the results of the reviews.

Compile a departmental draft training plan for the following year.

Pass the draft training plan to the Training Manager.

Directors/senior managers

Identify your own training needs and notify the Personnel Director, who will organize the training.

Training Manager

Discuss the various department plans with the relevant managers.

Draw up a company training plan for the following year.

Submit the plan to the Personnel Director before 15 December for approval.

6.2.2–4 VERSATILITY CHART

Page 1 of 1

Department/Section _____   Chart created _____

Employee name	Task											Individual's record last updated

Degree of skill/competence — Fully expert — Competent without supervision — Competent under supervision only — Very basic skills only — No skills

Signed _____   Date _____

Manager

6.2.2–5 VERSATILITY CHART (COMPLETED EXAMPLE)

Department/Section ___*Assembly*___   Chart created ___*15/10/2000*___

Employee name	Assemble X	Assemble Y	Assemble Z	Test A	Test B	Test C	Replace resin	Calibration	Cleaning	Line-change	Individual's record last updated
Isabel Aguilar		▧		▧		▧			▧		15/11 J.S 19/12 J.S
Lisa Moran	▧		▧			▧		▧	▧		
Arun Gupta	▧	▧	▧	▧		▧		▧	▧	▧	
Bob Blagojev				▧	▧	▧					1/12 J.S
John Browne		▧	▧			▧		▧			
Arrifin Susilo				▧		▧				▧	
Mike Small	▧	▧				▧	▧				
Sean Murphy	▧			▧		▧		▧			
Sarah Ho		▧				▧				▧	

Degree of skill/competence:

▦ Fully expert	▧ Competent without supervision	▨ Competent under supervision only	▤ Very basic skills only	☐ No skills

Signed ___*J. Smith*___   Date ___*15/10/2000*___
Manager

6.2.2–6 TRAINING EVALUATION SHEET *Page 1 of 1*

Course title _____

Date _____

Trainer _____

Please give your assessment of the course by rating it as follows:

Excellent: 4 Good: 3 Satisfactory: 2 Poor: 1

	Rating	Comment
The course overall		
Amount you learned from/achieved during the course		
Quality of the handout material		
Opportunity to participate, ask questions, etc.		
Balance between theory and practical aspects		
Were your personal objectives met?		
Is this a useful course for your colleagues?		

Is there any follow-up action you feel should be taken that would help you in implementing the material learned?

_____

_____

_____

_____

_____

_____

Signed _____

6.3–1 NOTES ON AN ISO 9000 MAINTENANCE SYSTEM   *Page 1 of 1*

LIST OF CRITICAL ITEMS OF PLANT

You need to be able to show that you have surveyed the entire process to identify where plant maintenance is critical to product quality. The result of this survey will then form the preventive maintenance checklist(s).

EQUIPMENT FILES

It is probably useful to open a file or maintenance log for each item on the list. Include in the file any 'specification' of process capability. For example, a particular machine should be operating at minimum rpm, amps, psi or dBA. There may be diagnostic tests to confirm if it is working properly. These should be listed. However, if this information is already in the equipment supplier's manual and easily accessible there is no need to write it out again.

CHECKLIST FOR WEEKLY/MONTHLY/ANNUAL MAINTENANCE TASKS

These are the preventive maintenance aspects of the maintenance activity. They can be added to as new items crop up, for example, from the corrective action procedure.

ANNUAL PLANT SHUT-DOWN CHECKLIST

In the case of a process which shuts down only once a year there are probably a number of maintenance tasks which must be done at that time. These should be listed on a checklist or plan.

Maintenance needs sometimes come to light at other times when it is not possible to action them. If these requirements are not recorded somewhere they may not get done when the opportunity arises.

LIST OF CRITICAL SPARES WITH MINIMUM STOCK LEVELS

There are probably some items that should be held in stock so that you will not have to compromise on quality the day you need a part but do not have a spare. These should be listed and somebody should be given the responsibility of ensuring that there is always a spare.

Note that there is no need to set up a total stock control system for maintenance parts just to satisfy ISO 9001 requirements.

RECORDS OF REPAIRS WORK

Much will depend here on what the company wants to record. A record of *significant* repairs should be kept, particularly where there has been a breakdown. Corrective action to prevent a recurrence should be taken and this should be recorded. The nature of this record is at the company's discretion.

It may not be practical or useful to complete a nonconformity report for every small incident. A note in a diary could be sufficient. However, if there is a recurring or chronic problem then it may warrant a more detailed investigation, and in that case a detailed report may be justified.

RULES FOR MAINTENANCE PERSONNEL IN THE PLANT

It may not be necessary to have detailed procedures for the maintenance done in your company. However, there are probably some restrictions you place on maintenance work, and these can be covered conveniently in simple rules, for example: 'Always report first thing to the local supervisor'; 'Never do any grinding, drilling or painting near exposed product'; 'Always tidy up after the job'; 'Never leave nuts, bolts or other loose small objects on ledges above production lines'; 'Always label clearly a job in progress'; 'Always complete the specified record'.

6.4–1 PHYSICAL CONDITIONS CHECKLIST – RESTAURANT   *Page 1 of 1*

Month _____

Week No.	1	2	3	4	5
Date					
All staff wearing proper clothing					
No staff suffering from illness, uncovered cuts, etc.					
Utensils for raw product not used for cooked					
Food protected from glass breakage					
No perishable food left standing at room temperature when not in use					
No food left uncovered on worktop or in store					
Work surfaces clean					
Surfaces sanitized per procedures					
Hand wash: hot water, soap, towels and nailbrush					
Waste containers available; covered; not full					
Cloths used properly					
Cold room clean; products stored properly					
Dry store clean					
Product and packaging stored off the ground					
Doors and windows protected from pests					
Raw and ready-to-eat food segregated properly					
Electric fly-killer units operating					
Fixtures and fittings clean					
Kitchen floor and walls clean					
Staff room clean					
Cleaning chemicals stored properly					
Sign					

Tick to indicate that the standard is met. Note any nonconformities overleaf.

6.5–1 PROCEDURE: REFERENCE LIBRARY

Page 1 of 1

Objective   To ensure that company personnel have access to information necessary for their tasks.

Scope   All books, magazines, and copies of legislation in the display cabinet in the Quality Manager's lobby. Each item is stamped 'Reference'.

The library contains items relating to quality, product safety, environmental impact, health and safety and personal development. The current list of items in the library is posted on the door of the cabinet.

Access to the library is via the Quality Manager. In his or her absence please contact the Laboratory Supervisor or the Production Manager.

Articles may be removed from the library, but should not be taken off-site.

All articles removed must be signed for, and should remain in the borrower's area until they are returned, so that they may be found easily if required suddenly.

No item removed from the library should be stored in locked lockers, as they cannot be retrieved if the locker holder is not on site.

6.8–1 QUALITY FAILURE COSTS – THE ICEBERG MODEL

The cost of quality failure is almost always significantly more than it appears at first. For that reason the iceberg is a useful analogy for communicating this as part of a quality awareness campaign.

The obvious visible cost relates to the value of product lost, or the cost of having to repeat a service contract because it was not done properly the first time. But there is much more to the loss than this.

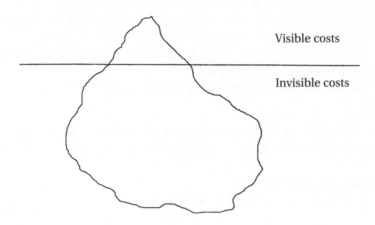

Visible costs

Invisible costs

SOME EXAMPLES OF INVISIBLE COSTS

The following are just a few examples of invisible costs that are easily understood and accepted, but are not often considered as part of the loss:

- Loss of morale among staff, resulting in more nonconformities and reduced productivity.
- Increased absenteeism, resulting in increased overtime costs.
- Loss of customer confidence, resulting in reduced orders.
- Management time spent investigating causes of problems.
- Interruption to processes while reject product is being identified and isolated.
- Cost of storing rejected product.
- Production time lost due to inadequate maintenance of equipment.
- Legal costs in the event of litigation or prosecution.

7.1.3.3–1 PROCEDURE FOR INTRODUCING PROCESS CHANGES

Objective   To ensure that changes to processes are properly assessed for their effect on product quality and other processes.

Scope   Changes to processing or storage conditions.
Introduction of new equipment.

PROCEDURE

Proposer of the change (manual 'owners' only)

1 Make sure that the full details of the proposed change are available.
2 Copy relevant procedures (significant ones only) and mark in the changes. *Follow the document control procedure!*
3 Identify any effects that the change might have outside its primary effect. Obtain external assistance in assessing the effect if in doubt.
4 Identify any procedures that will need to be changed as a result.

Quality manager

5 Carefully assess the proposed change for its overall impact. Consult as necessary.
6 If the change is beneficial with no unacceptable drawbacks, approve the change by signing the form.
7 Return the form to the proposer.
8 Table a copy of the form at the next management meeting.

Proposer

9 Implement all necessary changes to documentation.
10 Train personnel involved as necessary.
11 Inform other personnel as necessary.

RESPONSIBILITIES

The Quality Manager is responsible for ensuring that all changes submitted for approval are adequately assessed for possible impact before they are approved.

The proposer is responsible for ensuring that the proposed change is adequately defined, and for implementing the change after its approval. This includes initiating all necessary changes to documentation.

7.1.3.3–2 PROCESS CHANGE REQUEST FORM

Process involved	
Products affected	
Reference documentation attached Important: See Document Control Procedure (4.2–2)	

Details of proposed change
Reason for change (e.g. current problems, benefits)
Change has potential impact on:
Signed   Date

Change assessed for impact on	Impact (Y/N)	Action required
Product quality		
Product safety		
Other processes		
Cost		
Environment		
Occupational health and safety		
System documentation		
Other		

Comments

The above change is approved subject to any Action or Comments noted above.

Signed   _____   Date   _____

Quality Manager

7.2–1 PROCEDURE FOR HANDLING CUSTOMER ORDERS (PACKED PRODUCT)

Objective   To ensure that all customer orders for packed product are dealt with promptly, and completely.

Scope   Orders received by phone, mail, fax, or personal visit.

PROCEDURE

Taking the order

1 Enter the order on computer immediately. Fill in the specified details fully. Note particularly any special requirements by the customer.

2 Check availability of stock on computer.

3 If stock is not available inform customer of the lead time. This is indicated on the computer.

Sales office staff

4 Check all outstanding orders at the start of each day.

5 Schedule outstanding orders for delivery at the next available delivery run.

Dispatch Supervisor

6 Before the order is loaded into the van check it for the following:

- quantities match order quantities;
- batch codes and customer name are recorded on dispatch docket; and
- no evidence of damage to the product.

7 Complete the relevant inspection sections on the dispatch docket.

8 Return blue copy to the office.

7.2–2 HANDLING ORDERS FOR BULK PRODUCT (CUSTOMER CONTRACT REVIEW)

Objective   To ensure that all orders for bulk product are adequately reviewed so that its production can be planned and implemented to the customer's satisfaction.

Scope   Orders for bulk product from associate companies.

PROCEDURE

Once the Managing Director has approved the contract in principle, the review process is carried out under the direction of the daily production meeting.

Responsibility for the various stages of the customer contract review is as follows:

Approval to initiate contract review	Managing Director
Specification – availability and adequacy	Quality Manager
Availability of materials	Materials Manager
Production capacity	Production Director
Personnel availability	Personnel Director
Knowledge of production	Production Manager
Production plan/specific requirements	Production Manager
HACCP for this product	Quality Manager
Documentation	Production Manager, Quality Manager
Records	Production Manager, Quality Manager
Testing	Laboratory Manager
Delivery/transport arrangements	Materials Manager
Insurance arrangements	Financial Controller
Final approval to sign contract	Production Director

Each manager is responsible for documenting the relevant elements of review process adequately. All documents relating to the customer contract review are filed together and retained by the Quality Manager for later review, if required.

7.2–3 GUIDANCE ON LEGAL COMPLIANCE   *Page 1 of 1*

Objective   To ensure that all managers comply with the relevant legal requirements.
Scope   All Departments.
All staff.
All products, processes, materials and equipment.
All activities.

GUIDANCE

The persons listed below are responsible for ensuring that the company is aware of its legal obligations in the relevant legal area:

Product safety legislation	Quality Manager
Product liability legislation	Production Director
Environmental legislation	Production Director
Health and safety legislation	Quality Manager
Financial/company law	Financial Controller
Local by-laws	Financial Controller

METHOD

1 Obtain a list of legislation that may be relevant in our sector. Consult the company solicitor, Internet sites, industry sector organizations, etc.
2 Identify from the list any Act or statutory instrument that is relevant to our operation. Prioritize them intuitively.
3 Obtain copies of all legislation that you consider applicable.
4 Read through the legislation carefully, noting in the margin any paragraphs that may be problematic for us. Use a highlighter.
5 If we are fully compliant indicate this on the front page, sign and date it.
6 If we are not fully compliant, prepare a summary, quoting precise references, and indicate what action needs to be taken to reach compliance.
7 Pass the summary to the Managing Director, for discussion at the next Management Meeting.

7.2–4 PROCEDURE FOR CUSTOMER COMMUNICATION

Objective   To ensure that formal channels of communication with all customers operate to facilitate rapid reaction by the company.

Scope   Individual consumers, retail outlets and customers for bulk product.
Complaints, suggestions and requests for technical information or advice.
Amendments to orders and changes to requirements.

PROCEDURE

Individual consumers

The sales office operates a dedicated telephone help-line during office hours. The telephone number is printed on every pack and sales brochure. Any comments relating to the quality of product should be recorded. For convenience use the complaints form for this.

Retail outlets

Sales representatives should encourage retail outlets to communicate on all matters via the telephone ordering number. Any comments relating to the quality of product or service should be recorded. For convenience use the complaints form for this.

Corporate customers (bulk product)

Regular communication with these customers is maintained at several points. The Materials Manager, Quality Manager and Financial Controller should maintain regular contact with their counterparts. All comments that indicate significant positive or negative attitude towards the products or service should be recorded and used in the overall company measurement of customer satisfaction.

Guidelines on dealing with customers

(This is a summary of the material covered during training.)

1 Always be polite.
2 Your starting position should be that the customer is correct.
3 If the customer is clearly wrong, give them a way out without having to appear totally wrong.
4 Record the necessary details about the customer (use the complaints form, even for comments or suggestions).
5 If you need to contact the customer later, agree when you will do this. Record it on the form.
6 Contact them at the agreed time without fail, even if it is only a holding measure. If you cannot do it arrange for somebody else to make the contact.
7 Before finishing the contact finally establish whether the customer is satisfied with the result. If not, report the matter to the Customer Services Manager.

7.3–1 SIMPLIFIED DESIGN/DEVELOPMENT PROCESS FLOW CHART

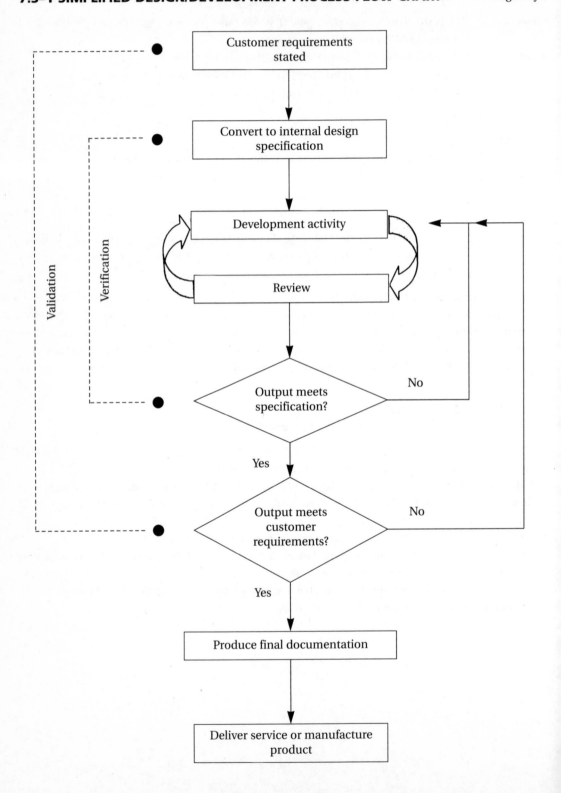

7.3–2 PROCEDURE FOR DESIGN/DEVELOPMENT OF NEW PRODUCTS   *Page 1 of 1*

Objective   To ensure that all new products are developed to meet customer requirements fully, in the most efficient manner.

Scope   Products developed for external contract customers.
Products developed as part of the company's product range.

The Product Development Manager is responsible for setting out a development plan for each individual development project.

PROCEDURE

1 Set up a channel of communication with the customer.
2 Check the requirements for the product provided by the customer. Make sure that criteria for final validation of the product are clear.
3 Make out an internal product brief. Include the inputs that may be necessary or appropriate (for example, codes of practice, legislation and documentation from similar products), criteria to be met at the verification stages, and the outputs that will be needed, including, but not confined to, specifications for product and raw materials, training requirements, process operating conditions and testing methods.
4 Agree with other managers on the assignment of responsibilities for all activities foreseen. For example:
  ● development work;
  ● defining production conditions;
  ● control of production trials;
  ● assessment of samples;
  ● developing specifications and procedures;
  ● providing raw materials; and
  ● training staff.
5 Set review dates. Alternatively define the conditions that will trigger a review. Specify who should attend reviews.
6 Define the points at which verification and validation are to be carried out, and the action to be taken at those stages.
7 The Product Development Manager must update the plan and incorporate firm dates for milestone activities in the latter stages of the development process.
8 When a product has been produced that meets the requirements of the product brief, the Product Development Manager must prepare the necessary documentation in the appropriate format for presentation to the Managing Director.
9 The Managing Director takes the final decision on the approval of the product.
10 Once the product has been approved the Quality Manager must incorporate the product fully into the quality management system documentation.

7.3.3–1 DESIGN/DEVELOPMENT VERIFICATION REPORT   *Page 1 of 1*

Project/product description _____ Ref. No. _____

Customer _____   Customer ref. _____

Attendance _____   _____

_____   _____

_____   _____

Deviations from brief

Action (modifications, etc.)

Signed _____   Date _____
       PD Manager

The output of the above project meets the requirements of the product brief.

Signed _____   Signed _____
     Customer Service Manager   Product Development Manager

Date _____   Date _____

7.3.3–2 PROCEDURE FOR DEVELOPING IN-COMPANY TRAINING COURSES

Objective   To provide a standard plan that ensures the most efficient development of training courses that meet client requirements fully.

Scope   All training courses developed for delivery in-company.

PROCEDURE

The consultant dealing with the client is responsible for planning and developing the course.

1 Meet the client to discuss requirements.
2 Make sure the objectives that will enable final validation of the course to be carried out are clear.
3 Gather the appropriate information necessary for planning, for example: exact topics required to be covered; number of people attending; current duties of people attending and relevant experience; facilities to be provided by the client; whether certification by end-of-course examination is required.
4 Make out an internal project brief. Set out the criteria to be met at the verification stage.
5 Identify inputs that may be necessary or appropriate. For example, documentation from other similar courses developed previously, codes of practice and legislation.
6 Prepare appropriate course material and handouts.
7 Define the outputs that will be needed, including, but not confined to, training aids, course material and handouts.

REVIEW AND VERIFICATION

Review and verification will take place on completion of the planning phase. The course programme should be assessed against the client's requirement by a second trainer. If it appears that the course designed may not meet the requirements, the course trainer must review and consider modifying the course programme.

VALIDATION

Validation will be carried out during the delivery of the course at appropriate times. These points should be highlighted in the trainer notes. If at validation stage it is clear to the trainer that client requirements are not being met, the trainer will have to establish a course of corrective action and modify the course immediately.

7.4.1–1 PURCHASING PROCEDURE   *Page 1 of 1*

Objective   To ensure that purchased materials that are relevant to product quality meet defined quality standards.

Scope   All materials and services listed in the List of Approved Suppliers ('Controlled items').

PROCEDURE

General

A purchase order (PO) must be made out for every item ordered. If necessary this may be done retrospectively for emergency telephone orders made with the approval of the department manager.

1 Check if the item to be ordered is a controlled item.
2 If so select a supplier from the List of Approved Suppliers.
3 Make out the PO. Be sure to include a precise description of the material ordered. Where there is a company specification make an accurate reference to the specification number. In the case of laboratory items take care to state the catalogue number (or precise grade) of material ordered.
4 When the PO is complete check the details against the requirements given by the person who requires the item, and then sign the PO.
5 Post or fax the PO to the supplier as soon as possible. If there is to be any delay in sending it out inform the person who requested the item immediately.
6 Send a copy of the PO to the person who will receive the material on arrival (stores supervisor, laboratory manager or maintenance supervisor).

Emergency purchases from non-approved suppliers

In an emergency it may be necessary to purchase a controlled item from a supplier not on the List of Approved Suppliers.

1 Get the Quality Manager to countersign the PO.
2 Make a note on the retained copies of the PO so that the user can check the item carefully on receipt.
3 The Quality Manager may decide to approve the supplier based on the experience with this material, subject to full evaluation of all aspects of quality. See procedure for approval of suppliers.

7.4.1–2 VERBAL ORDERS

Date	Supplier	Material and grade	Quantity	Date promised	Comments	Sign

7.4.1-3 INSPECTION OF INCOMING MATERIALS

Date	Supplier	Material	Lot no.	Condition of product	Temperature	Packaging	Cert. of analysis	Comments	Initials
Specification/standard required: see raw materials specifications manual									

Tick (✓) each relevant box to indicate that the delivery meets the standard. If not relevant insert a dash (—). Initial the last column when finished.

NOTE TO READER

The above form would be suitable for the situation where incoming inspection involves a small number of checks that can be done visually or very simply.

7.4.2–1 PROCEDURE FOR APPROVAL OF SUPPLIERS *Page 1 of 2*

Objective   To ensure that all suppliers of quality-critical materials and services have been properly assessed for their ability to meet requirements.

Scope   Suppliers of materials and services listed in the List of Approved Suppliers.

PROCEDURE

Purchasing Officer

1 Send a copy of the New Supplier questionnaire to the prospective supplier to be completed and returned. Attach a copy (uncontrolled) of the company specification and request agreement or comments, or a copy of the supplier's specification.

2 Pass the supplier's response to the Quality Manager.

Quality Manager

3 Assess the response and decide if further information is required. For example, samples may need to be tested. If none, then step 9 below.

4 Inform the Purchasing Officer if further information, samples, etc. are required.

Purchasing Officer

5 Request the material required by the Quality Manager.

6 Pass this on to the Quality Manager immediately it arrives.

Quality Manager

7 Assess the information received and test any samples.

8 Decide whether to proceed with the assessment of the supplier. If necessary instruct the Purchasing Officer to arrange an audit.

9 Make out a detailed set of requirements for the supplier, depending on the nature and criticality of the material to be purchased. This will include some or all of the following :

- process control and finished product testing to be carried out by the supplier (number of samples, test methods);
- controls to be exercised during manufacture, storage, transport;
- arrangements for visiting/auditing by us;
- information to accompany the deliveries (processing information, test results, certificates, etc.).

10 Decide on a suitable trial period.

Purchasing Officer

11 Finalize the agreement with the supplier, based on 9 above, and place an appropriately sized trial order.

Quality Manager

12 At the end of the trial period decide whether to add the supplier to the List of Approved Suppliers.

13 Update the List of Approved Suppliers.

NOTES

1 At the discretion of the Quality Manager, any of the above steps may be omitted or modified. However, the Quality Manager should make a brief note of the reason for this.

2 Both the Quality Manager and the Purchasing Officer must keep appropriate records of each of the steps above.

RESPONSIBILITIES

Deciding if the above procedure applies in any given case – Quality Manager.

Deciding whether to purchase from any particular approved supplier – Purchasing Officer.

7.4.2–2 PROCEDURE FOR REVIEW OF SUPPLIERS *Page 1 of 1*

Objective To ensure that suppliers are assessed regularly for ability to supply quality products and services.

Scope Suppliers, materials and services listed on the List of Approved Suppliers.

Target duration of review: 2 hours.

PROCEDURE

1 Prior to the Review the following summary information is gathered in relation to each supplier and each material supplied:

Information required	*By whom*
Conformance to specification	Quality Manager
Performance of the item in use	Production Manager
Nonconformity reports	Quality Manager
Customer complaint records	Customer Services Manager
Laboratory test results	Laboratory Manager
Physical condition of the materials on receipt	Materials Manager
Packaging in general	Production Manager
Corrective action by the supplier	Quality Manager

2 Include in the summary a list of any suppliers you would recommend for de-listing.
3 The review is carried out by the persons listed above, chaired by the Quality Manager.
4 The group reviews each supplier, and makes one of the following decisions on each:

- renew the approval;
- de-list the supplier; and
- continue to use the supplier for a limited period, but inform them that they must improve.

The final decision in each case is taken by the Quality Manager, *based purely on the confidence in the quality of the purchased item.* Costing is not to be taken as a factor, as this will be addressed by purchasing personnel at the time of placing the order.

5 The Quality Manager records the results of the review.
6 The Quality Manager updates the List of Approved Suppliers.

RESPONSIBILITIES

Ensuring that the review of suppliers takes place twelve-monthly – Quality Manager.

7.4.2–3 REVIEW OF SUPPLIERS (EXAMPLE)

Present: *Una Goggin*   *Mary Smith*
     Quality   Materials

    Jim Hennessy   *Frank Jones*
     Production   Purchasing

Date *16/12/2000*

Supplier	Material	Quality	Prod.	Handling	Decision
Fine Films plc	Shrink film	O.K	O.K	O.K	Approved
Generic Packs Ltd	Trays	O.K.	O.K	O.K	Approved
Paper Supplies Ltd	Trays	O.K	O.K	O.K	Approved
Acme Engineering	Widgets	Note 1	O.K.	O.K	Discontinue A.S.A.P!!
Techno Ltd	Calibration	O.K	O.K	O.K	Approved
Steel Suppliers Ltd	Cans and ends	O.K	O.K	Note 2	Approved
Superfood Supplies Ltd	Milk and cream	O.K	O.K	O.K	Approved

NOTES

1 Too many defects are being found in the incoming inspection. AE have been notified seven times this year about the problems. There is a serious risk that Quality Control will not pick up all the defectives.

2 The cans are coming in open end up. Covering sometimes damaged. We need to get them to either turn them upside down or improve the packaging.

Signed *Frank Jones*

7.5.1–1 ISO 9000 CONSULTANCY PROJECT COMPLETION REVIEW   *Page 1 of 1*

Client _____

Date of review _____

☐ All requirements of the standard addressed in procedures?

☐ Full audit completed and comprehensive corrective action list made out?

☐ Management review carried out?

☐ Internal audits carried out?

☐ Review of suppliers carried out?

☐ Managers fully aware of what they need to do in future?

☐ Manuals not causing any problems?

☐ Document control procedure not causing problems?

☐ CEO understands his/her role and is committed?

☐ CEO satisfied the system can work practically?

☐ Quality Manager satisfied the system can work practically?

☐ All relevant documents handed over?

☐ All relevant diskettes handed over?

☐ Quality Manager has full knowledge of steps necessary for certification?

This project has been completed.

Signed _____
                    Consultant

7.5.2–1 PROCEDURE FOR INSPECTION AND TEST STATUS   *Page 1 of 1*

Objective   To ensure that all materials are adequately labelled as to their status in regard to inspection and testing.

Scope   All raw materials to be incorporated into the product, packaging materials, intermediate products, bulk product and packed product.

PROCEDURE

General

Test status is defined on computer and all product is bar-coded. Movement of product through the process is controlled by reading the bar-code. A material which does not have the correct status will not be allowed to proceed to the next processing step.

Status codes used

NYT: not yet tested.
PAT: passed all tests.
RJR: rejected – return to supplier.
RJD: rejected – downgrade.

Raw materials

Raw materials are assigned an internal batch code on receipt and are entered on the computer. The computer prints out a bar-coded label for each pallet. A status of 'not yet tested' (NYT) is assigned automatically. For convenience an indicator yellow NYT sticker is affixed to prominent pallets.

On completion of the specified testing QC personnel change the computer status to either passed all tests (PAT) or reject: return to supplier (RJR).

Intermediate product

A batch number is assigned to each batch at start of mixing. The batch retains this code throughout the remainder of the process and packaging. Computer status of NYT is automatically assigned.

Use of materials is computer controlled. A material which has not been passed for use by the authorized function cannot be used.

Authority to change NYT to PAT status is as follows:

Raw materials	Laboratory Supervisor
Intermediate product	Laboratory Supervisor or Production Supervisor (defined on the relevant testing plan)
Bulk product	Laboratory Manager
Packed product	Laboratory Supervisor.

Product which does not conform to specification may be graded RJD (downgraded) or RJR (rework).

Authority to regrade 'RJD' or 'RJR' to 'NYT' or 'PAT' is restricted to the Quality Manager.

7.5.2–2 PRODUCT RECALL PROCEDURE

Objective   To ensure that all product which is a danger to customers, or which does not comply
with legal requirements is withdrawn from the market as quickly as possible.

Scope   All situations where a product recall is declared by the Managing Director.
All situations where a corporate product recall is declared.

PROCEDURE
The table summarizes the duties and responsibilities.

Task	Responsibility
Declare the recall	Managing Director
Control the detailed activities of the recall	Production Director
Notify the public health authorities	Quality Manager
Inform management	Production Director
Keep full records of all details during the crisis	Financial Controller
Identify the production run affected	Production Director
Notify all customers who may have received product from that run	Customer Services Manager
Identify whether external technical assistance is required	Quality Manager
Engage the services of a qualified external expert	Quality Manager
Decide whether the public need to be informed	Managing Director
Inform the media and carry out all communication with them	Managing Director
Make preparations for receipt and isolated storage of product returned from the market	Materials Manager
Make arrangements for the examination of returned product	Quality Manager
Decide when the crisis is over	Managing Director
Decide on the disposal of returned product	Quality Manager

GENERAL RULES TO BE OBSERVED DURING PRODUCT RECALL
1 Record all actions taken.
2 Ensure that no errors are made that allow recalled product to mix with other product.
3 Do not destroy any product. Retain all samples tested.
4 Nobody except the Managing Director may talk to any person outside the company about the recall
or its circumstances.
5 The sooner effective action is taken the more likely the situation can be controlled. Any delay in
taking effective action will probably result in a much worse situation.

*Remember: Companies have recovered from apparently catastrophic recall situations by managing the
problem effectively.*

7.5.2-3 INCOMING MATERIALS/TRACEABILITY RECORD

Material	Supplier	Lot no.	Date received	Comment	Sign	Used first in batch no.	Used last in batch no.

Tick (✓) each relevant box to indicate that the delivery meets the standard. If not relevant insert a dash (—). Initial the last column when finished.

NOTE TO READER

The above form combines the records of the receipt of materials and their usage in the process. In this case only minimal inspection on arrival is necessary. The first and last times that each lot is used in the process is recorded above. For this to be effective as a traceability record strict stock rotation must be observed (that is, only one lot is in use at any one time).

7.6–1 PROCEDURE FOR CONTROL OF MEASURING INSTRUMENTS   *Page 1 of 1*

Objective   To ensure that all instruments used for critical measurements are maintained in a suitable state and remain capable of measuring to the required accuracy.

Scope   Instruments used to provide information used in making a decision about product quality. These instruments are listed on the Laboratory Calibration Plan and the Factory Calibration Plan.

INSTRUMENTS

1 All measuring instruments should be treated with care and should not be subjected to any unnecessary stress. In particular, instruments should not be knocked or dropped.

2 When not in use instruments should be stored in the manner recommended by the manufacturer.

MEASUREMENT

Measurements should be carried out in the correct environment. Follow any instructions given in the relevant procedures. Where necessary, care should be taken to eliminate any vibration that might affect the accuracy of the result.

CALIBRATION STATUS

Calibration status is shown by means of a sticker on the instrument. This should always show the date on which the next calibration is due.

An instrument may only be used within the time in which the previous calibration is valid.

CALIBRATION

All instruments used to make a decision on product quality are calibrated according to a defined schedule set out in the relevant calibration plan.

An instrument does not need to be calibrated unless it, alone, provides information that is used to determine if the product complies with specification. So, where an instrument is used to control the process, but the product testing will subsequently be carried out to confirm product conformance then calibration is not, strictly, necessary.

The manager of each department is responsible for ensuring that all relevant instruments are included in the calibration plan and that all calibrations are carried out to schedule.

OUT OF CALIBRATION

When the *as found* result shows that the instrument had been out of calibration the following action must be taken:

1 Inform the Quality Manager immediately.

2 The Production Manager must immediately review all product released since the previous calibration. Establish if any released product was outside specification.

3 The Quality Manager must assess all product likely to have been outside specification, and decide whether to grant a waiver (see procedure for non-conforming product) or to recommend to the Managing Director that the product be recalled (see recall procedure).

7.6–2 CALIBRATION PROGRAMME (EXAMPLE)

Instrument	Serial no./ location	What measured	Acceptable error	Calibration frequency	By whom	Doc. ref.	Record	Action if out of calibration
Thermometer	A1025736	Temperature	0.5 °C	3 months	Lab	Q5/27	Lab calibration log	Remove from use. Report to Quality Manager. Check records since last calibration.
Pressure gauge	No. 1	Air pressure	1 psi	12 months	Approved external supplier	N/A	Certificate filed in Maintenance office	Remove and replace. Quarantine product for previous 6 hours. Report to Quality and Maintenance Managers IMMEDIATELY
Pressure gauge	No. 4	Air pressure	1 psi	6 months	Approved external supplier	N/A	Certificate filed in Maintenance office	Remove and replace. Quarantine product for previous 6 hours. Report to Quality and Maintenance Managers IMMEDIATELY

NOTE TO THE READER

In the above example there are two identical pressure gauges, yet it has been established that one needs more frequent calibration than the other. There may be other pressure gauges, numbers 2 and 3, perhaps, but presumably these do not require calibration because of the use to which they are put.

8.2.1.2–1 PROCEDURE FOR CUSTOMER SURVEYS

Objective   To gather customer feedback about the products and company service, including possible improvements.

Scope   · All packed products.

All retail sales outlets.

GUIDELINES ON CUSTOMER SURVEYS FOR SALES PERSONNEL

1 Select a different retail outlet each time.
2 Over the year ensure that you include approximately equal numbers of small, medium and large outlets.
3 Select the participants randomly from purchasers of our products. Take the first available person.
4 Complete the survey form fully.

PROCEDURE

1 Carry out a survey every month.
2 Return the survey form to the Customer Services Manager within two working days.
3 Note all comments, positive and negative, about the products, the company or the service.

CUSTOMER SERVICES MANAGER

1 Analyse the data contained in the survey reports and extract information relating to satisfaction, dissatisfaction and suggestions for improvement.
2 Prepare a summary report showing the overall satisfaction rating and a list of all negative comments and suggestions for improvement.
3 Copy the report to the Quality Manager and Managing Director.
4 Table the summary report for discussion at the next interim management review.

8.2.1.2–2 CUSTOMER SURVEY FORM   *Page 1 of 1*

Date _____   Retail outlet _____

Question 5–10 people purchasing the product. Ask the first available person. Do not select respondents.

Answer codes: 5 Agree strongly; 4 Agree; 3 No opinion; 2 Disagree; 1 Disagree strongly.

	Respondent									
	1	2	3	4	5	6	7	8	9	10
Our products are totally suitable for your requirements										
Our products perform as you expect them										
Our products are consistent in their quality										
Our products are suitably packaged										
Our products represent good value										
You receive sufficient information about the products										
Our products compare well with other similar products										
Our products have a good public image										
Our products will continue to be suitable for you in the future										
You would recommend our products to your friends										
You have a positive opinion of the company										
Have you any other comments on our products or the company? [Record comments overleaf]										

Signed _____

      Sales Representative

8.2.1.2–3 PROCEDURE FOR CUSTOMER COMPLAINTS   *Page 1 of 2*

Objective   To ensure that all genuine customer complaints are dealt with promptly, and that corrective action is taken to prevent a recurrence, where practicable.

Scope   Complaints received by phone, mail, fax or personal visit.

PROCEDURE

1 All complaints are referred initially to the Quality Manager (in his or her absence the Laboratory Manager).

Quality Manager

2 Assign the next complaint number, and enter the details on a two-part complaint form. Details should include, where possible:
   - customer name and address;
   - date purchased;
   - item complained of;
   - the nature of the complaint; and
   - any other relevant details reported.

3 *Note particularly if there is any mention of sickeness. If so inform the Managing Director and Customer Services Manager immediately.*

4 If a sample has been returned pass it immediately to the laboratory, with the blue copy of the complaint form.

Laboratory Supervisor

5 Check what laboratory testing is required by reference to the current Complaints Testing Plan.

6 Ensure that the sample is tested as soon as practicable, and stored cold (below 4°C) until it is tested.

7 Record the test results on the 'Laboratory' section of the complaints form.

8 Return the complaints form to the Quality Manager.

Quality Manager

9 Check the relevant records for the time of manufacture (records of production, cleaning, metal detector, etc.) for any indication as to the cause of the complaint. Check that the process was fully in control. If the process was not at all times in control, indicate if the conditions could have given rise to the complaint in question.

10 Complete the complaint form. Where corrective action can be identified enter this on the form.

11 Draft an appropriate technical answer for the Customer Services Manager on the complaint form. If the complaint has been justified indicate what steps the company is taking to prevent it happening again. Pass the complaint form to the Customer Services Manager.

Customer Services Manager

12 Record on the complaint form whatever action is to be taken by the relevant sales representative.

13 If a visit is not necessary reply to the customer by letter. If the complaint was justified, apologize and state what action is being taken to prevent a recurrence. If appropriate, reassure the customer about the hazard and risks.

14 Consider whether it is necessary to recover any stock from the market. Consult with the Quality Manager on this point.

15 Implement the Corrective Action Procedure to ensure that the risk of the problem arising again is reduced.

SAMPLES

Where a sample is received it should be marked clearly with the complaint number, and put into cold storage immediately. It should not be opened or tampered with in any way until the Quality Manager has examined it. Samples should be stored cold until tested, and frozen afterwards, where appropriate.

REFERENCES

7.5.2–2 Procedure for product recall.

8.5.2–1 Procedure for corrective action.

8.2.1.2–4 COMPLAINT FORM

Page 1 of 1

Date received _____ by _____ Complaint Ref. No. [_____]

Name of complainant _____

Address _____

Product _____

Purchased at _____ on _____ (date)

Nature of complaint

Signed _____
_____
Laboratory findings

Signed _____
_____
Investigation

Signed _____
_____
Corrective action

Signed _____
_____
Corrective action completed   Date _____ Signed _____

8.2.1.3–1 PROCEDURE FOR INTERNAL QUALITY AUDITS   *Page 1 of 1*

Objectives   To ensure that the quality system is assessed properly for adequacy and effectiveness. To ensure that any defects are highlighted and corrected.

Scope   All activities covered in any procedure in the quality system manuals.

PROCEDURE

Nominate auditors from panel of trained auditors	Quality Manager
Nominate lead auditor	Quality Manager
Arrange details with department manager	Lead auditor
Direct opening meeting	Lead auditor
Audit	Auditor
Check corrective action from previous audit	Lead auditor
Direct close-out meeting	Lead auditor
Written report to Quality Manager	Lead auditor
Corrective action	Department manager
Follow-up	Quality Manager

GENERAL GUIDANCE

Carry out the audit in accordance with the guidance given in training.

Use the current internal audit checklist. Tick off the items that have been audited. Leave any aspects that have not been audited unticked. Use the back of the sheets to record details of the aspects audited, as appropriate.

Check the status of previous non-compliances raised. These should have been implemented and monitored by the management team following the previous audit. Confirm with the Quality Manager that this has happened. If not, obtain a copy of the previous audit report and check that corrective action has been taken in all instances.

Note any specific instances of non-compliance with documented procedures or with ISO 9001.

The audit report should include:

- the scope of the audit (areas or functions audited; clauses of ISO 9001 audited);
- specific non-compliances;
- suggested corrective action, where appropriate; and
- instances where existing procedures are not fully effective to meet quality objectives.

Attach the actual audit checklist used in the audit, as a record of the scope of the audit.

The audit report should be given as soon as completed to the Quality Manager.

The daily operations meeting is used to monitor the progress on implementing corrective action.

RESPONSIBILITIES

The Quality Manager is responsible for ensuring that the audits are scheduled.

The Manager for the department audited is responsible for ensuring that agreed corrective action is taken within the specified timescale.

REFERENCES

8.5.2–1 Procedure for corrective action.
8.2.1.3–2 Checklist for internal quality audits.
8.2.1.3–5 Notes on internal auditing of quality systems.

8.2.1.3–2 ISO 9001 INTERNAL AUDIT CHECKLIST

PERMANENT FEATURES OF THE SYSTEM

The questions in this part of the checklist will usually not have to be considered at every audit, since they relate to aspects of the quality management system that are not likely to change in the short term.

4.1 General requirements

Have all processes and how they interact been identified and documented?
Are the methods for controlling and monitoring processes defined in the quality management system documentation?

4.2.2 Quality manual

Is there a quality manual?
Does it define the scope of the quality management system with justification for any exclusions?
Does it contain or refer to documented procedures?
Does it contain a description of the sequence and interaction of the processes of the quality management system?
Is it controlled under the document control procedure?

4.2.3 Control of documents

Is there a documented procedure for document control, and does it address:
a) approval of documents for adequacy prior to issue?
b) reviewing, updating and reapproving documents?
c) how revision status is shown?
d) availability of documents in the locations where they are needed?
e) documents of external origin (identification and control)?
f) control of obsolete documents (including any retained for reference)?

4.2.4 Control of quality records

Are quality records defined?
Are quality records maintained?
Is there a documented procedure for the identification, storage, retrieval, protection, retention time and disposal of quality records?

5.2 Customer focus

Is concern for meeting customer needs and expectations adequately addressed in the quality management system documentation?

5.3 Quality policy

Is the quality policy set by top management appropriate to the purpose of the organization?
Does it include a commitment to meeting requirements and to continual improvement?
Does it provide a framework for establishing and reviewing quality objectives?

5.4.1 Quality objectives

Is it documented how and when quality objectives are set?

5.4.2 Quality management system planning

Are the resources needed to achieve the quality objectives identified and planned?
Is the output of the planning documented?

Does quality planning include:

a) the processes of the quality management system?
b) the resources needed?
c) continual improvement of the quality management system?
d) planning for maintaining the integrity of the quality management system during periods of change?

5.5.1 Responsibility and authority

Are functions, their interrelations, responsibilities and authorities defined?
Have deputies been nominated, where appropriate or necessary?
Are they communicated throughout the organization?

5.5.2 Management representative

Has a member of management been appointed with responsibility and authority for:
a) ensuring the quality management system is maintained?
b) reporting to top management on the performance of the system, including needs for improvement?
c) ensuring that awareness of customer requirements is promoted throughout the organization?

5.5.3 Internal communication

Are channels of communication established?

5.6 Management review

Is the process of management review adequately described in the system documentation?

6.1 Provision of resources

Is there a defined method for ensuring that resource needs are reviewed and the necessary resources provided?

6.2 Personnel

Is there a method of ensuring that all personnel with defined responsibilities are competent?

6.3 Infrastructure

Is there a formal method for identifying what infrastructure is needed in order to meet requirements?
Is there a defined method of ensuring that essential equipment and structures are maintained adequately?

6.4 Work environment

Have the appropriate physical conditions standards for the work environment been defined?

7.1 Planning of product realization

Is the plan for product realization (or the method of planning it) described adequately in the system documentation?
Is the plan specific for the product or service, and does it incorporate:
a) quality objectives for the product, project or contract?
b) the realization processes?
c) documentation?
d) resources?
e) facilities?
f) verification and validation activities, and the criteria for acceptability?
g) records?

7.2.1 Identification of product requirements

Are customer requirements defined, including:

a) product requirements specified by the customer?

b) availability, delivery and support?

c) necessary product requirements not specified by the customer?

d) legal requirements?

7.2.2 Review of product requirements

Are all requirements reviewed prior to the commitment to supply a product to the customer?

Does the review address the following:

a) product requirements are defined?

b) the customer requirements are confirmed before acceptance where there is no written order?

c) differences between order and earlier tender?

d) ability to meet defined requirements?

Are the results of the review and subsequent follow-up actions recorded?

Where product requirements are changed is *all* relevant documentation amended?

Are all relevant personnel made aware of the changed requirements?

7.2.3 Customer communication

Are there formal channels of communication with customers relating to product information, enquiries, contracts or orders, feedback and complaints?

7.3 Design and development

Are design/development projects planned?

Does the plan for a project define:

a) the different stages of the project?

b) review, verification and validation activities?

c) responsibilities and authorities?

d) interfaces and communication between different groups involved?

7.4.1 Purchasing process

Is there a programme of control on purchasing?

Is the type and extent of control appropriate for each material/supplier involved?

7.4.3 Verification of purchased product

Are inspection and test requirements for incoming materials defined?

Are inspections or tests carried out at the supplier's premises? If so, are the arrangements for inspection, testing and release of the product defined and communicated to the supplier?

7.5.1 Operations control

Are there specifications for all products and services?

Is suitable equipment provided?

Is the equipment maintained in a suitable condition?

Are the appropriate measuring and monitoring devices available?

Are there adequate monitoring activities?

Is there a defined process for release, delivery and post-delivery activities?

7.5.2 Validation of processes

Are there any processes where the resulting output cannot be verified by subsequent measurement or

monitoring? If so, are these processes validated to demonstrate capability?
Are validation arrangements defined?

Do they include:

a) qualification of processes?

b) qualification of equipment and personnel?

c) use of defined methodologies and procedures?

d) requirements for records?

e) revalidation?

7.5.3 Identification and traceability

Is there a defined method of identifying materials (product and raw materials)?

Does the system permit traceability throughout the process to the extent defined as necessary?

7.5.4 Customer property

Does the organization hold any material owned by the customer?

If so, do procedures adequately address the control of this material?

Is all loss or damage required to be reported to the customer?

7.5.5 Preservation of product

Do procedures adequately address the physical protection of the product at all stages up to final delivery?

7.6 Control of measuring and monitoring devices

Are those measurements used to determine conformance to specification defined?

Are there appropriate measuring devices?

Are these devices adequately controlled and maintained?

Is measurement capability consistent with the measurement requirements?

Are they safeguarded from unauthorized adjustments?

Are they protected from damage and deterioration?

Is software used for measuring and monitoring of specified requirements validated prior to use?

8.1 Planning

Is there a method of ensuring that continual improvement is planned?

Does the plan include statistical techniques, where appropriate?

8.2.1 Customer satisfaction

Is there a formal documented approach to measuring the level of customer satisfaction?

8.2.2 Internal audit

Are internal audits carried out to a plan?

Does the plan reflect the status and importance of the activities and areas to be audited?

Are audits conducted by personnel other than those who perform the activity being audited?

Is there a documented procedure for audits, covering the audit scope, frequency and method?

Are responsibilities defined?

8.2.3 Measurement and monitoring of processes

Are there adequate methods for measuring and monitoring realization processes?

8.2.4 Measurement and monitoring of product

Is there a documented plan of inspections and tests of product?

Are all inspection and testing activities completed before product is released?

8.3 Control of non-conforming product

Is there a documented procedure to control all non-conforming product?

Has authority been assigned for making decisions regarding non-conforming product?

Is it defined what action is to be taken when defects are discovered after delivery?

Is there an adequate product recall procedure?

8.4 Analysis of data

Is there a formal approach to analysing data with a view to continual improvement of the processes, the system and conformance to requirements?

8.5.1 Continual improvement

Is there a plan for generating continual improvement of the quality management system?

Is continual improvement addressed in:

a) quality policy?

b) objectives?

c) audit results?

d) analysis of data?

e) corrective and preventive action?

f) management review?

8.5.2 Corrective action

Is there a documented procedure for corrective action?

Does the procedure require action that will prevent a recurrence?

Is corrective action reviewed subsequently to ensure it is permanently implemented?

8.5.3 Preventive action

Is there a documented procedure for preventive action?

Does it address the root causes of potential nonconformities?

Is preventive action reviewed subsequently?

ISO 9001 INTERNAL AUDIT CHECKLIST

IMPLEMENTATION ASPECTS OF THE SYSTEM

4.1 General requirements
Is all the information necessary to operate processes available?

4.2.2 Quality manual
Is the quality manual currently available to the appropriate people?

4.2.3 Control of documents
Has the document control procedure been implemented in all cases recently?
Are there any obsolete documents in use?
Are obsolete reference documents properly marked and stored?
Are there any uncontrolled instructions in use that should have been issued in the form of controlled documents?

4.2.4 Control of quality records
Are records legible, identified and easily retrieved?
Are records filled up properly and completely (no blanks)?
Are out-of-specification results highlighted and commented on?

5.2 Customer focus
Is there evidence of top management commitment to meeting customer needs and expectations?
Is there evidence of top management communicating the importance of customer focus throughout the organization?

5.3 Quality policy
Is there evidence that the quality policy has been communicated throughout the organization?
Is there evidence that it is understood throughout the organization?
Is it reviewed at appropriate intervals for continuing suitability?

5.4.1 Quality objectives
Are there currently quality objectives established by top management for relevant functions and levels within the organization?
Are they measurable and consistent with the quality policy?
Do they include the need to meet the requirements for the product?

5.4.2 Quality management system planning
Is there adequate evidence that planning is carried out to ensure that the quality management system is effective?
Has the quality management system been maintained during any recent periods of upheaval?

5.5.1 Responsibility and authority
Have all recent decisions regarding quality been taken by authorized persons?

5.5.2 Management representative
Is there evidence that the management representative monitors the quality management system?
Does the management representative report to senior management on the system?
Is there evidence that awareness of achieving customer satisfaction is being promoted?

5.5.3 Internal communication

Is there evidence that communication takes place throughout the organization regarding the performance of the quality management system?

5.6 Management review

Is the next management review scheduled?

Did the last review examine the suitability and adequacy of the quality management system for current needs, and its effectiveness?

Did it evaluate the need for changes to the system, including quality policy and quality objectives?

Was it carried out by senior management?

5.6.2 Review input

Did the last management review address:

a) current performance?

b) audits (internal and external)?

c) customer feedback?

d) process performance and product conformance?

e) status of preventive and corrective actions?

f) follow-up actions from earlier management reviews?

g) changes that could affect the quality management system?

5.6.3 Review output

Is there a record of the outcome of the last management review?

Did the output cover actions related to:

a) improvement of the quality management system?

b) improvement of product related to customer requirements?

c) resource needs?

Was the specified corrective action subsequently taken?

6.1 Provision of resources

Is there evidence that resources are provided in a timely manner?

6.2 Personnel

Have competency needs been identified for personnel whose duties could affect quality?

Has training (or other appropriate resource) been provided to satisfy those needs?

Has the effectiveness of all training been evaluated?

Have employees been made aware of the relevance and importance of their activities?

Are there appropriate records of education, experience, training and qualifications for all relevant persons?

6.3 Infrastructure

Are adequate facilities provided (e.g., workspace, associated facilities, equipment, hardware and software, transport, communication)?

Is there evidence that essential equipment is adequately maintained?

6.4 Work environment

Is the physical environment suitable for the work being carried out and adequate to ensure a quality output?

7.1 Planning of product realization

Is there a realization plan for the contracts or orders currently being processed?

7.2.1 Identification of product requirements

Are customer requirements (or an appropriate in-company specification) documented for current contracts?

7.2.2 Review of product requirements

Has a review been carried out (and recorded) for every recent contract or order?

7.2.3 Customer communication

Is there evidence that the customer can readily communicate with the company when necessary?

7.3.1 Design and development planning

Is there a product development plan on file for all recent projects?
Is there evidence that the plan was updated, as appropriate, as the project progressed?

7.3.2 Design and development inputs

Were inputs relating to product requirements defined and documented for recent projects?
Did the inputs include (as appropriate):
a) functional and performance requirements?
b) legal requirements?
c) information from previous similar designs?
Were inputs reviewed for adequacy prior to starting?

7.3.3 Design and development outputs

Were the outputs documented in a manner that enabled verification against the inputs?
Did the output:
a) meet the input requirements?
b) provide adequate information for product realization?
c) contain or make reference to product acceptance criteria?
d) define the essential characteristics of the product?
Are output documents approved prior to release?

7.3.4 Design and development review

Were planned reviews carried out during the process to:
a) evaluate the ability to fulfil requirements?
b) identify problems and propose follow-up actions?
Were all appropriate functions represented at the reviews?
Were the results of the reviews and subsequent follow-up actions recorded?

7.3.5 Design and development verification

Was the output verified against the inputs?
Were the results of the verification and subsequent follow-up actions recorded?

7.3.6 Design and development validation

Was the resulting product validated to confirm that it was suitable for intended use?
Were the results of the validation and subsequent follow-up actions recorded?

7.3.7 Control of design and development changes

Were changes identified, reviewed, documented and controlled?

Were the effects of the changes evaluated?

Were *all* changes verified and validated, as appropriate, and approved before implementation?

Were the results of the review of changes and subsequent follow-up actions documented?

7.4.1 Purchasing process

Have all current regular suppliers been approved?

Was the last review of suppliers carried out when it was supposed to be done?

Were the results of the review recorded and acted upon?

7.4.2 Purchasing information

Do purchasing documents contain adequate information describing the product to be purchased?

Are purchasing documents reviewed for adequacy of product specification prior to posting?

7.4.3 Verification of purchased product

Have all specified tests and inspections been carried out on materials currently in use or recently used?

Has appropriate action been taken in cases of nonconformity?

7.5.1 Operations control

Are specifications for the current products available where needed?

Are work instructions available close to where the tasks are carried out?

7.5.2 Validation of processes

Have all processes currently used been validated?

Have any changes been made to processes that might necessitate revalidation?

Have changes to the process (or new equipment introduced) been evaluated and approved?

7.5.3 Identification and traceability

Are all materials currently in stock adequately identified?

Is the status of all materials with respect to inspection and testing adequately identified? (Physically check the stock.)

Can materials be traced? (If possible, pick an instance of non-conforming product from stock and trace backwards.)

7.5.4 Customer property

Are there records of all customer-owned material currently in stock?

7.5.5 Preservation of product

Are all materials properly stored and handled?

Is there any sign of damage to materials currently in stock?

7.6 Control of measuring and monitoring devices

Is there a current calibration plan?

Have all the listed devices been calibrated within the specified calibration period?

Are there calibration records for all listed instruments?

Are any non-listed instruments used to make a decision on product quality?

Do all external calibration certificates contain the necessary information (e.g., traceability; as-found values)?

Has appropriate action been taken in relation to product if devices were found to be out of calibration?

8.1 Planning

Is there evidence that activities have been planned recently with a view to improving the quality management system and conformity of product?

8.2.1 Customer satisfaction

Has the level of customer satisfaction been measured recently?

Was this result analysed to see what action should be taken?

8.2.2 Internal audit

Have internal audits been carried out as required by the current plan?

If not, have the audits been re-scheduled?

Are there adequately detailed records for all recent audits?

Were the audits carried out by trained auditors?

Were the results reported to senior management?

Has the corrective action been carried out?

8.2.3 Measurement and monitoring of processes

Is there a current plan for monitoring the realization process?

Were the specified checks carried out and recorded for recent contracts or orders?

Were the results within specification? If not, was appropriate action taken in respect of the product involved?

8.2.4 Measurement and monitoring of product

Was recent product adequately inspected or tested to verify conformance with specification?

Were the results recorded?

Were all instances of results outside specification highlighted and the appropriate action taken?

Do the records indicate who released the product?

8.3 Control of non-conforming product

Is all non-conforming product currently in stock adequately identified as such?

Are there adequate records of the disposal of all recent non-conforming product?

Where product waiver was granted was this in accordance with the contract or order?

Where non-conforming product was reworked was it reinspected?

8.4 Analysis of data

Is there evidence that appropriate data is collected and analysed to evaluate the performance of the quality management system?

Does the data include information on:

a) customer satisfaction?

b) conformance to customer requirements?

c) characteristics of processes, product and their trends?

d) suppliers?

8.5.1 Continual improvement

Is there evidence that the above analysis is used for improvement of the system?

8.5.2 Corrective action

Is corrective action recorded for *all* recent instances of non-conforming product?

Does all corrective action taken recently address the root causes of the problems?

Is the corrective action taken likely to prevent recurrence of the same problems?

8.5.3 Preventive action

Has any effort been made recently to identify potential problems?

Has any preventive action been taken recently?

Has all preventive action been recorded?

Have procedures been amended, where appropriate?

8.2.1.3–3 ISO 9001 INTERNAL AUDIT PLAN FOR YEAR 2001 (EXAMPLE) *Page 1 of 1*

	Senior mgt	Prod.	QA	Stores	Admin
1.2 Permissible exclusions		▩		▩	▩
4.1 Quality management system	▩	▩		▩	▩
4.2.2 Quality manual					
4.2.3 Document control					
4.2.4 Record control					
5.1 Management commitment		▩		▩	▩
5.2 Customer focus		▩		▩	
5.3 Quality policy					
5.4 Objectives & planning					
5.5.2 Responsibilities and authority					
5.5.3 Management representative		▩		▩	▩
5.5.4 Internal communication					
5.6 Management review		▩		▩	▩
6.1 Provision of resources					
6.2 Human resources					
6.3/6.4 Facilities & work environment	▩				
7.1 Production planning	▩				
7.2 Customer requirements and communication	▩			▩	
7.4 Purchasing	▩	▩			
7.5.1/ 7.5.5 Operations control & preservation of products	▩		▩		▩
7.5.2 Process validation	▩				
7.5.3 Identification & traceability	▩				
7.6 Measuring devices	▩				▩
8.1 Planning of monitoring activities					
8.2.1 Customer satisfaction	▩			▩	
8.2.2 Internal audits					
8.2.3 Measurement of process performance	▩				
8.2.4 Product testing	▩			▩	▩
8.3 Non-conforming product					
8.4 Analysis of data					
8.5.1 Continual improvement					
8.5.2 Corrective action					
8.5.3 Preventive action					

Sections 1–5: w/c 5 Feb; Sections 6 and 8: w/c 7 May; Section 7: w/c 3 Sept.

Signed *Una Goggin*   Date *15 Dec. 2000*

Quality Mgr

8.2.1.3–4 NOTES ON THE INTERNAL AUDIT PLAN
(HELP DOCUMENT 8.2.1.3–3)

The plan presented is based on a small manufacturing company. All personnel work in one of five departments.

The blank boxes represent clauses of ISO 9001 which need to be audited in particular departments. The hatched boxes represent audit elements which are considered to be not relevant to the particular department. This company does not have a product development function (7.3) nor does it handle customer-supplied materials (7.5.4), so these clauses do not appear. In this plan the clauses relating to the management representative (5.5.3) are dealt with in the audit of senior management and do not need to be audited in other sections of the company.

Permissible exclusions are audited under senior management only. That does not imply that such exclusions only apply to senior management, it means that any decisions on excluding clauses of the standard are taken by senior management, and this is therefore the appropriate place to audit this aspect in respect of the entire organization.

Similarly, with regard to customer satisfaction (8.2.1) it is not implied that only the Quality Assurance and Administration functions are interested in this. Simply from an auditing point of view these are the two places where it is considered most useful to audit in this particular company.

On the other hand, all departments need to be active in such areas as document control, nonconformity, preventive action and human resources, and these activities have to audited in all areas.

When the audits represented by all the blank boxes have been carried out the entire standard and all activities should have been audited. If any gaps remain then the matrix needs to be adjusted.

Audits can be carried out 'vertically' or 'horizontally'. A vertical audit entails auditing a particular department against all the clauses of the standard. A horizontal audit entails auditing all departments against a single clause. Some clauses are more suited to one approach than the other. For example, the horizontal might be more appropriate for internal communication, whereas a vertical audit in a production department would cover aspects such as document and record control, measuring devices and analysis of data.

The physical location of departments may also affect the approach you take. If they are physically separated it may be simpler to do all audits as vertical ones.

Help document 8.2.1.3–3 represents the template for an annual audit plan. The individual elements should be scheduled and the dates planned for the audits written in. When an element has been completed the box can be ticked and the audit date entered. The completed sheet will then represent the record of the full audit cycle and should be filed away for reference.

8.2.1.3–5 NOTES ON INTERNAL AUDITING OF QUALITY SYSTEMS

Procedure: Ref. 8.2.1.3–1.

Audit: A systematic independent and documented process for obtaining evidence and evaluating it objectively to determine the extent to which the quality policies, procedures and requirements are fulfilled.

OBJECTIVES OF THE ISO 9000 INTERNAL AUDIT

1 To confirm the system complies with the requirements of ISO 9001.
2 To confirm that the documented procedures are being implemented.
3 To identify nonconformities, that is, any instances where requirements are not met or procedures not followed.

AUDITING

It is important to point out to the auditee at the outset that the audit is intended to be a service to him or her. Its objective is to help him or her identify problems that might not be noticed by the people in the area. Reporting a non-compliance should not be taken as a personal criticism, since it is usually caused by some problem within the system that facilitates an error on the part of an individual.

Carrying out the audit involves:

1 Asking questions, for example:
   a) Who ...? Who is responsible for doing that?
   b) What ...? What happens when the customer complaints?
   c) Why ...? Why is that box put to one side?
   d) When ...? When was the last supplier review?
   e) Where ...? Where is it stated that reject product can be reworked?
   f) How ...? How do you know that this is the current version?
2 Examining procedures, work instructions, drawings, plans.
3 Examining records.
4 Looking at physical activities and items.
5 Interviewing people.

You must see the evidence. A verbal description is usually not adequate if it is not backed up by documentation. To prevent long explanations and descriptions *ask to see the procedure or record in question.*

LOOK ABOUT YOU!

There is a lot of information all around, which can give an auditor leads to follow.

● There may be product samples lying around. (Why is this sample getting special attention? Is this a non-conforming product? Is the nonconformity properly recorded? Is the sample properly labelled? How will the decision about it be made?)
● Check memos on noticeboards, for example, about changes to procedures because of problems. (What is the problem? Is the nonconformity recorded properly? Should the documented procedure have been changed? Has the person who issued the memo the authority to make the change?)
● There may be seldom-used equipment in a corner. (What is the function of this equipment? Does it require a written procedure? Has somebody been trained in its use?)

Questions like these will often reveal significant nonconformity or weaknesses in the system.

TRACEABILITY EXERCISE

Where the operation involves a product, a traceability exercise can give a good overview of the system. Locate an example of nonconforming product in the store or warehouse and record the details. Trace this product back through the process, paying special attention to the decisions that were taken along the way. Note how the nonconformity was recorded and investigated. If there are any weaknesses in the system they are most likely to manifest themselves when the system is under pressure, as in the case of nonconforming product.

THE THREE BASIC RULES

During the audit remember these rules and check to see that they are followed:

1 No inspection without recording.
2 No recording without review.
3 No review without action.

THE AUDIT REPORT

The audit report should contain the following:

- an indication of the scope of the audit – what parts of the standard, and what departments were covered;
- a list of specific non-compliances. Be specific about the details.

In addition the auditor should try to assess how effective the procedures are in helping to achieve the stated objectives and, if appropriate, make suggestions for improvement.

GENERAL

Always act in a professional manner when auditing. Be sensitive to the other's positions and worries. Deal only in facts. Do not let interpersonal difficulties cloud your objectivity.

Do not make criticisms in the report. The auditor's function is to report the facts. Leave it to somebody else to criticize, if that is necessary.

There must be no surprises for the auditee when the report appears.

There must be no dispute over the facts themselves, though there may be disagreement afterwards over the *significance* of a particular non-compliance.

8.2.1.3–6 ISO 9001 INTERNAL AUDIT REPORT (COMPLETED EXAMPLE)   *Page 1 of 2*

Date of audit: 9.2.2001   Auditor: Ida Clare

Areas audited: Purchasing, Product Development, Maintenance and Customer Services

ISO 9001 clauses/requirements audited: See items ticked on the attached audit checklist.

	Details	NCR Ref.	Completed
	Purchasing		
1	Suppliers' performance is rated but procedure P002 doesn't mention this.		
2	Supplier audits are mentioned in P002 but there is no explanation of when or how this is done.		
3	There are different assessment/approval procedures for different samples (P003, P009). Does this make sense?		
4	One of the three sample test report forms is not included in the manual.		
5	Specification S057 (13.10.99) has not been signed.		
6	Two pallets of GrittexM were found in the store. The supplier is not approved and there is no approved specification for this material.		
7	Shouldn't copies of all nonconformity reports relating to purchases be sent to the Purchasing Manager?		
	Product Development		
8	Approximately 80% of the product specifications are approved and on computer at this stage.		
9	A file of purchasing specifications is held in the Product Development department. It was not clear whether these were duplicates of specifications in Purchasing Department, since the numbering system is different.		
10	Formulations and specifications show (inconsistently) imperial and metric quantities. This may cause confusion and lead to error.		
11	Specifications do not show page number on page 2.		
12	It is not clear how purchasing specifications are introduced, approved, etc.		
13	Only the Product Development Manager has access to the computer holding product specifications. This is not covered in the Manuals.		

	Maintenance		
14	The daily check on the chlorine cylinders is not described in the Maintenance Manual, and records of the check are not kept.		
	Customer Services		
15	Complaint records are retained for 3 months (blue copy) and 2 years (yellow copy). Quality Manual states that records should be kept for 4 years.		
16	Complaint C99-017: 'Customer not happy with response. Georgina to call'. It was not possible to verify if this happened. Similarly C00-002 – 'Rep. to call'.		
17	It is not clear that corrective action is taken in relation to all complaints (i.e., investigation of cause, and action to prevent a recurrence).		
	General		
18	Nonconformity reports are not always raised as required by procedure Q015. Two instances on weekly reject report for 15.1.2000 (items 5 and 12) did not have corresponding NCRs.		
19	Weekly summary of reject product is now produced, but this is not mentioned in any manual.		

Signed _____*Ida Clare*_____   Date   *11/2/01*

8.2.2–1 PROCESS CONTROL INSPECTION PLAN

Process step	Sample	Inspection/Test	Frequency	By	Target limits	Critical limits	Method
Mixing	Completed mix	Total solids	One sample per mix	Operator	48–52%	45–55%	PC012
		pH	One sample per mix	Operator	6.5–6.8	6.2–7.0	PC005
Heat treatment	Heated mix	Viscosity	One sample per mix	Operator	See current spec. at control panel		PC013
Spray-drying	Dry powder ex chute	Bulk density	One hour after start of drying	Laboratory	0.48–0.52 g/ml	0.45–0.55 g/ml	L023
		Moisture	Every hour	Automatic	2.5% min.	4.5% max.	N/A

If any result is found to be outside the target limits take immediate action to correct the problem.

If a result goes outside the Critical limits it is likely that non-conforming product will result. Inform the manager immediately.

8.2.3–1 PRODUCT RELEASE PROCEDURE

Objective   To ensure that all relevant and available information is evaluated before product is released for dispatch.

Scope   All bulk and packed finished product.

PROCEDURE

1 Check the following records for confirmation that the product was manufactured within normal conditions:

   a) raw material input record;

   b) production process control record;

   c) finished product testing results;

   d) nonconformity reports for the production date.

2 If any abnormality was reported, investigate the circumstances and assess if there may have been any impact on product quality. If necessary consult the production operator or supervisor involved.

3 Sign the Production process control record in the appropriate space.

4 Staple the first three documents listed above together.

5 File the record in the product history filing cabinet.

6 Change the computer status for the batch from NYT (not yet tested) to PAT (passed all tests).

AUTHORITY

All product fully within specification may be released by the Laboratory Manager.

Product outside specification in any respect must be referred to the Quality Manager. See 'Procedure for non-conforming product', reference 8.3.1–1.

8.2.3–2 PRODUCTION RECORD/PRODUCT RELEASE

Page 1 of 1

Production date _____ Product _____ Batch no. _____

Pre-Start-up checks
(Tick to indicate checked
and OK)

❏ Mixer clean
❏ Machine A clean
❏ Tank B empty

❏ Conveyor belt speed correct
❏ Machine C set correctly
❏ Temperature of D > 150°

Sign _____

Ingredients used

Ingredient	Amount added	Sign	Ingredient	Amount added	Sign
Ingredient 1	5 kg		Ingredient 3	500 grams	
Ingredient 2	10 kg		Ingredient 4	57.7 litres	

For ingredient batch numbers consult the Incoming materials/traceability record.

Process control inspections

	Spec.	8.00	11.00	14.00	16.00
Temperature of mix	65–75				
Check E	Max 60 sec.				
Wrapping OK?	Not torn or creased				
Metal detector checked	Rejects both test pieces				

Comments/incidents
Any relevant Incident Reports? Yes/No

The above product was manufactured to company standards.

Signed _____   Date _____
     Supervisor

Finished product inspection   Date:

Test	Spec.	Result	Sign
Test F	2.05–3.55		
Inspection G	No cloudiness		

The above product is released for dispatch and sale.

Signed _____   Date _____
     Laboratory Manager

8.3.1–1 PROCEDURE FOR NON-CONFORMING PRODUCT *Page 1 of 1*

Objective   To ensure that non-conforming product is physically prevented from inadvertent use, and that it is disposed of in an appropriate manner.

Scope   Any batch of product, or any part of a batch of product which does not meet the product specification on physical, organoleptic, microbiological or packaging characteristics.

PROCEDURE

1 The person discovering the nonconformity records the details on a nonconformity report and gives it to the Quality Manager. In the case of routine (planned) inspection or testing it is sufficient to note the nonconformity on the normal record sheet.

2 The Quality Manager gathers the information on the product, which will enable a decision to be made. This may involve (as he or she considers appropriate):
   a) testing further samples to determine the extent of the nonconformity;
   b) comparison with other batches;
   c) literature searches;
   d) consultation with the customer;
   e) consultation with external experts.

3 The Quality Manager consults the Materials Manager before making a decision on disposal of the product.

4 The options available for disposal of product are:
   a) waiver (release as conforming product) – this may only be considered if it is certain that the consumer will not be affected in any way. In the case of bulk product the approval of the customer must be obtained;
   b) rework – according to the reworking procedure, and only at a level which will not adversely affect the final product;
   c) sale as regraded product – only if the product is fully suitable for its new purpose;
   d) destruction.

5 The Quality Manager records the decision on the nonconformity report and adjusts the computer status.

6 The Quality Manager sends a copy of the report to the Stores Supervisor.

7 The Stores Supervisor arranges for the disposal, and records the full details on the nonconformity report when it is dispatched.

8 The Stores Supervisor sends the nonconformity report to the Quality Manager.

9 The Quality Manager ensures that the corrective action procedure is implemented to prevent a recurrence of this nonconformity.

8.3.2–1 NON-CONFORMING PRODUCT WAIVER REQUEST (PRODUCT FOR RETAIL SALE)

Product _____ Batch no. _____ Date of manufacture _____

Details of nonconformity

Details of similar product released in the past. Include any feedback or customer reaction to that product.

Likely effect of the nonconformity on product performance and customer satisfaction

Probability of nonconformity being detected by testing or otherwise

Is there a customer contract for this product? Is waiver permitted by the contract?

Signed _____   Date _____
            Quality Manager

The above product is approved for release subject to the following restrictions:

Signed _____   Date _____
            Managing Director

8.4–1 GUIDANCE ON ANALYSIS OF DATA

Objective   To ensure that all managers examine data objectively in order to obtain maximum information about trends.

Scope   Data relating to quality of output.

Data relating to the performance of the processes.

Data relating to the performance of suppliers.

Data relating to customer satisfaction and dissatisfaction.

POSSIBLE SOURCES OF DATA

Data can take many forms. The following are some examples that may be relevant in your area:

- surveys and questionnaires;
- measurements taken on processes and products;
- records from previous periods;
- the number of occurrences or non-occurrences of something;
- sample testing; and
- trial runs of products or services.

THE ANALYSIS

Do not substitute opinion for objective data.

Do not lose focus. When you have come to a conclusion that can be usefully applied start taking action.

Look for connections between the data and the physical reality.

Try to find root causes of problems, not the superficial causes.

ANALYSIS TOOLS

The following are some of the tools that may be appropriate in the analysis of collected data:

- brainstorming;
- flow charts;
- bar charts;
- run charts;
- cause-and-effect analysis;
- Pareto analysis;
- cumulative sum graphs; and
- moving average graphs.

Further information on the above tools is available in the Reference library or from the Quality Manager. The Quality Manager is available to offer advice on the most appropriate methods for analysing data.

ACTION

Prioritize the corrective or preventive action. Start with the action that will have most effect for the effort involved.

RECORDS

Keep brief records of the data analysis exercise – date, persons involved, raw data analysed and conclusions reached.

8.5.2–1 PROCEDURE FOR CORRECTIVE ACTION   *Page 1 of 1*

Objective   To ensure that any significant problems are adequately investigated so that they are prevented from recurring, as far as practicable.

Scope   Incidents that could have led to, or did lead to, non-conforming product.
Incidents where a failure of the quality system occurred.

Note This procedure does not apply to the normal process adjustment that is made for purposes of process control. It would apply, however, in the case of a process control variable that is persistently difficult to maintain within the target range.

PROCEDURE

1 The person raising the nonconformity report places a copy in the production meeting in-tray as soon as possible after the problem is noticed.

2 The nonconformity report is discussed at the next production meeting. The Quality Manager ensures that an adequate investigation takes place.

3 When the full facts are known and agreed, the chairperson assigns corrective action to an individual. This action should help prevent, or reduce the likelihood of, a recurrence.

4 Details of the corrective action taken are documented on the nonconformity report. If appropriate, procedures should be amended, or new procedures written.

5 The nonconformity report is raised at each production meeting until the matter is fully resolved.

RESPONSIBILITY

Each person is responsible for reporting nonconformities that he or she discovers.

The Quality Manager is responsible for ensuring that each one is properly investigated and corrective action taken.

The manager in the affected department is responsible for taking the corrective action and ensuring that the action is maintained permanently.

8.5.2–2 NONCONFORMITY/CORRECTIVE ACTION REPORT
Page 1 of 1

Details of nonconformity

Signed _____

Investigation

Signed _____

Corrective action to be taken

Signed _____

Corrective action completed: Date _____   Signed _____

Corrective action reviewed: OK?   Yes/No

Signed _____   Date _____

8.5.3–1 PROCEDURE FOR PREVENTIVE ACTION   *Page 1 of 1*

Objective   To ensure that potential causes of nonconformity are identified before they arise, and are prevented.

Scope   All activities, all processes, all departments and staff.

PROCEDURE

Review the process flow chart for each process under your control. If there is no flow chart list out the individual steps.

1 For each step in the process identify any aspect that could give rise to customer dissatisfaction.
2 If necessary, consult with internal or external experts.
3 Include in the assessment any analysis of key data that has been carried out since the previous risk assessment.
4 Where appropriate preventive action can be taken assign the necessary tasks and ensure that they are carried out.
5 Record brief details of the tasks and items that have been risk-assessed, and any preventive action implemented or recommended.
6 Where preventive action requires authorization present the risk assessment record to the next operations meeting.

RESPONSIBILITY

Each manager is responsible for carrying out a risk assessment of all processes under his or her control at least annually.

8.5.3–2 HACCP PLAN (EXTRACT)

CCP no.	Step	Hazards	Control measure	Monitor	Target and limits	Corrective action	Doc. ref.	Record ref.
5	Storage in chill	Temperature rise – growth	Temperature control	Operator check product core temperature weekly	Max 5 °C	Adjust thermostat	P2/11	Q1/7
				Operator check air temperature daily	Target 4 °C Max. 8 °C	Adjust thermostat Call supervisor	P2/11	Q1/8
			Maintenance	Supervisor check records weekly	Maintenance done to schedule	Schedule maintenance	P3/6	Q2/4
		Growth due to age	Strict stock rotation procedure	Supervisor check stock daily	No product older than that currently in use	Re-training/awareness	P2/10	Q3/2
		Cross-contamination	Strict storage procedures	Supervisor check daily	All product stored per procedure	Quarantine any suspect product Re-training/awareness	P2/10	Q3/2
N/A	Food removal from chill	Contamination from staff	Protective clothing	Supervisor observe daily	All staff properly attired	Instruct staff	P1/2	Q3/2
			Health controls	Supervisor observe daily	Nobody coughing or complaining of stomach problems	Remove from food handling duties	P1/1	Q3/2
					No uncovered cuts	Cover immediately with appropriate dressing		
			Hand-washing	Supervisor inspect facilities daily	Soap, towels, nailbrush, hot water in place	Replace missing items	P1/3	Q3/2
				Supervisor observe staff	Staff washing hands when appropriate	Instruct staff	P1/3	Q3/2

8.5.3–3 PYRAMID MODEL OF NONCONFORMITY STATISTICS   *Page 1 of 1*

It is a fact, proven by numerous studies covering many thousands of accidents, that there is a definite ratio between the numbers of serious accidents, minor accidents and so-called 'near misses'. Furthermore, the ratio is fixed, and no amount of intervention can change it. The actual ratio varies from study to study, but is remarkably consistent, around 1:30:300.

The only way we can influence the occurrence of accidents is to prolong the time it takes for the accidents to happen. For example, one company might have one serious accident, 30 minor accidents and 300 near misses in six months, while another company might only have those numbers over a ten-year period.

The value of this concept is in the prevention of accidents. The normal reaction to a serious accident is to prevent that accident recurring. This is corrective action, and is, of course, essential. However, if you consider the logic of the ratio being fixed you can see that by reducing the number of near misses the number of minor and serious accidents automatically falls! Thus preventive action taken in reaction to near misses is equally effective and much more cost effective.

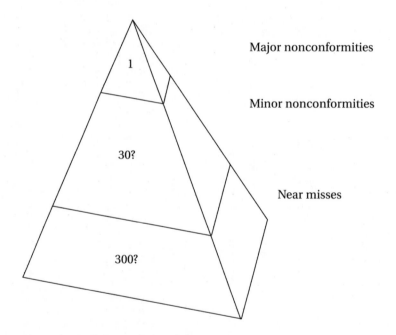

Does a similar situation obtain in relation to quality? Experience suggests strongly that it does, though the shape of the pyramid and the actual ratios are unknown.

For every time you have a serious product rejection situation you have numerous instances of smaller amounts rejected. What you probably do not realize is that there are very many indicators all around of errors that go unpunished by not causing rejection of product, due purely to chance.

If you say that you never have major quality problems, but that you frequently have small amounts rejected, it may be that you are steadily building up the pyramid and will eventually cap it with a major loss of product.

This can only be prevented effectively by attention to detail and acting to correct the numerous small breaches of procedures that occur in every organization.

Index

The Index contains principally references occurring in the main text. This enables the reader to identify the relevant clauses in the standard, and from there further references to the topic may then be easily located in the sample quality manual, implementation checklists and Help documents.